BEST OF THE

APPALACHIAN TRAIL

TRAIL 3RD EDITION

DAY HIKES

LEONARD M. ADKINS &
VICTORIA AND FRANK LOGUE

MENASHA RIDGE PRESS
Your Guide to the Outdoors Since 1982

APPALACHIAN TRAIL
CONSERVANCY®

The Best of the Appalachian Trail: Day Hikes

Copyright © 1994, 2004, 2018 by Leonard M. Adkins and Victoria and Frank Logue
All rights reserved
Printed in the United States of America
Published by Menasha Ridge Press and the Appalachian Trail Conservancy
Distributed by Publishers Group West
Third edition, first printing

Project editor: Kate Johnson
Cartography and cover design: Scott McGrew
Text design: Leslie Shaw
Cover photo: John Wollwerth/Shutterstock
Interior photos: As noted on page and as follows: pages 14, 58, 68, and 86, Lafe Low; pages 38, 98, 112, and 150, Leonard M. Adkins; pages 122 and 140, Matt Willen; pages 188 and 214, Victoria and Frank Logue

Library of Congress Cataloging-in-Publication Data

Names: Adkins, Leonard M., author. | Logue, Victoria, 1961- author. | Logue, Frank, 1963- author.
Title: The best of the Appalachian Trail : day hikes / Leonard M. Adkins, Victoria and Frank Logue.
Description: Third Edition. | Birmingham, Alabama : Menasha Ridge Press, [2018] | Victoria Logue appears as
    principal author on previous edition's published title page. | "Distributed by Publishers Group West"
    —T.p. verso. | Includes index.
Identifiers: LCCN 2017050202| ISBN 9781634041454 (paperback) | ISBN 9781634041461 (ebook)
Subjects: LCSH: Hiking—Appalachian Trail—Guidebooks. | Trails—Appalachian Trail—Guidebooks.
    Backpacking—Appalachian Trail—Guidebooks. | Appalachian Trail—Guidebooks.
Classification: LCC GV199.42.A68 L646 2018 | DDC 796.51/0974—dc23
LC record available at lccn.loc.gov/2017050202

MENASHA RIDGE PRESS
An imprint of AdventureKEEN
2204 First Ave. S., Ste. 102
Birmingham, AL 35233
menasharidge.com

Appalachian Trail Conservancy
PO Box 807
Harpers Ferry, WV 25425
appalachiantrail.org

BEST OF THE
APPALACHIAN
TRAIL
3RD EDITION

DAY HIKES

DEDICATION

Dedicated to the thousands of volunteers, past, present, and future,
who make our ramblings on the Appalachian Trail possible.
Your efforts are appreciated and do not go unnoticed.
—Leonard

In memory of Hulda Kramp Kelly: a great lady,
a good friend, and the best grandmother a girl could have.
—Victoria

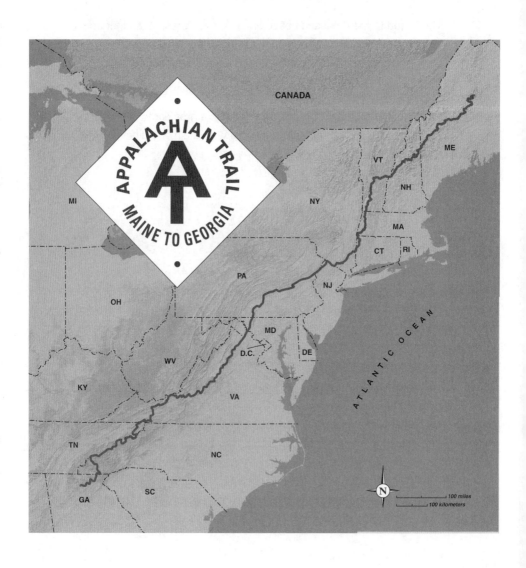

CONTENTS

(continued)

CONTENTS

(continued)

ACKNOWLEDGMENTS

A book is never the work of the author or authors alone. We wish to acknowledge and thank the many people who took time out of their busy schedules to assist us.

Leonard would like to thank Michael Alper, Batona Hiking Club; Nancy D. Anthony, Natural Bridge Appalachian Trail Club; David Boone, AMC Connecticut Chapter; Jeff Buehler, Susquehanna Appalachian Trail Club; Cosmo Catalano Jr., AMC Berkshire Chapter; Daniel D. Chazin, New York–New Jersey Trail Conference; V. Collins Chew, Tennessee Eastman Hiking Club; Kitty Farley, Mount Rogers Appalachian Trail Club; David Field, Maine Appalachian Trail Club; Rita Floriani, Blue Mountain Eagle Climbing Club; Doris Gove, Smoky Mountains Hiking Club; Mark Hedee, Old Dominion Appalachian Trail Club; Edward F. Kenna, Jr., Philadelphia Trail Club; Christine Lauriello, Cumberland Valley Appalachian Trail Club; Howard McDonald, Carolina Mountain Club; Andrew Norkin, AMC White Mountains Trails manager; Herbert Ogden, Green Mountain Club; the late Charles Parry, Roanoke Appalachian Trail Club; Bill Rogers and James Newman, Tidewater Appalachian Trail Club; Lee Sheaffer, Potomac Appalachian Trail Club; Cynthia Taylor-Miller; the late Vaughn Thomas, Piedmont Appalachian Trail Hikers; Melanie Wertz, Cumberland Valley Appalachian Trail Management Association; and Barbara Wiemann, Allentown Hiking Club—thank you for being valuable sources of information. Any errors that may remain are ours and not yours.

Brian B. King, ATC Publisher—thanks for your support through the many years.

Dr. Stephen Lewis, Caroline Charonko, Terry Cumming, and Susie Surfas—thank you for the many extra years of trail life you have given me.

Nancy Adkins—love you forever, Mom.

Kathleen, John, Tim, and Jay Yelenic—love you too.

Laurie—who could ever have imagined I would find you? You are my perfect companion through the trails of life.

Victoria and Frank would like to thank Vic Hasler of the Tennessee Eastman Hiking and Canoeing Club for his invaluable input; Bill Van Horn of the Nantahala Hiking Club for his help with the hikes in that club's section of trail; and Tom Weaver of the Carolina Mountain Club and Pete Buak of the Georgia Appalachian Trail Club for their assistance.

Leaves of red, orange, and yellow rustled in the wind and broke loose from their branches. The soft sound made by thousands of leaves as they fell onto the already littered forest floor could barely be heard over the burbling, pattering, and splashing sounds from Little Black Branch. The small creek runs alongside the Appalachian Trail on a hike from Forest Service Road 10 to Little Rock Pond. We walked over to the stream to show our daughter, Griffin, the water she heard just off the trail. In a wide, shallow pool, red maple leaves circled around and around, caught in an eddy. The wet leaves seem iridescent, lit by the sunlight streaming through the trees on that crisp October morning.

That short, easy hike was the perfect way to spend the morning. There was plenty of time for Griffin to get down and walk on her own, and the pond surrounded by Vermont's peak foliage was a breathtaking sight.

This book was written to introduce you to just that kind of experience—the best day hikes on the 2,190-mile Appalachian Trail.

HISTORY OF THE APPALACHIAN TRAIL

The idea for a trail running the length of the Appalachian Mountains was first considered in the early part of the 20th century. The Appalachian Trail, as we know it, was the vision of Benton MacKaye (rhymes with "sky") and others who had been thinking about the concept for more than 10 years. In 1921, MacKaye took the initiative and launched the project through an article in *The Journal of the American Institute of Architects.*

In that first article, MacKaye wrote about the purpose of the Trail, "There would be a chance to catch a breath, to study the dynamic forces of nature and the possibilities of shifting to them the burdens now carried on the backs of men. . . . Industry would come to be seen in its true perspective—as a means in life and not as an end in itself."

MacKaye's original intent was to construct a trail from "the highest peak in the North to the highest peak in the South—from Mount Washington [New Hampshire] to Mount Mitchell [North Carolina]." He envisioned a fourfold plan including the trail, shelters, community camps, and food and farm camps. The camps never came about. And although MacKaye's larger economic plan for the Appalachian Trail never gained support, his main purpose—an opportunity for American families to commune with nature—is the reason for the Trail's continued existence.

Within a year after MacKaye's article appeared in the architectural journal, the New York–New Jersey Trail Conference began work on a new trail with the goal of making it part of the Appalachian Trail. In the Hudson River Valley, the new Bear Mountain Bridge would connect a planned section in New England with Harriman State Park and eventually with the Delaware Water Gap in Pennsylvania.

In 1925, MacKaye and others formed the Appalachian Trail Conference to guide the project to completion. By 1936, Myron H. Avery, who would be chairman of the Appalachian Trail Conference for 22 years, had finished measuring the flagged route of the Appalachian Trail. He became the first 2,000-miler one year before the completion of the Trail.

On August 14, 1937, Civilian Conservation Corps (CCC) workers cleared the final link of the 2,025-mile (the length at that time) Appalachian Trail. On a high ridge connecting Spaulding and Sugarloaf Mountains in Maine, a six-person CCC crew cut the last 2 miles of trail. The finished route of the Appalachian Trail was not as originally envisioned by MacKaye: the final product was longer, stretching from Georgia's Mount Oglethorpe (the southern terminus of the eastern Blue Ridge) to Katahdin in what is now Maine's Baxter State Park.

The Trail did not remain complete for long. The next year, a hurricane demolished miles of trail in the northeast, while the decision to connect Skyline Drive (under construction at the time) with the Blue Ridge Parkway displaced another 120 miles of trail in Virginia. The Trail was not made continuous again until 1951, after the world had settled down from World War II.

In 1968, President Lyndon B. Johnson signed the National Trails System Act and designated the Appalachian Trail as the first National Scenic Trail. The act charged federal agencies with the task of buying lands to protect the trailway from encroaching development, but 10 years passed before the government acted and began protecting the Trail lands. 99% of the 2,190 miles of the Appalachian Trail were under protection within some form of public lands. The Appalachian Trail Conservancy (ATC) is now leading a coalition of private and public entities that are trying to protect all the most significant viewsheds of the A.T.

Perhaps the most amazing aspect of the world's largest greenway is that, prior to their construction by federal crews and the CCC, the Trail routes were conceived and selected by private citizens. As a testament to the volunteers' involvement, the federal government delegated much of the management of the Trail to a private nonprofit group—the ATC—even after the footpath was brought under federal protection.

SELECTING A HIKE

When we set out to pick the best of the A.T., we decided that although the hikes could use side trails, they would have to mostly be on the Trail proper to qualify for the book. But a few hikes in this book bend that rule—these were so spectacular that although they use little of the Trail, we just couldn't leave them out.

The hike descriptions in this book often suggest more than great hikes, however. The information provided will also tell you, for example, good times to hike in the area or when to avoid hiking there.

To help you pick out a hike that offers just what you're looking for, several easy-to-find pieces of information are located at the top of each hike description: the hike rating, the distance and configuration, and icons denoting major attractions along the way. At the beginning of each chapter, this same information, along with the hike name and page number, is also presented in a quick-reference table format.

ICONS

Each hike has one or more icons that show the major attractions along the way. The icons are intended to give you easy-to-identify symbols that you can use when you flip through the book looking for a hike.

mountain peak

scenic view/ photo opportunity

pond or river

waterfall

historical area

bird-watching

wheelchair access

RATINGS

The hikes are rated as *easy, moderate,* or *strenuous.* Easy hikes have little elevation gain or loss and are no more than 10 miles long. Moderate hikes have no long, steep climbs or descents but may have some short, steep grades or long, gradual ascents. Strenuous hikes are steep and sometimes long—they should not be attempted by inexperienced hikers or people in poor physical condition.

LENGTH AND HIKE TIMES

A good way to gauge hiking time is to allow a half hour for each mile to be hiked, as well as an additional hour for each 1,000 feet of elevation gained. This pace allows for a leisurely hike with some time to stop at overlooks and other points of interest. The hikes in this book can certainly be done faster or slower, but this formula will give you an idea of how long you will need to walk.

EQUIPMENT FOR DAY HIKES

One of the benefits of day hiking (as opposed to backpacking) is that you are relatively unburdened by equipment. There are a few things, however, that every well-prepared day hiker should have, as well as a few optional items that you might want to take along to make your trip more enjoyable.

You need to be dressed in comfortable clothes that don't constrict your movement too much. For many hikes in this book, a sturdy pair of shorts or pants, a shirt, and good walking shoes or hiking boots will be adequate. You will also need a day pack or fanny pack to carry what little gear you need. For all but the shortest of hikes (a mile or less), you should carry at least a quart of water and raingear, such as a rainsuit, poncho, or umbrella.

Items you may want to consider carrying in your pack include a small first aid kit, a lighter or matches, toilet paper and a trowel, and a map or guidebook. We also suggest that you carry only a photocopy of the pages you need from this book when you hike rather than the entire book.

If you're going to be hiking at high altitudes or above tree line, carry warm clothing, because the temperature on the mountaintops can be much lower than in the valleys. Other items you may want to carry in your pack include a camera (if you're not exclusively using your phone); binoculars; wildlife guides; and a filter, pills, or drops if you expect to treat water from a spring or stream.

BOOTS

Hiking boots range in price from $50 to $500 and are generally divided into three categories: *heavyweight, mediumweight,* and *lightweight.* Heavyweight boots weigh more than 4 pounds and are generally designed for technically demanding climbs on ice (usually with crampons), snow, or rock. You won't need heavyweights for the hikes in this book unless, say, you choose to climb Katahdin in the dead of winter.

Mediumweight boots, which weigh 2–4 pounds, are made almost entirely of leather, though many incorporate tough fabric as well. Mediumweights are ideal for the broadest range of hiking situations.

Lightweight boots, which weigh less than 2 pounds, are generally made with a combination of leather and a breathable fabric. Lightweights are tough enough to handle any hike in this book.

When purchasing hiking boots, the most important factor to keep in mind is fit—even the most expensive boots will make you miserable if they don't fit properly. Fitting is best done in person, in a store; buy online only if you know the company has a good return policy. Heavyweight and mediumweight boots require that you break them in before you head out into the woods. Lightweight boots generally need no breaking in, but even these can be purchased too small or too big, too narrow or too wide, so be prepared with moleskin to treat hot spots before blisters develop (see page 11 for more on blister care).

DAY PACKS

Because most day packs are made in the same teardrop style, the important thing to look at is how well the pack is made. Inexpensive day packs can be purchased at any discount store, but if they are poorly padded and have little support, you won't have hiked a mile before you regret the purchase.

Because of advances in fabric technology, hikers have dozens of well-made day packs to choose from these days. We suggest reading online reviews for the packs you are interested in. Make sure that the shoulder straps are secure—this is the first place where day packs fall apart, because you carry the weight on your shoulders as opposed to your hips. To prevent ripping, a number of day packs have extra reinforcement where the shoulder straps connect to the sack.

Another feature to look for is padding on the back of the pack. The more padding there is, the less likely you'll be poked and prodded by the objects inside the pack.

Other features to look for in day packs include convenient loading through a top or front panel, pockets for smaller items (some day packs also feature a special loop to hold keys), a waist strap to keep the pack from bouncing against your back, padded shoulder straps, and lash points for extra gear. Many day packs now feature hydration packs that have various-sized reservoirs to hold water and an attached tube that allows you to easily sip while hiking. Day packs vary greatly in price, but the best ones tend to be between $50 and $200, and most manufacturers feature a variety to choose from.

FANNY PACKS

Fanny packs can be used on day hikes in place of a day pack, but they aren't as comfortable as day packs: they don't distribute the weight as well and usually cannot carry as much as you might like to bring. They can be used along with a day pack or alone (if you have a partner carrying a day pack).

Some hikers use fanny packs worn in reverse, snug across their bellies with the strap fastened in the small of the back. Cameras, water, snacks, data books, maps, guides, or whatever you need can be quickly accessed using this method.

When purchasing a fanny pack, make sure that the belt is well padded for comfort and the sack is sturdy enough to carry the load you intend for it. Some fanny packs will sag if heavy objects are placed in them. Also, if the fabric is thin, you may get poked and prodded by the objects inside.

EQUIPMENT CHECKLIST

- ➤ Bandanna(s)*
- ➤ Camera/spare smartphone and memory cards/film*
- ➤ Compass*
- ➤ Cell phone (for emergencies only; keep it turned off when not in use)
- ➤ Day pack and/or fanny pack
- ➤ Filter or other water treatment*
- ➤ First aid kit (including moleskin and space blanket)*
- ➤ Food and water for length of hike
- ➤ GPS unit*
- ➤ Hiking boots
- ➤ Hiking stick*
- ➤ Insect repellent and sunscreen*
- ➤ Maps and guidebooks*
- ➤ Pocketknife*
- ➤ Raingear
- ➤ Sunglasses*
- ➤ Sweater or coat*
- ➤ Toilet paper and trowel for burying waste**

optional or seasonal equipment
**optional, depending on length of hike and availability of facilities along the way*

WATER TREATMENT

Staying well hydrated is essential for hikers. If you're day hiking, we recommend that you carry all of the water you need, but if you anticipate needing more, be aware that you *must* treat water from any source along the A.T. unless it has been guaranteed safe to drink. The incidence of waterborne illnesses has been rising among A.T. hikers because they have either become lazy about treating their water or are unaware that they should do so. Fortunately, a wide variety of treatment methods exist, from boiling to iodine pills to gravity filters. As with other outdoor gear, check out product reviews and advice online before making your choice.

MINIMUM IMPACT

Minimum-impact camping is a philosophy summed up by the National Park Service as "Take nothing but pictures, leave nothing but footprints." The following sections discuss measures you can take to help eliminate traces of your presence along the Trail. This isn't so much a list of rules as it is a way of living that is becoming increasingly important to adopt. If these techniques are not used by everyone (and currently they're not), the A.T. will lose its natural beauty. Nature is resilient, but its ability to fight back is limited. A little effort goes a long way toward improving the world we're escaping to. If everyone pitches in, we'll be able to enjoy our backcountry experiences even more.

CARRY OUT ALL OF YOUR TRASH

Pack it in, pack it out, and you're already one giant step toward improving the environment you love. Keep a garbage bag handy for storing your trash—and that means everything, even organic material. Yes, orange peels, apple cores, and eggshells are natural and biodegradable. So why not toss them into the brush? Because they don't break down *instantly:* it takes five months for an orange peel, for instance, to rot and become one with the earth.

Few things are worse than heading into the woods to relieve yourself and discovering a trail of toilet paper, proving that you weren't the first to have this idea at this spot. Soggy used TP is one of the uglier reminders of human presence.

Likewise, following trails littered with cigarette butts is disheartening. If you want to smoke, that's your prerogative, but don't think of the outdoors as one big ashtray. Not only are cigarette butts ugly to look at, but it takes just a single stray spark to start a forest fire.

CARRY OUT TRASH LEFT BY OTHERS

Sadly, many people who wouldn't dare throw trash on the ground at home feel no compunction about doing so in the outdoors. And unfortunately, the users and abusers of America's trails outnumber the enviro-conscious. We have to make up for their ignorance and sloth by picking up after them.

You can make the outdoors an even better place by stopping occasionally to pick up other people's trash. As for nastier stuff like used toilet paper and discarded food, you can at least take a minute to cover it with leaves, moss, dirt, and twigs. Pick up trash, and you'll find you feel a lot better about yourself.

SWITCHBACKS

Stay on designated trails. Switchbacks are there for a reason: they slow down erosion on steep climbs. It may seem easier to scramble up the hillside to the next section of trail, but if too many people did that, rain would start using the newly exposed earth as a watercourse, washing away both trail and mountain in its wake. You may curse the person who blazed it and those who attempt to keep it passable for you, but remember that just about any trail you hike was built and maintained by volunteers.

WASTE MANAGEMENT

There's more to being green than just packing out your trash—properly discarding the remnants of nature's call keeps the wilderness not only cleaner but prettier, too. Always, always, always (we can't say it too many times) dig a hole 6–8 inches deep for solid waste, and make sure that you choose a spot at least 200 feet from the nearest water source. If you're hiking alongside a stream, *climb up.*

Urinating on rocks or gravel is preferable to bushes or dirt—urine contains salts that can attract wildlife, which may then dig up the spot where you've relieved yourself. Many hikers bring along a wide-mouthed plastic bottle or portable urinal; a flat-bottomed resealable cooking bag is a great option if you're trying to conserve space in your pack.

TRAIL MAINTENANCE

Give back to the Trail and the hiking community by becoming involved in trail maintenance. Maintaining a section of existing trail and helping out with blazing new trails are good ways to pay back the outdoors for the good times you have had there. Trails are beginning to crisscross the entire country, and there is sure to be a new or old trail somewhere near you. Contact your local trail clubs to see what you can do to help out. Most backpacking shops can tell you about clubs in your area.

The entire Appalachian Trail is maintained by volunteers. To find out more about the clubs that maintain the A.T., contact the Appalachian Trail Conservancy (see Appendix, page 224).

FINDING SOLITUDE

Many hikers retreat to the Appalachian Trail seeking a wilderness experience, only to find themselves sharing a crowded section of trail with more hikers than they bargained for. Here are a few tips for finding a little alone time on America's most popular long-distance trail.

- **Start your hike early in the morning.** We once took this advice to the extreme and enjoyed the best hike of our lives for the effort. We started climbing Katahdin at 2:30 a.m. and arrived at Baxter Peak by 5:30 a.m. in time for the sunrise. The view was spectacular, and we didn't share the summit with another hiker. That was on a Labor Day weekend, when later in the day, hikers marched in a long, single file from Baxter Peak to Pamola Peak. By making an extra effort to get up early (and hike the tricky section of trail in the dark), we had the peak to ourselves on perhaps the busiest day of the year. If you hike in the dark, be prepared. A headlamp or flashlight is absolutely necessary. And don't attempt difficult sections of trail in the dark if you are not experienced enough to do so.

- **Hike during the off-season.** Roan Highlands on the Tennessee–North Carolina state line gets very crowded during the peak bloom of its rhododendron garden. In June, visitors flock to see the awesome spectacle—thousands of big Catawba rhododendrons in bloom at once—but we've camped alone on the summit during the winter. We didn't see the rhododendrons, but the snow-covered mountain was a magnificent sight.
- **Discover your own special places.** After enjoying the hikes in this book, branch out and discover more of the Trail on your own. To help you in your search, the Appalachian Trail Conservancy publishes a set of 11 guidebooks (buy them at atctrailstore.org) that covers the entire 2,190-mile footpath, mile by mile.

SAFETY

Trouble is rare on the Appalachian Trail, but theft is not uncommon. Cars parked at trailheads may be targeted for break-ins because thieves know that the owner will be away for a while. Conceal anything worth stealing, or better yet, leave valuables at home. Also, do not leave any notes on your car stating where you are going and how long you intend to be gone. You might as well advertise for car theft.

You're unlikely to run into troublesome humans on the A.T., but if you do encounter someone who gives you a bad feeling, keep moving.

When it comes to the weather, it's neither impossible nor necessarily uncomfortable to hike in rain or snow or intense heat; nevertheless, you would be wise to take certain precautions. Clothing suitable to the situation is important: raingear for rain; layered clothing for snow and cold weather; and lightweight, porous clothing for hot days. Appropriate clothing can go a long way toward preventing both hypothermia and hyperthermia.

Some of the hikes in this book take in sections of trail that are located above tree line or in other exposed areas. In some cases, alternative bad-weather routes are available, but in others, they're not. If inclement weather is a probability, it may be best to take a rain check until the storm passes. For hikes above tree line, bring raingear just in case, because storms can form suddenly at high elevations.

Getting lost is rarely a problem on the A.T., but anyone can become distracted and miss a blaze that indicates a turn. The Appalachian Trail is marked with white blazes at least every 0.25 mile, and usually more often. Most trail maintainers try to blaze so that you can see the next blaze as soon as you've passed the previous one—if you've walked for more than five minutes without seeing a blaze, it would be wise to backtrack until you see a blaze before continuing on your way.

LIGHTNING

Lightning kills more people each year than any other natural disaster, including earthquakes, floods, and tornadoes. If you get caught on the A.T. during a lightning storm, you can reduce your chances of being struck: Avoid bodies of water and low places where water can collect. Avoid high places, ridges, open places, tall objects, metal objects, rock outcrops, wet caves, and ditches. If possible, find a stand of trees and sit with your knees pulled up to your chest, head bowed, and arms hugging knees.

FIRST AID

The risk of serious injury on a day hike is not high, but being unprepared would be tempting fate. You can still get stung by a bee; twist an ankle; or develop blisters, hypothermia, or heatstroke. The following information will give you some ideas about how to deal with these situations if they arise.

HYPOTHERMIA Shivering, numbness, weakness, and drowsiness are the first signs of hypothermia, or subnormal body temperature. These symptoms are followed by mental confusion/poor judgment, slurred speech, failing eyesight, and unconsciousness. The most serious warning sign of hypothermia occurs when the shivering stops: that means death is near.

Fortunately, hypothermia can be easy to treat if you catch it early. As long as you're able to keep moving, your body will continue to try to warm itself, but if you or a friend can't go any farther, do your best to warm up by other means. In the case of a day hike, this may mean nothing more than hurrying back to your car, stripping yourself of wet clothes, and turning the heater on.

HYPERTHERMIA At the other extreme, this ailment develops in three stages: *heat cramps, heat exhaustion,* and *heatstroke.* The best treatment for hyperthermia is prevention. If you're hiking in extremely hot weather, drink as much water as you can stomach, as dehydration usually leads to heat-related ailments. If you need a break, sit in the shade, drink some more water, and give your body a few minutes to cool off.

If your legs or abdomen begin to cramp, you're on your way to heat exhaustion and heatstroke. Find some shade and sip water slowly; in the case of heat cramps, add a bit of salt to the water if you have it on hand. Rather than continue hiking, you should call it a day.

Heat exhaustion can follow heat cramps. Although the body temperature remains fairly normal, the skin is pale, cool, and clammy; you may also feel faint, weak, nauseated, and dizzy. Again, sit in the shade, sip water, and lower your head between your knees to relieve the dizziness. You can also lie down, loosen your clothes (or take them off if you're not shy), and elevate your feet about 1 foot. Bathe in cool water if any is available. If you or an overheated friend feels nauseated or starts vomiting, do your best to get medical help right away.

With heatstroke, the skin becomes hot, red, and dry and the pulse rapid and strong. Unconsciousness is common. The victim should be undressed and bathed in cool water until the skin temperature is lowered, but do not overchill the victim, which can be as dangerous as overheating. Seek medical attention as soon as possible.

BLISTERS Blisters develop slowly and can make you miserable. As soon as you feel a hot spot—that is, a place on your foot that feels as if it is being rubbed more than other places—cover it with moleskin. If not treated properly, blisters can become infected. If you do get a blister, leave it unbroken; if it is already broken, treat it like an open wound, cleansing and bandaging it. Do not continue to hike if you are in too much pain.

BEE STINGS Although most insects (other than black flies, deer flies, and ticks) will try to avoid you, bees and wasps—yellow jackets in particular—are attracted to food, beverages, perfume and scented toiletries, and brightly colored (or dark) clothing. Yellow jackets nest anywhere that provides cover: logs, trees, even underground. And they don't mind stinging more than once! If you're sensitive to stings, carry an oral antihistamine to reduce swelling; a topical antihistamine, such as Benadryl, will help reduce itching. If you know that you could have a life-threatening allergic reaction to a sting, carry a prescription EpiPen or Ana-Kit (which contains a couple of injections of epinephrine plus antihistamine tablets), and seek medical attention as soon as possible if you get stung.

OTHER PESTS Deer, bears, boars, moose, raccoons, snakes, skunks, and porcupines live all along the A.T. These animals rarely cause problems for hikers, but if you do encounter them, do not approach them. Backing away slowly until they leave the area is the best way to avoid a confrontation.

Bee stings, as previously discussed, present an immediate and potentially fatal problem, but there are other insects to watch out for: no-see-ums, black flies, deer flies, horse flies, mosquitoes, and ticks. The first five insects produce itchy, painful bites that can be treated with a topical or oral antihistamine (or both, depending on how badly you react). Wearing protective clothing, including a hat, will put the bugs at a disadvantage, but it may be impractical or uncomfortable, especially in hot weather. If you prefer to use insect repellent instead, choose a product containing at least 35% DEET.

When it comes to pests along the A.T., ticks are the biggest concern, particularly in the Northeast, because they can carry Lyme and other diseases. Exercise caution when hiking through tall grass and underbrush in the spring, summer, and early fall, as warmer temperatures caused by climate change have increased the tick population. The deer tick, which carries Lyme disease, is tiny—about the size of a pinhead. It takes a while for a tick to become embedded, so do a thorough check at the end of the day to catch the tick before it catches you. Look carefully, because deer ticks can be hard to spot. Make sure to check behind ears, between toes, and in the groin, as ticks like warm, tight spaces.

Wear a hat and a long-sleeved shirt, and tuck the cuffs of long pants into your socks to discourage ticks. Too uncomfortable? Use a repellent with permethrin, and stick to the center of the trail to avoid brushing against branches and shrubs. Ticks, like mosquitoes, are attracted to heat and have been known to wait for months for a hot body to pass by. Wearing light-colored clothing will help you spot them easily.

If a tick attaches itself to your body, the best way to remove it is to grasp it as close to the skin as possible and then just pull it off. Then carefully wash the bite with soap and water. After you remove the tick, keep an eye out for the symptoms of Lyme disease—fever, headache, and pain and stiffness in joints and muscles—or for signs that might indicate other diseases, such as flulike symptoms or swelling and infection at the site of the bite. If left untreated, Lyme disease can produce lifelong muscular and nervous system impairment, brain damage, and, in 10% of victims, chronic, crippling arthritis. If you think you may be infected with Lyme disease, see your doctor.

Lyme disease affects more than 30,000 people a year, but be aware that more than a dozen tick-borne diseases exist (for example, Powassan virus, which is on the rise). Tick season runs April–October, with a peak of May–July.

HANTAVIRUS While infection with this rodent-borne virus—which can cause an often-fatal respiratory illness—is possible in the eastern United States, it's a much bigger concern in the West. It is also rare and difficult to contract: You must (1) have direct contact with the feces or urine of deer mice/white-footed mice or rice rats/cotton rats, or (2) you must breathe airborne particles containing their droppings.

Federal and state authorities have trapped and tested mice in A.T. shelters in southwest Virginia, where a thru-hiker contracted the disease in the early 1990s, without finding evidence of the disease. To be safe, though, do your best to avoid contact with rodents and their waste, which can carry other diseases besides hantavirus.

DOGS

From the *Leave No Trace Southeast Skills and Ethics* booklet:

"Wildlife and pets are not a good mix—even on a leash, dogs harass wildlife and disturb other visitors. . . . The best option is to leave dogs at home. Obedience champion or not, every dog is a potential carrier of diseases that infect wildlife."

If you decide to take your dog along anyway, please note the following:

- Dogs are prohibited in the following places along the Trail: **Baxter State Park** in Maine, the **Trailside Museum and Wildlife Center** at **Bear Mountain State Park** in New York (an alternative walk-around route is available here), and **Great Smoky Mountains National Park** in North Carolina and Tennessee.

- Dogs must be leashed wherever the A.T. passes through **National Park Service** lands, including/in addition to the following places: **Delaware Water Gap National Recreation Area** in New Jersey and Pennsylvania, the entire state of **Maryland, Harpers Ferry National Historical Park** in West Virginia, and along the **Blue Ridge Parkway** in Virginia. All that said, simply keeping your dog leashed at all times is the best strategy to avoid run-ins with wildlife, other dogs, and other hikers.

- Keep your dog away from water sources, and dispose of its waste as you would your own (see page 8).

MAINE

Hike	Page	Distance (mi)	Configuration	Time (hr)	Difficulty	Features
1. Katahdin	16	10.4	round-trip	9.5	★★★	mountain peak, scenic view, waterfall
2. Baxter Ponds Loop	18	5.1	loop	2.5	★	scenic view, pond or river
3. Little and Big Niagara Falls	20	2.6	round-trip	1.5	★	pond or river, waterfall, historic area, bird-watching
4. Gulf Hagas	22	8.2	round-trip	5.0	★★	scenic view, waterfall
5. Barren Ledges	23	4.5	round-trip	3.0	★★★	scenic view, pond or river, waterfall
6. Pleasant Pond Mountain	25	3.2	round-trip	2.0	★★★	mountain peak, scenic view, pond or river
7. Avery and West Peak of Bigelow	26	5.4	round-trip	5.5	★★★	mountain peak, scenic view
8. West Peak of Bigelow and The Horns	28	9.2	round-trip	8.0	★★★	mountain peak, scenic view, pond or river
9. Sugarloaf Mountain	30	5.8	round-trip	4.0	★★★	mountain peak, scenic view, pond or river
10. Saddleback Mountain	31	10.4	round-trip	8.0	★★★	mountain peak, scenic view, pond or river
11. Moxie, Long, and Sabbath Day Ponds	32	7.4	round-trip	3.75	★★★	pond or river, bird-watching
12. Dunn Notch and Falls	34	2.0	round-trip	1.25	★	waterfall
13. Baldpate Mountain	34	7.8	round-trip	6.0	★★★	mountain peak, scenic view
14. The Eyebrow	36	2.2	round-trip	1.5	★★	scenic view
15. Speck Pond	37	9.6	round-trip	8.5	★★★	scenic view, pond or river

DIFFICULTY ★★★ strenuous ★★ moderate ★ easy   CONFIGURATION ⟋ round-trip ↻ loop

mountain peak   scenic view   pond or river   waterfall   historic area   bird-watching

THE APPALACHIAN TRAIL IN MAINE is more rugged and remote than in any of the other 13 trail states. The northern terminus of the A.T. is at Baxter Peak, on top of Katahdin in Baxter State Park. From that peak, you can look to the southwest and see the Maine lake country that the A.T. crosses. The Trail in Maine traverses several prominent mountains, including the twin peaks of the Bigelow Range, the Crockers, Saddleback, Old Blue, the Baldpates, and the Mahoosuc Range. In the Mahoosucs, the A.T. features what is often described as the "toughest mile." This section through Mahoosuc Notch is a testament to the trail builders' imagination and a hiker's stamina: here the A.T. goes over and under an incredible boulder-filled notch. (Mahoosuc Notch is beyond the scope of this book—see *The Best of the Appalachian Trail: Overnight Hikes*.) The A.T. continues over Goose Eye and Mount Carlo on its way to the Maine–New Hampshire state line.

1 KATAHDIN

STRENUOUS | 10.4-mile round-trip | 9.5 hours

From Katahdin's Baxter Peak, the surrounding lakes shimmer in the sunlight thousands of feet below. Katahdin affords one of the most expansive wilderness views east of the Mississippi River and one of the most outstanding hikes on the A.T. Katahdin, known by the Abenaki Indians as *Kette-Adene,* meaning "greatest mountain," is not part of a range of mountains. Instead, the gray granite monolith towers alone over the central Maine forests. The A.T. follows the Hunt Spur Trail from Katahdin Stream Campground along the route used in 1804 by Charles Turner Jr., who made the first known ascent of the peak.

Katahdin is the crown jewel of Baxter State Park. Maine's governor, Percival Baxter, championed the idea for the park. Yet during his five terms in the state legislature and one term as governor, he failed to convince his colleagues to create the park. In 1931, after his term as governor ended, he bought more than 6,500 acres on and around Katahdin and gave the land to the state. By the time of his death in 1969, Baxter had extended his initial grant to more than 201,000 acres and had created the largest park east of the Mississippi devoted solely to wilderness use. As a condition of the grant,

Laurie and Leonard M. Adkins celebrate on Katahdin at the end of one of their thru-hikes.
Photo: Leonard M. Adkins

Baxter maintained that the area "forever be left in its natural wild state." In Baxter State Park, recreational use is secondary to wilderness preservation.

Katahdin is a difficult day hike, but the walk is well worth the effort. Leave early and carry plenty of warm clothes and raingear no matter what weather is expected below. Despite the difficulty, this hike is extremely popular. One year, we climbed the mountain on Labor Day weekend with what seemed like a continuous line of hikers along the route. Like all backcountry areas, the mountain is less crowded during the week than on weekends. For more information, contact the park at 207-723-5140 or baxterstatepark.org.

THE HIKE

From the trailhead at Katahdin Stream Campground, follow the A.T. north. Hike along Katahdin Stream 1.2 miles and reach the 50-foot cascade, Katahdin Stream Falls. After passing the falls, the Trail continues its moderate ascent another 1.6 miles before passing through The Boulders. The Boulders are tricky to traverse, even in good weather. Steel bars driven into the rock offer hand- and footholds to help you climb up and over the jumbles of rocks and begin the steady, steep ascent of Hunt Spur.

Just over 3.5 miles from Katahdin Stream Campground is The Gateway, the rim of the tableland. It is a large, relatively flat boulder field left by the glacier that planed off the top of the mountain. Reach Thoreau Spring, named for the famous philosopher whose attempted ascent of Katahdin ended here, at 4.2 miles. The spring does not offer a reliable source of water in dry weather. From Thoreau Spring, 1.0 mile of easy to moderate climbing along the boulder field leads you to Baxter Peak, the northern terminus of the A.T.

The return trip will go faster, but allow plenty of time to get off the mountain.

TRAILHEAD DIRECTIONS
Take I-95 to Exit 244 (Millinocket). Turn onto ME 157 West, and drive 11.3 miles. Turn right onto Katahdin Avenue, and drive just 0.2 mile; then turn left onto Bates Street. After 0.8 mile, Bates Street becomes Millinocket Road; continue 7.4 miles. Millinocket Road becomes Baxter Park Road; continue 8.7 miles. At the Togue Pond Gate, take a slight left onto Park Tote Road. Drive about 8 miles to the Katahdin Stream Campground.

GPS TRAILHEAD COORDINATES N45° 53.206' W68° 59.950'

2 BAXTER PONDS LOOP

EASY | 5.1-mile loop | 2.5 hours

This loop (the Grassy Pond Trail) is an easy leg-stretcher in Baxter State Park, which uses the A.T. You will pass four small ponds and, in good weather, will be afforded excellent views of Katahdin and other lesser peaks in the area from Daicey Pond. If you are planning on visiting Baxter Park with children, the Ponds Loop is your best bet for an enjoyable afternoon.

One of the most thrilling things that may happen to you on this hike is to turn a corner of the Trail just in time to catch a bull moose raising its head out of a pond. You might even hear it before you actually see it, as gallons upon gallons of water roll off a massive set of antlers, drip down the muscular neck, and splash loudly back into the pond. During the summer, a moose's favorite food is aquatic vegetation, such as water lilies and pondweeds, so you might also see a long strand of foliage hanging from its mouth. Long legs and short necks make it difficult for moose to eat or drink in shallow water, and this is why you will sometimes come upon them kneeling down.

Canoe racks at the west end of Daicey Pond   *Photo: Mary Alley*

THE HIKE

Walk from the campground back to the A.T. and follow it north 0.5 mile. You will be skirting the north shore of Daicey Pond. In another 0.5 mile, keep right to continue along the shore of Daicey Pond.

At 1.3 miles, the A.T. turns away from the shore of the pond to follow an old tote road. Almost 2 miles after leaving the campground, a side trail leads 0.1 mile to the south end of Grassy Pond. Pass the outlet of Grassy Pond and continue through a swamp on bog bridges.

At mile 2.2, reach the park's perimeter road, which is about 0.1 mile from Katahdin Stream Campground. Turn left onto the road and follow it 0.7 mile before making a left to follow the 0.1-mile trail that skirts Tracy Pond, with fine views of the Doubletop Mountains. In another 0.3 mile, you will skirt the shore of Elbow Pond and cross its outlet.

From the outlet, hike another 0.5 mile to the junction with the A.T. Follow the white blazes around the north shore of the pond and return to Daicey Pond Campground.

TRAILHEAD DIRECTIONS

Take I-95 to Exit 244 (Millinocket). Turn onto ME 157 West, and drive 11.3 miles. Turn right onto Katahdin Avenue. Drive 0.2 mile; then turn left onto Bates Street. After 0.8 mile, Bates becomes Millinocket Road; continue 7.4 miles. Millinocket Road becomes Baxter Park Road; continue 8.7 miles. At the Togue Pond Gate, take a slight left onto Park Tote Road. Drive 10 miles; then turn left onto the Daicey Pond Road. Drive a little over a mile; you will cross the A.T. just before you reach the Daicey Pond Campground.

GPS TRAILHEAD COORDINATES   N45° 52.882' W69° 01.792'

Flat rocks provide perches on which to enjoy Big Niagara Falls. *Photo: Leonard M. Adkins*

3 LITTLE AND BIG NIAGARA FALLS

EASY | 2.6-mile round-trip | 1.5 hours

A walk to a waterfall is always a nice way to spend a few leisurely hours in the morning or afternoon. This easy outing, which brings you to two falls, is made even more enjoyable by the abundance of birds often seen (or at least heard) going about their daily lives in the mixed hardwood/coniferous forest. Black-capped chickadees and several types of woodpeckers, such as pileated, downy, and hairy, are some of the most common.

Although Little and Big Niagara Falls may be small compared to some waterfalls coming down mountainsides, Nesowadnehunk Stream is wide, and its volume of water makes for impressive scenes. The rapid current precludes swimming, but there are many large, flat rocks on which to sunbathe and dangle your feet in the cooling water. This is an easy hike with just a bit of an uphill grade on the return.

THE HIKE

Walk from the campground back to the A.T. and turn left. A side trail to the right at 0.9 mile leads to the Toll Dam across Nesowadnehunk Stream. From the late 1800s to mid-1900s, the waterway played a major role in Maine's timber industry, because logs were floated downstream to the West Branch Penobscot River. The dam, first built in 1879, helped control water flow for the log drives.

A few hundred feet south of the dam side trail is another pathway to the right, leading in less than 100 yards to Little Niagara Falls. Stanchions, used as part of the 1800s apparatuses to get logs over the falls, are still visible. Anglers claim that the pools just below the falls provide some of the best brook trout fishing in the park.

At 1.1 miles into the hike is a short side trail to a spring; less than 0.2 mile later is the Trail, right, to Big Niagara Falls. Certainly larger than its counterpart upstream, the falls drop noisily into their basin, with large granite outcrops providing grandstand seats from which to watch the spectacle. Return to the campground by retracing your steps along the A.T.

TRAILHEAD DIRECTIONS

Take I-95 to Exit 244 (Millinocket). Turn onto ME 157 West, and drive 11.3 miles. Turn right onto Katahdin Avenue. Drive 0.2 mile; then turn left onto Bates Street. After 0.8 mile, Bates Street becomes Millinocket Road; continue 7.4 miles. Millinocket Road becomes Baxter Park Road; continue 8.7 miles. At the Togue Pond Gate, make a slight left onto Park Tote Road. Drive 10 miles; then turn left onto the Daicey Pond road. Drive a little over a mile; you will cross the A.T. just before you reach the Daicey Pond Campground.

GPS TRAILHEAD COORDINATES N45° 52.882' W69° 01.792'

4 GULF HAGAS

MODERATE | 8.2-mile round-trip | 5 hours

The Gulf Hagas day hike bends the rule about hikes in this book primarily following the A.T. Of the 8.2 miles, only 2.6 are on the A.T. The Gulf's deep slate canyon made it easy to bend the rule. It is a wilderness area of astounding beauty and can only be reached via the A.T.

Gulf Hagas Brook cuts its way through the canyon in a series of spectacular waterfalls. The pools below the falls create a number of swimming holes that hearty hikers may want to sample. You'll want to take care though: several of the descents from the Trail to the brook are quite steep and rocky. The easiest falls to reach for swimming are at the top and bottom of the Gulf Hagas Loop. This loop makes an especially good fall foliage hike if you're not interested in swimming.

THE HIKE

From the parking lot on the St. Regis Logging Road, take the side trail 0.2 mile north to the A.T. and reach the ford of the West Branch of the Pleasant River. The cold river water is usually only knee-deep, which makes for a relatively easy crossing. The rocks can be slippery, though, and you will need to go slow and be sure of your footing to avoid falling.

One mile beyond the river ford puts you in the center of the Hermitage, a stand of 100-foot white pines owned by the Maine Chapter of the Nature Conservancy. This type of tree was once used for the masts of sailing ships.

Just 1.5 miles from the parking lot, reach the junction with the Gulf Hagas Trail. Turn onto it. The Gulf Hagas Trail is a loop hike of 5.2 miles that begins and ends at this junction. Go a few feet and bear left to begin the loop. (You could cut the hike short by hiking out and back on a portion of the Gulf Hagas Trail instead of completing the loop.)

Hike 0.5 mile to a side trail leading 0.1 mile to a worthwhile view of the canyon at Hammond Street Pitch. Here the Gulf is more than 90 feet deep. Just over 0.25 mile farther, the Trail turns right, and another side trail leads to a view of the canyon.

Hike another 1.0 mile to a short side trail leading to the base of Buttermilk Falls, and another 0.5 mile to Stair Falls. The trail reaches the head of the Gulf in 0.75 mile and turns sharply right, leaving the river behind. In 0.25 mile, reach the Pleasant River

Road. Descend back to the starting point of the loop at its junction with the A.T. and return to the St. Regis Logging Road via the A.T. and the parking lot side trail.

TRAILHEAD DIRECTIONS

Take I-95 to Exit 199 (ME 16/Alton/LaGrange/Milo). Turn left onto ME 16 West, and drive 24.2 miles into Milo. Turn right onto Main Street (signs for ME 11). In just a few hundred feet, veer left onto ME 11, and drive 12.5 miles. Turn left onto Ebeemee Road/Katahdin Iron Works Road, and drive 6.5 miles to the Katahdin Iron Works Gate. (There might be a fee.) After passing through the gate, take the first right to stay on Katahdin Iron Works Road, and drive 3.4 miles. Stay left at the fork to stay on Katahdin Iron Works Road; then drive another 3.1 miles. Leave your car in the parking area 6.7 miles from the Katahdin Iron Works Gate.

GPS TRAILHEAD COORDINATES N45° 28.644' W69° 17.194'

5 BARREN LEDGES

STRENUOUS | 4.5-mile round-trip | 3 hours

A drive on a backcountry road, a stream ford, a shelter and a waterfall inside a deeply shaded gorge, a steep climb on what could be slippery trail, and a spectacular view of mountains and lakes. You would be hard-pressed to find a shorter hike more representative of what longer hikes in Maine can encompass.

Barren Ledges is located on the southern end of the 15-mile-long Barren-Chairback Range, and the southward-facing view from its open rock slopes can be breathtaking. To the east, the rounded mass of Boarstone Mountain rises sharply from Lake Onawa's southern shore. Almost directly below Barren Ledges is flat Bodfish Intervale, a wide valley believed to have once been underwater and a part of Lake Onawa.

THE HIKE

Follow the A.T. north and ford Long Pond Stream in 0.1 mile. (The stream is usually no more than knee-deep. However, you should not attempt it if the water is up, as rocks may be slippery and footing uneven.)

The view from Barren Ledges   *Photo: Leonard M. Adkins*

A short side trail to the left at 0.8 mile leads to Slugundy Gorge and Falls. At 0.9 mile is the side trail to the Long Pond Stream Lean-To, which overlooks its namesake waterway.

Beyond the lean-to you will climb steeply, gaining 800 feet in a bit more than a mile, and reaching a short side trail to a viewpoint atop Barren Slide. Continue 0.2 mile to arrive at the vista from Barren Ledges. Many people try to be here early to watch the sunrise. Retrace your steps along the A.T. to return to your car.

TRAILHEAD DIRECTIONS

Take I-95 to Exit 157 (US 2/ME 11/Newport/Skowhegan). Turn right onto ME 11, and drive 6.5 miles. In Corinna, continue onto ME 7, and drive 8.2 miles. Turn left onto ME 23 North, and drive 11.1 miles. Turn left onto ME 15 North/ME 6 West, and drive 1 mile. Turn right onto ME 150 North/Blaine Avenue, and drive 8.7 miles. MN 150 will curve to the right, but follow the sign for Willimantic and continue straight onto Norton Corner Road. Drive 6.9 miles, during which Norton Corner Road becomes Mountain Road. At the fork go right to stay on Mountain Road, and drive 2.9 miles. Turn left to stay on Mountain Road, and drive 1.6 miles to the Barren Mountain trailhead on the A.T.

GPS TRAILHEAD COORDINATES N45° 25.045' W69° 25.221'

6 PLEASANT POND MOUNTAIN

STRENUOUS | 3.2-mile round-trip | 2 hours

The climb to the top of Pleasant Pond Mountain gets a *strenuous* rating because you will climb more than 1,100 feet in only 1.3 miles. Yet what a reward you reap for this effort! Once on top, which is above tree line, you can wander about the broad plateau, walking across large slabs of slate, marveling at the 360° vista.

Look northward and you will see Big Squaw Mountain, the Barren–Chairback Range, and White Cap Mountain. On very clear days, if you have very sharp eyes, you can make out the summit of Katahdin, more than 140 trail miles away. To the east is Moxie Bald Mountain, and to the west are Sugarloaf, Bigelow, and Pierce Pond Mountains. Beyond Pleasant Pond and Moxie Mountain to the south are the flatter lands of Maine receding toward the coast.

There is also the added attraction of being able to take a swim in Pleasant Pond near the beginning and end of the hike.

THE HIKE

Follow the A.T. northward, coming to Pleasant Pond Lean-To in 0.3 mile. If you want to take a swim, you can follow the side trail at 0.5 mile, which goes right about 300 yards to a sandy beach along the shore of Pleasant Pond.

Beyond this point, the hike becomes a steep ascent, passing first through a mixed forest and then one of evergreens, before climbing above tree line to obtain the open summit at 1.6 miles. You might find remnants of an old fire tower as you walk, but also be looking for the geological history of the mountain etched into the rock. The slate beneath your feet gained its smooth surface as the glacier from the last ice age slid across it 25,000–14,000 years ago. The small grooves and notches are where rocks and other debris were ground across the slate as the glacier advanced and then receded. Return the way you came, possibly stopping for a swim to cool off and clean away any trail grime.

TRAILHEAD DIRECTIONS

From I-95, take Exit 133 (US 201) North. Turn left onto US 201 North, and drive 14.4 miles. Turn right onto Island Avenue/Main Street to continue on US 201 North. After 0.3 mile, turn left onto Court Street, and drive one block. Turn left onto High

Street, and drive one block again. Turn right onto Madison Avenue, which will quickly become US 201 again; drive 38.3 miles. In the town of Caratunk, turn right onto School Street, which will almost immediately become Pleasant Pond Road. Drive 3.2 miles and bear left at the fork. The roadway will soon become gravel. At the intersection about 1.5 miles later, continue straight, and leave your car in the parking area near the north end of Pleasant Pond.

GPS TRAILHEAD COORDINATES N45° 16.321' W69° 55.403'

7 AVERY AND WEST PEAK OF BIGELOW

STRENUOUS | 5.4-mile round-trip | 5.5 hours

This hike uses very little of the A.T., but it is another exception to the rule. The Bigelow Range is possibly the most outstanding in Maine. Bigelow is known as Maine's Second Mountain, next to Katahdin. The long, east–west range consists of six major peaks and a number of minor ones. The most spectacular are Avery (East) and West Peaks, followed closely by the Horns. This hike also uses the Firewardens Trail. Although it provides the shortest route to Avery and West Peaks, it is also the steepest ascent and descent.

View of Flagstaff Lake from Avery Peak
Photo: Chris M. Morris/Flickr/CC BY 2.0
(creativecommons.org/licenses/by/2.0)

Avery (East) Peak of Bigelow was named in honor of Myron H. Avery, a Mainer who was chairman of the Appalachian Trail Conservancy from 1931 to 1952. Avery was instrumental in the development of the A.T., particularly in Maine, where he all but single-handedly flagged and cut the route.

The views from Avery rank right up there with those from Katahdin, and eagle-eyed hikers might spot that particular mountain on a crystal-clear day, as well as New Hampshire's Mount Washington to the southwest. Both Avery Peak and West Peak feature an above-tree-line alpine area. These areas are home to the rare yellow-nosed vole, along with other interesting small animals. The plants found on these peaks are similar to those found atop Katahdin and New Hampshire's Mount Washington.

THE HIKE

From the parking area on Stratton Brook Pond Road, follow the blue-blazed Firewardens Trail northeast along an old tote road. Ascend gradually 1.2 miles to the junction with the blue-blazed Horns Pond Trail to the left. Ascend steeply along the Firewardens Trail. The final 0.75 mile to Bigelow Col is incredibly steep, gaining about 1,300 feet in elevation.

At the floor of Bigelow Col, reach the junction with the A.T. Campsites are available for those who wish to spend the night. Hike 0.5 mile north on the A.T. to the summit of Avery Peak (elevation 4,088'). En route to the summit, a small spring provides water for the col. From the summit of Avery Peak, hikers will find one of the most outstanding views in the northeast. The Barren–Chairback Range, White Cap, and Katahdin can all be seen to the northeast, while the Crockers, Saddlebacks, and Mahoosucs can be viewed stretching away to the southwest. On especially clear days, you can also see Mount Washington and the White Mountains of New Hampshire to the southwest. The border mountains of Canada are 30 miles to the northwest. Below, and paralleling the Bigelow Range, is Flagstaff Lake. The spillway elevation of the lake is at 1,146 feet.

Return to the col and follow the A.T. 0.25 mile south to the open summit of the West Peak of Bigelow. At an elevation of 4,150 feet, the views are similar to those found atop Avery Peak. Return once again to Bigelow Col and follow the Firewardens Trail to Stratton Brook Pond Road.

TRAILHEAD DIRECTIONS

From I-95, take Exit 130 (ME 104/Main Street/Waterville). Turn onto ME 104 North, and drive 13 miles. Turn right onto US 201A North, and drive 7.6 miles. Turn left onto Main Street, and drive 0.5 mile. Turn right to stay on Main Street, and drive 4.7 miles (during which Main Street becomes 201A North). Turn left onto ME 16 West, and drive 8.3 miles. Turn left to stay on ME 16 West, and drive another 7.6 miles. Turn right onto ME 16 West/ME 27 North. Drive 18.4 miles and then turn right onto Stratton Brook Pond Road. (You will have crossed the A.T. on ME 27 approximately 0.7 mile before reaching Stratton Brook Pond Road.) Drive about 1 mile on the gravel road to where it intersects the A.T. To use the Firewardens Trail, continue another mile to the trailhead and parking area.

GPS TRAILHEAD COORDINATES N45° 06.671' W70° 19.839'

8 WEST PEAK OF BIGELOW AND THE HORNS

STRENUOUS
9.2-mile round-trip, including optional side trip to North Horn | 8 hours

This loop hike uses very little of the A.T., but it provides the best of both worlds by allowing the hiker a whirlwind tour of the Bigelow Range, with spectacular views from both the West Peak of Bigelow and South Horn. A side trail leads 0.25 mile to the summit of North Horn, 0.5 mile north of Horns Pond. The mountain tarn with its two lean-tos is a good stopping place for a picnic lunch (if you begin your hike early in the day).

A tarn is defined as a small mountain lake or pond, especially one found in a cirque, a rounded bowl carved out by glacial action. As you stand next to the pond, surrounded by the extremely steep mountain walls rising to the Horns, there is no doubt as to what shaped the topography.

This hike also uses the Firewardens Trail. Although it provides the shortest route to West Peak, it also has the steepest ascent and descent. This loop with the Horns Pond Trail not only provides a greater enjoyment of the Bigelows but also allows a more gradual descent than on the Firewardens Trail.

In 1976, the people of Maine saved most of the Bigelow Range (33,000 acres) from development. A state referendum decided the fate of the Bigelows, and the citizens of Maine voted (by a narrow, 3,000-vote margin) to make them a wilderness preserve. The preserve protects 17 miles of the A.T. (the entire mountain range and a buffer zone).

THE HIKE

From the parking area on Stratton Brook Pond Road, follow the blue-blazed Firewardens Trail northeast along an old tote road. Ascend gradually 1.2 miles to the junction with the blue-blazed Horns Pond Trail to the left.

Ascend steeply along the Firewardens Trail. The final 0.75 mile to Bigelow Col is incredibly steep, gaining about 1,300 feet in elevation. At the floor of Bigelow Col, reach the junction with the A.T. Campsites are available for those who wish to spend the night.

From the floor of Bigelow Col, take the A.T. south. This will lead you to the open summit of the West Peak of Bigelow after a 0.25-mile ascent. Here, at an elevation of

4,150 feet, the views are spectacular. The Barren–Chairback Range, White Cap, and Katahdin can all be seen to the northeast. The Crockers, Saddlebacks, and Mahoosucs can be viewed stretching away to the southwest. On especially clear days, Mount Washington and the White Mountains of New Hampshire can also be seen to the southwest. The border mountains of Canada are slightly more than 30 miles to the northwest. Below, and paralleling the Bigelow Range, is Flagstaff Lake. The spillway elevation of the lake is at 1,146 feet.

Upon descending West Peak, traverse the crest of the range about 1 mile; then ascend the cone-shaped dome of South Horn. From the small but open summit (elevation 3,831'), there is a view of Horns Pond directly below the crest of the range.

From the summit, the Trail descends steeply toward the pond. Hike 0.1 mile to the junction with a side trail that leads 0.25 mile to the summit of North Horn (elevation 3,815'). Hike another 0.5 mile and reach Horns Pond Lean-Tos on the shore of Horns Pond, one of the most outstanding tarns in the state of Maine.

Another 0.25 mile brings you to the junction of the Horns Pond Trail, which heads south. Follow the Horns Pond Trail, descending moderately 1.0 mile before skirting a beaver pond. Continue a gradual descent through hardwoods, following an old logging road another 1.4 miles to the junction with the Firewardens Trail. Follow the Firewardens Trail another 1.2 miles to the parking area.

TRAILHEAD DIRECTIONS

From I-95, take Exit 130 (ME 104/Main Street/Waterville). Turn onto ME 104 North, and drive 13 miles. Turn right onto US 201A North, and drive 7.6 miles. Turn left onto Main Street, and drive 0.5 mile. Turn right to stay on Main Street, and drive 4.7 miles (during which Main Street becomes 201A North). Turn left onto ME 16 West, and drive 8.3 miles. Turn left to stay on ME 16 West, and drive another 7.6 miles. Turn right onto ME 16 West/ME 27 North. Drive 18.4 miles and then turn right onto Stratton Brook Pond Road. (You will have crossed the A.T. on ME 27 approximately 0.7 mile before reaching Stratton Brook Pond Road.) Drive about 1 mile on the gravel road to where it intersects the A.T. To use the Firewardens Trail, continue 1 mile to the trailhead and parking area.

GPS TRAILHEAD COORDINATES N45° 06.671' W70° 19.839'

9 SUGARLOAF MOUNTAIN

STRENUOUS | 5.8-mile round-trip | 4 hours

At 4,237 feet, Sugarloaf Mountain is Maine's second-highest peak. The A.T. went over the summit prior to the 1970s, when it was relocated to avoid ski resort development. This hike uses a 0.6-mile side trail to attain the mountaintop for a grand vista, which on clear days can reach from Mount Washington in New Hampshire to Katahdin in Maine's Baxter State Park—a distance of more than 300 trail miles.

Views of the nearby ridgelines include Crocker Mountain to the north, the Bigelow Range to the northeast, Mount Abraham to the south and—somewhat to the west—Spaulding Mountain and Poplar Ridge. (The final link of the Appalachian Trail was completed on a shoulder of Spaulding Mountain in 1937.)

There is no doubt this is a strenuous route suitable only for experienced hikers. First is the ford of the South Branch of the Carrabassett River, which can be difficult and dangerous during high water. Then there is a steep climb on open slopes to the junction with the side trail to the summit, which gains another 700 feet in 0.6 mile. In all, the elevation gain is more than 2,000 feet in less than 3 miles.

The descent on the return can be equally difficult, because the Trail is narrow in places where it crosses open terrain, and some people may experience an uncomfortable feeling of exposure.

THE HIKE

Follow the A.T. south from the road, fording the South Branch of the Carrabassett River at 0.1 mile, and begin to climb almost immediately through a mixed forest. The trees soon fade away and you are walking upon an open slope with low-growing vegetation as you come to the top of a deep ravine at 0.9 mile.

Cross a small stream at 1.7 miles, turn left onto the Sugarloaf Mountain Trail at 2.3 miles, and reach the summit at 2.9 miles. If you are here during the week in summer, you may have no companions other than an array of communication towers, buildings, and the apparatus for the resort's ski lift. Retrace your steps to finish the hike.

TRAILHEAD DIRECTIONS

Take I-95 to Exit 112B and turn onto ME 27 North. Drive 24.6 miles. Turn left onto US 2, and drive 9.5 miles; then turn right onto Main Street (signs for ME 27). Drive

3 miles, during which Main Street becomes ME 27 North. Turn right to stay on ME 27 North, and drive 35.9 miles. Turn right onto the (possibly) unsigned gravel Caribou Valley Road (about 1 mile west of the Sugarloaf USA access road). The conditions of Caribou Valley Road vary greatly from time to time, and it may not always be possible to drive the 4.4 miles to the A.T. crossing.

GPS TRAILHEAD COORDINATES N45° 02.364' W70° 20.680'

10 SADDLEBACK MOUNTAIN

STRENUOUS | 10.4-mile round-trip; 8 hours

Saddleback Mountain is one of the best day hikes in the state. On this hike, you will find a tremendous rock outcrop, two mountain ponds, and an above-tree-line climb. Piazza Rock, a large granite slab jutting from the side of a cliff, and the surrounding slab cave system are located on two short side trails. (If your time is limited or you are hiking with others who are not in the best shape, you could decide to do a day hike just to these two destinations. The outing would be an easy round-trip of 3 miles.)

Beyond the side trails, the A.T. skirts the banks of Ethel and Eddy Ponds, two lovely mountain ponds at the base of Saddleback, and then ascends the 4,116-foot mountain. The tough climb is well worth the effort because the 360° view from the summit is magical.

THE HIKE

From the trailhead on ME 4, follow the A.T. north. In 0.1 mile, you will cross Sandy River on a footbridge. In another 1.7 miles, the Trail reaches Piazza Rock Lean-To. A short side trail beside the shelter leads to the overhanging Piazza Rock. Another side trail, located 0.2 mile farther north on the A.T., leads to the Caves, a slab cave system. Both side trips are well worth the effort, but perhaps save them for your return from Saddleback to ensure that you have enough time for the above-tree-line section of this day hike.

From the lean-to, hike 0.7 mile to the shore of Ethel Pond. In another 0.5 mile, you will pass through a boggy section called Mud Pond, and 0.5 mile past the bog, you will reach the shore of Eddy Pond. Beyond Eddy Pond, the Trail ascends steeply up the slopes of Saddleback Mountain. The Trail is above tree line for the last 1.1 miles. Be extremely careful in this section. You are very exposed on the mountain and need to be prepared for severe weather. Make a quick retreat if a storm develops, as the mountain offers no protection from the elements.

From the summit of Saddleback Mountain at 5.7 miles, you can see Bald Mountain, East Kennebago Mountain, Jackson Mountain, the Bigelow Range, and many other neighboring mountains and ponds. To return, follow the A.T. south to ME 4.

TRAILHEAD DIRECTIONS

From I-95 near Augusta, take Exit 113 (ME 3/Augusta/Belfast). At the two traffic circles, follow signs for ME 3 West. Drive 1.1 miles on ME 3 West; then turn right onto ME 27 North/New Belgrade Road, and drive 22.4 miles. Turn left onto US 2 West, and drive 9.5 miles. At the light in Farmington, turn left to stay on US 2 West another 0.4 mile. Then turn right onto Oak Street, which quickly becomes Town Farm Road. Drive 3.4 miles; then turn left onto ME 4 North/Fairbanks Road, and drive 7.6 miles. Make a slight left to stay on ME 4 North; then drive 19.4 miles to where it intersects the A.T., at the Piazza Rock Trailhead. The parking area will be on your left.

GPS TRAILHEAD COORDINATES N44° 53.221' W70° 32.413'

11 MOXIE, LONG, AND SABBATH DAY PONDS

MODERATE | 7.4-mile round-trip | 3.75 hours

The ponds of Maine are some of its most beautiful places, and on this hike you experience not just one, but three. The flora and fauna are also representative of the state's variety. The hike begins in a hardwood forest whose floor is dotted with trout lily and spring beauty just as the weather begins to warm after winter. At a bit higher elevation, in the spruce and fir forest, be on the lookout for a spruce grouse or a Canada jay. In New England, the spruce grouse is often called a partridge. The Canada jay has earned the nickname "camp robber" because it has been known to be brave enough to boldly hop into camp and make off with bits of food from a hungry hiker's plate. Moose and loons are often seen in or around all three ponds.

Long Pond provides a view of a large expanse of sky.   *Photo: Leonard M. Adkins*

The great scenery and gentle terrain—there are only a few short uphills—make this the perfect place to introduce friends to the pleasures of hiking without subjecting them to the rigors of a more rugged topography. Swimming opportunities abound, and you might even decide to stay overnight at the shelter overlooking Sabbath Day Pond.

THE HIKE

Follow the A.T. northward, reaching the forested summit of Spruce Mountain at 0.8 mile, and arriving near the north shore of Moxie Pond at 1.6 miles.

Rise to an overlook of Long Pond on Bates Ledge at 2.7 miles, and come to a sandy beach along the pond's edge at 3.4 miles. You reach the day's destination, Sabbath Day Pond, with its waterside lean-to, at 3.7 miles. Return the way you came.

TRAILHEAD DIRECTIONS

From US 2 in Rumford, turn onto ME 17 West/Roxbury Road and drive about 26 miles. The A.T. parking area is about 0.5 mile north of the Bemis Stream trailhead, on the south side of the road.

GPS TRAILHEAD COORDINATES N44° 50.162' W70° 42.596'

12 DUNN NOTCH AND FALLS

EASY | 2-mile round-trip | 1.25 hours

This short, woodsy hike leads to the impressive Dunn Notch Falls. The West Branch of the Ellis River drops through the notch in two waterfalls. The Trail crosses the river between the upper and lower falls, both of which can be reached by side trails. The lower falls is a 60-foot double waterfall dropping sharply into the gorge below.

THE HIKE

Walk south on the A.T. from East B Hill Road. The Trail will cross a brook and enter Dunn Notch. At mile 0.8, reach the West Branch of the Ellis River. An old tote road leads down to the bottom of the lower falls. By following the river upstream 0.2 mile, you can reach the upper falls. Return to East B Hill Road by retracing your steps.

TRAILHEAD DIRECTIONS

From US 2 in Rumford, turn onto ME 17 West/Roxbury Road, and drive 2.6 miles. Turn left onto Black Bridge Road, and drive 0.1 mile to cross the Swift River; then turn right onto ME 120 West, and drive 12.3 miles to the town of Andover. Continue 8.1 miles (ME 120 West becomes Newton Street, then Upton Road, then East B Hill Road) to the trailhead, where the A.T. crosses East B Hill Road.

GPS TRAILHEAD COORDINATES N44° 40.069' W70° 53.585'

13 BALDPATE MOUNTAIN

STRENUOUS | 7.8-mile round-trip | 6 hours

On this day hike, you will climb out of Grafton Notch to cross the West Peak of Baldpate Mountain (elevation 3,680') with its partially open summit. From West Peak, you will drop sharply into the sag between the mountain's two peaks and then climb to the cairn marking the summit of the East Peak (elevation 3,812'). The climb involves areas where you will have to use your hands to negotiate some steep inclines. There is a more than 2,000-foot elevation difference between Grafton Notch and the peaks of Baldpate. The open summit on the East Peak and the fine 360° views of the surrounding western Maine mountains are well worth the work it will take to reach the summit.

An optional side trip on your return hike down the mountain will take you to Table Rock. The 1.5-mile trail passes an overlook with steep cliffs falling away to the notch below. The trail continues on to meet the A.T. before it crosses ME 26.

THE HIKE

From the trailhead in Grafton Notch, follow the A.T. north. In 0.1 mile, reach the junction with the Lower Table Rock Trail. Continue along the A.T. another 0.75 mile to the Upper Table Rock Trail. Hike 1.4 miles past the Upper Table Rock Trail junction and, near Baldpate Lean-To, cross a small stream at the base of Baldpate. For the next 0.75 mile, climb sharply up the mountain, gaining more than 1,000 feet in elevation. At mile 3.0, reach the summit of the West Peak of Baldpate; then drop steeply into the sag between the West and East Peaks. From the West Peak, it is 0.9 mile to the open summit of the East Peak of Baldpate Mountain.

On your return trip to Grafton Notch, heading south on the A.T., there is an optional side trip to Table Rock. Take the Upper Table Rock Trail, follow it to the rock, and then continue along the Lower Table Rock Trail to its junction with the A.T. The side trip will add 0.75 mile and approximately half an hour. The view is worth the side trip if you have the time.

TRAILHEAD DIRECTIONS

From Rumford, drive on US 2 West about 16.5 miles to Newry. Turn right onto ME 26 North, and drive 12.1 miles. The parking lot in Grafton Notch is right off ME 26, on the left.

GPS TRAILHEAD COORDINATES N44° 35.419' W70° 56.787'

Looking into Grafton Notch   *Photo: Leonard M. Adkins*

14 THE EYEBROW

MODERATE | 2.2-mile round-trip | 1.5 hours

This short but steep hike leads to a viewpoint overlooking the sheer cliffs that drop to Grafton Notch. The hike uses the A.T. and the Eyebrow Trail to form a loop to this outstanding view. The hike is rated as moderate because, though the total distance is short, the climb out of the notch is quite steep, gaining 800 feet in elevation in just over 1 mile.

THE HIKE

From the trailhead at Grafton Notch on ME 26, follow the A.T. south. In 0.1 mile, reach the lower end of the Eyebrow Trail. Continue following the A.T. 1.1 miles to the junction with the upper end of the Eyebrow Trail. Follow the Eyebrow Trail and reach the Eyebrow in 0.1 mile. After taking in the fine view, return via the Lower Eyebrow Trail. This section of the trail will lead you back to the A.T. in 0.75 mile. The Lower Eyebrow Trail joins the A.T. 0.1 mile from the parking area.

TRAILHEAD DIRECTIONS

From Rumford, drive on US 2 West about 16.5 miles to Newry. Turn right onto ME 26 North, and drive 12.1 miles. The parking lot in Grafton Notch is right off ME 26, on the left.

GPS TRAILHEAD COORDINATES N44° 35.419' W70° 56.787'

15 SPECK POND

STRENUOUS | 9.6-mile round-trip | 8.5 hours

At nearly 3,500 feet in elevation, Speck Pond is a beautiful tarn located between Old Speck and Mahoosuc Arm. The pond has a good swimming area near the campsite on the north shore. The Appalachian Mountain Club keeps a maintainer at the trail shelter and campsite and charges a fee for overnight use. On the way up, you could take an optional 0.6-mile round-trip to the summit of Old Speck for views of Grafton Notch, the Mahoosuc Range, and other western Maine mountains. On the return trip, you can take the Eyebrow Trail to the Eyebrow and enjoy spectacular views from the 800-foot cliffs to the notch below. Be sure to allow plenty of time for your return trip on this long but beautiful day hike.

THE HIKE

From the trailhead at Grafton Notch on ME 26, follow the A.T. south. In 0.1 mile, reach the lower end of the Eyebrow Trail and continue on the A.T. Hike another 1.1 miles to the junction with the upper end of the Eyebrow Trail. Continue along the A.T. and reach the junction with the side trail to the summit of Old Speck at mile 3.5. This trail leads 0.3 mile to the wooded summit and observation tower on Old Speck. Continue along the A.T. from the intersection and descend steeply 1.3 miles to Speck Pond. Return to the trailhead by way of the A.T. north.

An option on the return trip is to follow the Eyebrow Trail from its upper junction down to its lower terminus on the A.T., just 0.1 mile from the parking area at Grafton Notch. It is 0.1 mile to the Eyebrow from the upper junction and another 0.75 mile to the lower terminus.

TRAILHEAD DIRECTIONS

From Rumford, drive on US 2 West for about 16.5 miles to Newry. Turn right onto ME 26 North, and drive 12.1 miles. The parking lot in Grafton Notch is right off of ME 26, on the left.

GPS TRAILHEAD COORDINATES N44° 35.419' W70° 56.787'

NEW HAMPSHIRE

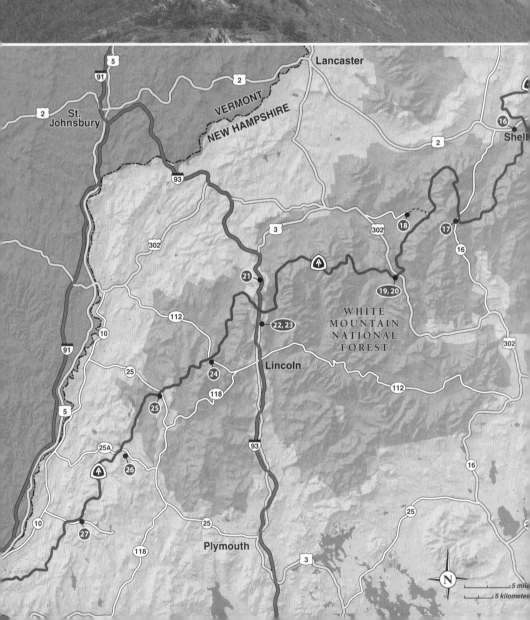

Lancaster

VERMONT
NEW HAMPSHIRE

St. Johnsbury

Shell

WHITE MOUNTAIN NATIONAL FOREST

Lincoln

Plymouth

N

5 miles
5 kilometers

Hike	Page	Length (mi)	Configuration	Time (hr)	Difficulty	Features
16. Mount Hayes	40	6.6	round-trip	4.0	★★	mountain peak, scenic view
17. Wildcat Mountain	41	6.0	round-trip	5.0	★★★	mountain peak, scenic view, pond or river
18. Mount Washington	43	10.0	round-trip	8.5	★★★	mountain peak, scenic view
19. Webster Cliffs	45	6.6	round-trip	6.0	★★★	scenic view
20. Ethan Pond	46	5.8	round-trip	4.75	★★★	scenic view, pond or river
21. Mount Lafayette and Mount Lincoln	48	9.6	round-trip	9.5	★★★	mountain peak, scenic view
22. Mount Liberty	49	8.4	round-trip	7.0	★★★	mountain peak, scenic view
23. Lonesome Lake	51	7.4	round-trip	4.5	★★	mountain peak, pond or river, waterfall
24. Mount Moosilauke	52	7.6	round-trip	7.5	★★★	mountain peak, scenic view, waterfall
25. Wachipauka Pond	53	4.2	round-trip	2.5	★★	pond or river
26. Mount Cube	54	7.0	round-trip	6.0	★★★	mountain peak, scenic view
27. Smarts Mountain	56	7.6	round-trip	6.0	★★	mountain peak, scenic view

DIFFICULTY ★★★ strenuous ★★ moderate ★ easy   CONFIGURATION ⟋ round-trip

▲ mountain peak   👓 scenic view   ≋ pond or river   ⟋ waterfall

39

FROM THE MAHOOSUC RANGE ON the Maine–New Hampshire state line, the Appalachian Trail in New Hampshire runs west over the rugged Carter–Moriah and Wildcat Ranges to Pinkham Notch. From the notch, the Trail heads into the northern Presidential Range with miles of above-tree-line trail. This is a very rugged and remote section of trail in the White Mountains National Forest, which attracts thousands of visitors each year. Many visitors underestimate the ruggedness of the terrain. The weather can quickly turn severe in these high elevations: even if the weather down below is expected to be nice, be prepared for the worst when hiking in the Whites. Mount Washington can get snow year-round.

As the A.T. crosses the White Mountains, it goes over some of the area's best-known peaks, including Mount Madison, Mount Washington, Mount Lafayette, Franconia Ridge, Kinsman Mountain, and Mount Moosilauke. From the Whites, the Trail traverses Mount Cube and Smarts Mountain on the way to Hanover. It passes by Dartmouth College, home of the Dartmouth Outing Club, which maintains a portion of the Trail here and in Vermont. The A.T. leaves the state at the Connecticut River.

16 MOUNT HAYES

MODERATE | **6.6-mile round-trip** | **4 hours**

Mount Hayes is the place to hike to in early spring and late fall. About 2,000 feet lower in elevation than the surrounding Northern Presidential and Carter–Moriah Ranges, its open, 2,555-foot summit provides a platform from which to look up to those higher peaks, which are often covered in snow, while Mount Hayes is free of any frozen precipitation.

Rising from the Androscoggin River Valley, the hike, which gains approximately 1,500 feet in 3 miles, begins by winding through stands of paper birch and passing by several views of the river below and the mountains above.

THE HIKE

Follow the Appalachian/Centennial Trail north from the parking area, watching for white blazes to guide you through several turns within the first few hundred feet of hiking. Pass a couple of viewpoints and drop to a small stream at 0.7 mile. The Trail soon breaks out of the trees, and stone cairns point the way as you ascend open slopes along the eastern side of Mount Hayes.

The best views of the journey occur at 2.8 miles on the eastern summit of Mount Hayes. You could turn back here, but just so that you can have the satisfaction of reaching the mountain's highest point, continue across open slopes another 0.3 mile to where the Centennial Trail comes to an end, at the junction with the Mahoosuc Trail. A left onto the Mahoosuc Trail will bring you to the top of the mountain in an additional 0.2 mile. Retrace your steps to the trailhead.

TRAILHEAD DIRECTIONS

From I-93 in Vermont, take Exit 1 (VT 18/US 2/St. Johnsbury). Turn onto VT 18 North (signs for US 2), and drive 0.4 mile. Turn right onto US 2 East, and drive 23.9 miles. At the fork, veer right to stay on US 2 East and cross the bridge into New Hampshire. At the traffic circle, take the first exit to stay on US 2 East, and drive 0.8 mile. At the fork, go left to stay on US 2 East, and drive 23.2 miles. Turn right to stay on US 2, and drive 4.8 miles; then turn left onto North Road, and drive 0.5 mile. Turn left onto Hogan Road, and drive 0.7 mile to the trailhead.

GPS TRAILHEAD COORDINATES N44° 24.0359' W71° 07.621'

17 WILDCAT MOUNTAIN

STRENUOUS | 6-mile round-trip | 5 hours

The Carter–Moriah Range is both rugged and wild. This particular hike is especially exhilarating because it passes an eerily beautiful boggy area along the Ellis River and Lost Pond before ascending Wildcat Mountain. Wildcat features five peaks, but this hike will take you to only two—Peaks East and D. Atop Peak East (elevation 4,046'), you will pass near the Wildcat Mountain Gondolas. In season, the gondola can be taken back down to NH 16. Most of the ski trails descend to NH 16 as well.

The peaks get progressively higher as you head northward. If you feel you have the time and energy, it is another strenuous 1.8 miles to Peak A of Wildcat Mountain (elevation 4,380').

THE HIKE

From the Appalachian Mountain Club Visitor Center in
Pinkham Notch, the A.T. north
crosses NH 16 and follows the
Lost Pond Trail to a wooden
bridge over a small bog. Ascending slightly from the Ellis River,
pass around the eastern shore of
Lost Pond, and continue along
the outlet stream. Just under
1 mile from Pinkham Notch,
turn left onto the Wildcat Ridge
Trail. To the right, the Wildcat

View from Wildcat Mountain   *Photo: D.R.Davis*

Ridge Trail leads 0.1 mile to NH 16 and Glen Ellis Falls.

Hike another 0.25 mile and begin the steep ascent of Wildcat Mountain. Use extra
care when climbing, especially when reaching the ledges of the mountain. From the
lower ledges at mile 1.4, ascend to the middle ledges and pass a side trail to the left
that leads to a spring. Reach the upper ledges at mile 2.4.

In another 0.1 mile, ascend the lower Peak East of Wildcat, and 0.25 mile later,
reach the summit of Peak East (elevation 4,046'). The Trail swings northward and
descends slightly, bypassing the terminal building of the Wildcat Mountain Gondolas.
From the terminal building, ascend northeast to Peak D (elevation 4,063'), where
there are views of Tuckerman Ravine to the left and Huntington Ravine to the right.
There are also great views of the northern Presidential Range.

Return via the A.T. (Wildcat Ridge Trail and Lost Pond Trail) to NH 16 at Pinkham
Notch. Or, if the gondolas are in operation, you can ride back down to the highway.

TRAILHEAD DIRECTIONS

From I-93, take Exit 36 for NH 141 (So Franconia). Drive 0.4 mile on NH 141 East;
then turn left onto US 3 North, and drive 11.5 miles. Turn right on NH 115 North,
and drive 9.7 miles. Turn right onto US 2 East, and drive 12.5 miles to Gorham. Turn
right onto Main Street, and drive 1.4 miles. Turn right onto NH 16 South, and drive
10.7 miles. The Pinkham Notch Visitor Center will be on your right.

GPS TRAILHEAD COORDINATES N44° 15.424' W71° 15.159'

18 MOUNT WASHINGTON

STRENUOUS | 10-mile round-trip | 8.5 hours

There are only 2.5 miles of the A.T. on this outing, but it is the shortest loop hike you can take to Mount Washington and is possibly the least steep way to reach the mountain's summit.

At 6,288 feet, Mount Washington is New England's highest peak. The views from its summit are in proportion to the grandeur of the mountain. The 360° vista takes in the Green Mountains of Vermont to the west, the ridgelines along the United States–Canada border to the north, the Mahoosuc Mountains of Maine to the east, and, on clear days, the Atlantic Ocean more than 70 miles to the south.

This hike should not be undertaken lightly. It is an arduous journey with a steep climb and a traverse of more than 4 miles above tree line across fields of felsenmeer—huge rocks and boulders that have been broken into jagged pieces by the freezing and thawing of water in their joints. Mount Washington is purported to have the worst weather in the world (trail signs warn about this as you climb). Days that appear sunny and warm when you start the hike can quickly turn cold, wet, and windy. Always carry enough clothing to protect you in these conditions.

THE HIKE

Cross the road from the parking area and follow the combined Jewell/Boundary Trail to cross the Ammonoosuc River. An easy ascent brings you to an intersection where you stay right to continue along the Jewell Trail. Pass by a side trail that leads to the Cog Railway at 1 mile, continuing to climb, sometimes steeply, with the trees getting progressively smaller and the trail rockier.

Reach treel ine at 3 miles and then come to the combined A.T./Gulfside Trail at 3.7 miles. Turn right and pass the Mount Clay Loop Trail. (In 2003, the New Hampshire legislature renamed Mount Clay in honor of Ronald Reagan, but the U.S. Board on Geographic Names later rejected the name.) Pass by the Westside Trail at 4.1 miles, and stay right where the Great Gulf Trail descends left at 4.6 miles. Soon leave the Gulfside Trail and follow the A.T. across the cog railway tracks to turn left and ascend along the combined A.T./Trinity Heights Connector Trail.

Reach the top of Mount Washington (the site of a weather station, restaurant, parking lot, and railway station) at 6.1 miles, and begin to descend its southwestern

Leonard M. Adkins atop Mount Washington's 6,288-foot summit   *Photo: Laurie Adkins*

side along the combined Crawford Path–A.T. Stay on the white-blazed A.T., passing between two of the Lakes of the Clouds and reaching the Lakes of the Clouds Hut at 6.9 miles. (Drinks and snacks available in season.)

Walk behind the hut and descend steeply on the Ammonoosuc Ravine Trail. On the way down is a short side trail to the Gorge, with waterfalls and base pools. The Trail also goes by Gem Pool and runs along the Ammonoosuc River before returning you to your car at 10.0 miles.

TRAILHEAD DIRECTIONS

From I-93, take Exit 36 for NH 141 (So Franconia). Drive 0.4 mile on NH 141 East; then turn left onto US 3 North, and drive 9.4 miles. Turn right onto US 302 East, and drive 4.4 miles. Turn left onto Base Station Road, and drive about 5 miles to the trail-head parking, which is about 0.2 mile before the entrance to the Mount Washington Cog Railway.

GPS TRAILHEAD COORDINATES   N44° 16.038' W71° 21.694'

Grafton Notch as seen from Webster Cliffs   *Photo: Leonard M. Adkins*

19 WEBSTER CLIFFS

STRENUOUS | 6.6-mile round-trip | 6 hours

The panorama from Webster Cliffs will take your breath away, or what little you have left after the steep ascent from Crawford Notch. Crawford Notch is named in honor of Abel and Ethan Allen Crawford, the father-son team that carved out the first trail to the summit of Mount Washington. After cutting the path in 1819, the Crawfords went on to establish the first hostelries for tourists in the notch that now bears their name.

Timothy Nash discovered the notch while hunting moose in 1777. Because there was no pass through the White Mountains at the time (you had to go around them), Nash's discovery made passage through the rugged mountains possible. Almost immediately, a road was built that crossed the Saco River (which flows through the notch) 32 times. Although passage was difficult, it was easier than traveling all the way around the Whites. The first item to be ported through the new passage was a keg of rum that is said to have ended up considerably lighter when it reached the other end.

In 1825, Samuel Willey opened a hostel in Crawford Notch. The following year, he and his entire family were killed when a ton of debris fell from the mountain wall and demolished the hostel. The slide (which helped shape the geophysical aspect of the notch) did not slow the activity in the notch. Summer tourists still flocked to the area, and the road remained a prime commercial route. The Willey House site and the Willey Slide are still visible just 1 mile north of the A.T.'s crossing in the notch.

THE HIKE

From Crawford Notch on US 302 (elevation 1,277'), the A.T. follows the Webster Cliffs Trail east. A short distance from the road, the A.T. crosses a bridge over the Saco River then climbs steeply, winding through a hardwood forest. At mile 1.8, reach Webster Cliffs. For the next 1.5 miles, the Trail follows the cliffs to the summit of Mount Webster (elevation 3,910'). To return to Crawford Notch, follow the A.T.– Webster Cliffs Trail south to US 302.

TRAILHEAD DIRECTIONS

From I-93, take Exit 36 for NH 141 (So Franconia). Drive 0.4 mile on NH 141 East; then turn left onto US 3 North and drive 9.4 miles. Turn right onto US 302 East, and drive 8.4 miles. Turn right into the entrance for the AMC Highland Center at Crawford Notch.

GPS TRAILHEAD COORDINATES N44° 10.267' W71° 23.285'

20 ETHAN POND

STRENUOUS | 5.8-mile round-trip | 4.75 hours

Located along the edges of the Pemigewasset Wilderness, this hike takes you across a low point in the Willey Range (elevation 2,907') before reaching Ethan Pond. Although the elevation rise is relatively gradual, there is still a gain of more than 1,500 feet in the trip to Ethan Pond. This elevation gain alone makes the trip a notch over moderate when it comes to the energy expended.

Pretty Ethan Pond is home to both moose and bear. Many have been spotted there, so keep an eye out. Tamarack, also called the eastern larch, lines the shores of the pond.

THE HIKE

From US 302 in Crawford Notch, follow the A.T. south up Willey House Station Road. Ascend the path to the right of the parking area, cross over railroad tracks, and take the combined A.T.–Ethan Pond Trail into the woods.

At mile 0.5, reach the intersection of the Arethusa–Ripley Falls Trail, which heads left 0.3 mile to Ripley Falls, 2.5 miles to Arethusa Falls, and 4.0 miles back to US 302.

Moose have been seen grazing in Ethan Pond.   *Photo: Leonard M. Adkins*

Continue along the A.T. and ascend rather steeply, then more gradually, 0.5 mile. At mile 1.6, reach the junction with the Kedron Flume Trail on the right, which descends steeply to the Willey House on US 302.

In another 0.25 mile, the A.T.–Ethan Pond Trail turns left and the Willey Range Trail goes straight. Continue on the A.T. and reach the height of the land in 0.25 mile. Begin a slight descent along a former logging road and, just over 1 mile later, reach the side trail to Ethan Pond. To return to Crawford Notch, follow the A.T.–Ethan Pond Trail north.

TRAILHEAD DIRECTIONS

From I-93, take Exit 36 for NH 141 (So Franconia). Drive 0.4 mile on NH 141 East; then turn left onto US 3 North, and drive 9.4 miles. Turn right onto US 302 East, and drive 8.4 miles. Turn right into the entrance for the AMC Highland Center at Crawford Notch.

GPS TRAILHEAD COORDINATES N44° 10.267' W71° 23.285'

Looking into Franconia Notch   *Photo: Leonard M. Adkins*

21 MOUNT LAFAYETTE AND MOUNT LINCOLN

STRENUOUS | 9.6-mile round-trip | 9.5 hours

This day hike is in one of the more spectacular sections of the Whites. It uses very little of the A.T., but it definitely had to be an exception to our rule. Both Mount Lafayette and Mount Lincoln are above tree line, reaching over 5,000 feet in elevation—tree line occurs on Franconia Ridge at approximately 4,200 feet. Above this elevation, only Krummholz (stunted spruce) and other alpine vegetation exist. Because this vegetation is extremely vulnerable to erosion (caused in a large part by foot traffic), please remain on the established trail.

Beginning at Cannon Mountain Tramway parking lot on US 3, this day hike uses the Greenleaf Trail as well as the A.T. The park encompasses the Basin, a glacial pothole 20 feet in diameter carved in granite at the base of a waterfall more than 25,000 years ago, and the Flume, a natural chasm more than 800 feet long with walls of granite 60–70 feet high and 12–20 feet wide. The Old Man of the Mountains, for which Profile Clearing was named, was a rock formation that fell from the mountainside in 2003.

THE HIKE

From US 3 at the Cannon Mountain Tramway parking lot, take the Greenleaf Trail 2.7 miles to Greenleaf Hut. From the hut, hike another 1.1 miles to reach the summit of Mount Lafayette (elevation 5,260'). You will see the remains of the summit house foundation just below the summit.

From the summit of Mount Lafayette, make a right onto the A.T. and hike another mile to the top of Mount Lincoln (elevation 5,089'). The walk along this ridge is absolutely spectacular, but it can be dangerous in inclement weather. The ridge is exposed to the full force of storms, which can happen suddenly and violently. Conditions can include hurricane-force winds and freezing temperatures (even in the summer). Be prepared. Bring along raingear and a warm coat or sweater in your day pack for emergencies. Head for Greenleaf Hut if the weather turns threatening.

Return to US 3 via the A.T. and the Greenleaf Trail.

TRAILHEAD DIRECTIONS

From I-93, take Exit 34B for Cannon Mountain Tramway/Old Man Historic Site. Turn onto Tramway Drive, following signs for the Cannon Mountain Tramway, and drive 0.3 mile to the parking lot.

GPS TRAILHEAD COORDINATES N44° 10.134' W71° 40.926'

22 MOUNT LIBERTY

STRENUOUS | 8.4-mile round-trip | 7 hours

This hike involves a tough climb to the summit of Mount Liberty (elevation 4,459'). You will be richly rewarded at the peak with a commanding view of Mount Lincoln, Mount Lafayette, the rest of Franconia Ridge, and other peaks in the White Mountains. On days when there seems to be a single file of hikers heading up from Profile Clearing to Mounts Lafayette and Lincoln, this hike offers a chance to get away from the heaviest crowds. The hike uses the A.T. until you are 0.25 mile from the summit. An optional return route takes you to the summit of Mount Flume and returns to US 3 via the side trail to the Flume.

Along Franconia Ridge   *Photo: Leonard M. Adkins*

THE HIKE

From the parking area at US 3 in Franconia Notch, take the 0.8-mile Whitehouse Trail to its junction with the A.T. Follow the A.T. north. In 0.6 mile, reach the junction with the Flume side trail. Continue on the A.T., climbing sharply 2.0 miles to Liberty Springs Campsite. Water is available from the spring located near the Trail at the campsite.

From the campsite, the Trail climbs steeply 0.3 mile to the junction with the Franconia Ridge Trail. Turn right onto that trail and reach the summit of Mount Liberty in 0.3 mile. After enjoying the views from Liberty, hike the 0.3 mile back down to the A.T. and return to your car via that trail.

The optional return is to continue on the Franconia Ridge Trail from Mount Liberty 0.9 mile to the summit of Mount Flume (elevation 4,327'). From the summit, follow the Flume side trail 3.4 miles down the mountain to its junction with the A.T. The Flume side trail descent off Mount Flume is quite steep for the first 0.5 mile but eases as you reach Flume Brook. From the junction with the A.T., it is 0.6 mile south to the trailhead at US 3. This return route adds 2.1 miles to your round-trip, but you get to climb Mount Flume and enjoy a nice walk along Flume Brook.

TRAILHEAD DIRECTIONS

From southbound on I-93, take Exit 34A and merge onto US 3. The Liberty Springs at Whitehouse parking area will be on your left in 0.2 mile. From northbound on I-93, take Exit 34A and merge onto US 3. The Liberty Springs at Whitehouse parking area will be on your right in 0.9 mile.

GPS TRAILHEAD COORDINATES N44° 06.033' W71° 40.934'

23 LONESOME LAKE

MODERATE | 7.4-mile round-trip | 4.5 hours

You will cross over two beautiful brooks—Whitehouse and Cascade—on this hike to Lonesome Lake. Set against the backdrop of Profile Mountain, the lake is a tarn that sits high on the side of Cannon Mountain.

The elevation change from the trailhead to the lake is more than 1,000 feet, but the Trail is well graded and the climb is moderate. Lonesome Lake can make for a good hike with children old enough for a trail that offers some challenges along the way.

THE HIKE

From the parking area on US 3, follow the 0.8-mile Whitehouse Trail to its junction with the A.T. Follow the A.T. south and cross under US 3. Hike 0.25 mile to Whitehouse Brook, which you cross on rocks. Hike another 1.1 miles to the junction with the Basin–Cascades Trail. Continue to follow the A.T., which will cross and then follow alongside Cascade Brook as you continue to climb up to Lonesome Lake.

From the Basin–Cascades Trail, it is 0.5 mile to the junction with the Kinsman Pond Trail. Continue to follow the A.T. alongside Cascade Brook, hiking another 0.9 mile to Lonesome Lake. Lonesome Lake Hut is 0.1 mile beyond the lake. The Appalachian Mountain Club operates the hut, where water is available and some refreshments are sold in season.

The return hike is north on the A.T. to the Whitehouse Trail, which you follow to the parking area on US 3.

TRAILHEAD DIRECTIONS

From southbound on I-93, take Exit 34A and merge onto US 3. The Liberty Springs at Whitehouse parking area will be on your left in 0.2 mile. From northbound on I-93, take Exit 34A and merge onto US 3. The Liberty Springs at Whitehouse parking area will be on your right in 0.9 mile.

GPS TRAILHEAD COORDINATES N44° 06.033' W71° 40.934'

Beaver Brook on Mount Moosilauke *Photo: Leonard M. Adkins*

24 MOUNT MOOSILAUKE

STRENUOUS | 7.6-mile round-trip | 7.5 hours

If you look up the words *beautiful* and *big* in your thesaurus, you find dozens of adjectives that could be used to describe Mount Moosilauke, which means "high bald place" in the language of the Pemigewasset Indians. But all of those words fall short in describing this imposing bald mountain that stands over the southwest corner of the White Mountains.

A carriage road to the open summit of Moosilauke was built in the mid-1800s. It led to Prospect House, a hotel on top of the massif. Dartmouth College bought the hotel in 1920 and maintained it as a hostel until 1942, when it burned down. The road is long since abandoned and the summit is free from development, but Mount Moosilauke still boasts the commanding view that attracted visitors more than a century ago.

This is a challenging hike and should not be taken lightly. There is a 1,000-foot gain in elevation for every mile of the uphill part of the hike. Allow ample time for your return trip because the descent can be tricky in places.

THE HIKE

From the trailhead at Kinsman Notch on NH 112, follow the A.T. south. The Trail climbs gradually for the first 0.5 mile, where, to the right of the Trail, you will see the lowest of a series of falls on Beaver Brook. At this point, the Trail begins its very steep climb out of Kinsman Notch.

For most of the next 0.5 mile, you will be alongside, or at some points almost in, Beaver Brook as you climb to pass the side trail to Beaver Brook Shelter at mile 1.5. Pass by the Asquam Ridge Trail at 1.9 miles and the Benton Trail at 3.4 miles. Climb another 0.4 mile to the open summit of Mount Moosilauke. Ruins of the old hotel are visible around the summit. The old carriage road can be seen leading to the South Peak of Moosilauke. There are outstanding views in all directions, particularly to the northeast, where the peaks of the White Mountains are prominent.

The return hike is back down the A.T. to Kinsman Notch.

TRAILHEAD DIRECTIONS

From I-93, take Exit 32 (NH 112/Lincoln/N Woodstock). Turn onto NH 112 West, and drive about 6.8 miles to the A.T. crossing. Parking (*note:* national-forest fee area) is available at the trailhead.

GPS TRAILHEAD COORDINATES N44° 02.532' W71° 47.327'

25 WACHIPAUKA POND

MODERATE | 4.2-mile round-trip | 2.5 hours

Wachipauka Pond is a nice place to take a swim on a warm afternoon. The water is cool and the surrounding scenery pleasing to the eye. The hike, which starts in a forest of maple, birch, and beech, has only one climb of 500 feet, and that is accomplished within the first mile.

There is also the option of extending the journey by following the former route of the A.T. to a viewpoint on the summit of Webster Slide Mountain.

THE HIKE

From the parking area, take the combined A.T.–Wachipauka Pond Trail south, soon following a woods road as it climbs over the northern slope of Wyatt Hill. Begin to descend about 1 mile later. You will reach Wachipauka Pond, which is at first visible through the trees, at 2.0 miles. Continue another 0.1 mile to a short side route, which will bring you to the shore of the pond.

If you want more hiking after your dip, continue south on the A.T., passing by Hairy Root Spring and turning right onto the ascending Webster Slide Trail. You reach the top of the mountain, with views of the pond and Mount Moosilauke, about 1 mile from the pond (adding 2 miles to the overall length of the hike). Retrace your steps back to your car.

TRAILHEAD DIRECTIONS

From I-93, take Exit 32 (NH 112/Lincoln/N Woodstock). Turn onto NH 112 West, and drive about 3.2 miles. Turn left onto NH 118, and drive 13 miles. Turn right onto NH 25 West, and drive 4.4 miles to the trailhead and parking.

GPS TRAILHEAD COORDINATES N43° 59.447' W71° 54.077'

26 MOUNT CUBE

STRENUOUS | 7-mile round-trip | 6 hours

From the southern summit of Mount Cube, you can see the Connecticut River Valley and the solitary summits of Smarts Mountain and Mount Ascutney. A short side trail takes you to the northern peak of Mount Cube, where, from its open ledges, you will find views of Mount Moosilauke and the White Mountains. This hike also features a short stroll along a New Hampshire bog before it ascends over mixed terrain, passing several brooks along the way. There is an elevation gain of nearly 2,000 feet, which makes this hike rather tough.

THE HIKE

The hike begins at NH 25A, near Upper Baker Pond. A short distance from a highway bridge, enter the woods on the A.T. at the southern side of the highway. After crossing

Mount Cube South summit   *Photo: Leonard M. Adkins*

a small swamp, begin to ascend on abandoned logging roads. At mile 0.5, you will cross a gravel logging road and continue your ascent.

Hike another 1.3 miles, cross Brackett Brook, and start your ascent of Mount Cube via switchbacks. Hike another 1.5 miles to the saddle between the summits of North and South Cube, where a short side trail to the right leads 0.3 mile to the open summit of North Cube for outstanding views of the Whites.

The A.T. continues left and soon reaches the summit of South Cube (elevation 2,909'), where you will find views of the Connecticut River Valley, Smarts Mountain, and Mount Ascutney. Return via the A.T., heading north.

TRAILHEAD DIRECTIONS

From I-93, take Exit 26 (US 3/NH 25/NH 3A/Plymouth/Rumney). Continue onto NH 3A South, and drive 4 miles. Turn right onto NH 25 West, and drive 11.7 miles. Turn left onto NH 25A West, and drive 4.2 miles to the A.T.; parking will be on the left.

GPS TRAILHEAD COORDINATES N43° 53.960' W71° 58.627'

27 SMARTS MOUNTAIN

MODERATE | 7.6-mile round-trip | 6 hours

This hike over open, rocky ledges leads to the summit of Smarts Mountain, where you will find wonderful views of the New Hampshire countryside.

THE HIKE

From the parking lot on Lyme–Dorchester Road, follow the A.T. north to begin an immediate ascent of Lambert Ridge. (The 3.6-mile Smarts Mountain Ranger Trail, which leads right to the summit of Smarts, is an alternative to make the hike a loop and is about the same distance as returning by the A.T.)

Hike about 0.75 mile to the first series of open ledges on the spine of Lambert Ridge. One mile later, descend Lambert Ridge, cross a stream, and begin your ascent of Smarts Mountain. Hike another 0.9 mile to the junction of the Smarts Mountain Ranger Trail. These two trails join, and you will continue on them until you reach the summit. In about 0.25 mile, the Trail makes a sharp right and ascends steeply to the summit.

Pass the short side trail leading to the Smarts Mountain tent site in 0.1 mile. Water is available from an intermittent spring just beyond the Trail junction. Hike another 0.1 mile and pass just east of the summit of Smarts Mountain (elevation 3,240'). The Smarts Mountain Ranger Trail ends here.

From here, you can also see the Firewardens Cabin, now maintained as a shelter by the Dartmouth Outing Club. Water is available from the Mike Murphy Spring, 0.2 mile north of this cabin on a blue-blazed side trail.

Return via the A.T. or the Smarts Mountain Ranger Trail.

TRAILHEAD DIRECTIONS

From I-91 (in Vermont), take Exit 14 (VT 113/US 5/Thetford). Turn right onto VT 113 East, and drive 1.4 miles. Turn right onto US 5 South, go 0.1 mile, and then turn left back onto VT 113 East, which quickly becomes East Thetford Road as you enter New Hampshire. Drive 1.8 miles; then veer right onto Dorchester Road. Drive 3 miles to a fork in the road (and Dorchester Road's first junction with the A.T.). Take the left (northern) fork another 1.7 miles to the parking lot at the A.T.–Smarts Mountain Ranger Trail junction.

GPS TRAILHEAD COORDINATES N43° 47.844' W72° 04.329'

Near the summit of Smarts Mountain   *Photo: Lafe Low*

VERMONT

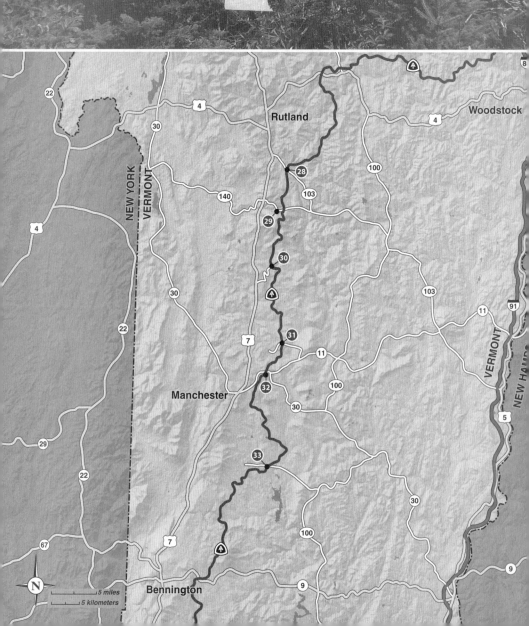

Hike	Page	Length (mi)	Configuration	Time (hr)	Difficulty	Features
28. Clarendon Gorge	60	0.2	↗	0.1	★	〰
29. White Rocks Cliff	61	4.6	↗	2.5	★★	👓
30. Little Rock Pond	62	4.8	↗	2.5	★	〰
31. Styles Peak	64	3.2	↗	2.0	★★	⛰ 👓
32. Prospect Rock	65	9.8	↗	6.0	★★	⛰ 👓
33. Stratton Mountain	66	7.6	↗	6.0	★★	⛰ 👓

DIFFICULTY ★★★ strenuous ★★ moderate ★ easy   CONFIGURATION ↗ round-trip

⛰ mountain peak   👓 scenic view   〰 pond or river

FROM THE CONNECTICUT RIVER at the New Hampshire–Vermont state line, the A.T. passes from east to west, crossing lowland hardwood forests and climbing steep hills dotted with pastures. The area from the Connecticut River to Sherburne Pass features stone walls, cellar holes, and other remnants of the farms that once dominated this area, which is now reverting to forest.

The A.T. then joins the Long Trail near Sherburne Pass, where it heads more than 100 miles south to the Vermont–Massachusetts state line. Following the Long Trail, it climbs the Killington and Pico Peaks of the Coolidge Range, part of the Green Mountains. The A.T. reaches its highest point in Vermont just below Killington Peak (elevation 4,235'). It descends again to rolling hills and farmlands, and crosses Clarendon Gorge on a suspension bridge before climbing back into the Green Mountains.

From here, the A.T. traverses the main ridge of the Green Mountains. It also crosses several peaks, including Stratton Mountain, said to be the Trail's birthplace. From Stratton, the Trail continues to Glastenbury Mountain before descending near Bennington. It then climbs to follow a ridge 14 miles until it meets the Vermont–Massachusetts state line.

28 CLARENDON GORGE

EASY | 0.2-mile round-trip | less than 10 minutes

The walk to take a swim in Clarendon Gorge is so short that we thought about not including it in this book. However, it is such a wonderful experience that excluding it would have been a disservice. It is so easy an outing that even those who are out of shape can handle it. It is an excellent introduction for first-time hikers. There are very few places on the A.T. you can reap such a marvelous and rewarding payback for the small amount of energy you will expend and the few minutes of time you will invest walking to this destination.

The gorge is popular and may be crowded on the weekends. Also, do not swim if the water is high: lives have been lost here.

THE HIKE

Walk south on the A.T., cross the bridge over the gorge, and take the pathway down to the water. (Please do not create new trails.) You can choose to swim in the narrow

View of Clarendon Gorge from the suspension bridge   *Photo: Jeriko Fox*

gorge, where you can sit in potholes created by the erosive action of Mill River and let the swirling waters relax you with nature's own whirlpool, or you can sunbathe on the flat rocks situated in the shallower water above the gorge. Return via the A.T.

TRAILHEAD DIRECTIONS

Take I-91 to Exit 8 (VT 131/US 5/Windsor/Ascutney). Turn onto VT 131 West, and drive 15.8 miles. Turn right onto VT 103 North, and drive 20.4 miles to the trailhead parking area on the left.

GPS TRAILHEAD COORDINATES N43° 31.272' W72° 55.509'

29 WHITE ROCKS CLIFF

MODERATE
4.6-mile round-trip, including the road walk on VT 140 | 2.5 hours

White Rocks Cliff, reached by a short side trail from the A.T., is a popular day-hike destination. The expansive view is the reason why so many come here. Directly below the wide quartzite cliffs, a talus slope bordered by a spruce forest leads the eye into the deep valley carved by the erosive waters of Otter Creek. The small town of Wallingford lies to the northwest along the banks of the creek. The Adirondacks of New York are on the western horizon.

THE HIKE

Walk westward a few yards to the A.T., cross VT 140, and use a bridge to get across Roaring Brook. Step over Sugar Hill Road in 0.3 mile and ascend through a hemlock forest to cross Bully Brook. Stay left on the A.T. where the Keewaydin Trail joins from the right at 1 mile. A blue-blazed trail on the left at 1.8 miles leads to Greenwall Shelter in 0.2 mile.

Continue to ascend on the A.T., but turn right onto the White Rocks Cliff Trail at 2.1 miles. A steep, rocky descent of 0.2 mile brings you to the cliffs, where you might get to watch a dozen or more turkey vultures soar on thermals rising from the valley floor. Retrace your steps to return to the trailhead.

TRAILHEAD DIRECTIONS

Take I-91 to Exit 8 (VT 131/US 5/Windsor/Ascutney). Turn onto VT 131 West, and drive 15.8 miles. Turn right onto VT 103 North, and drive 14.2 miles. Turn left on VT 140 West, and drive 4.8 miles; then turn right onto Van Wyck Road, reaching the parking area in 0.2 mile.

GPS TRAILHEAD COORDINATES N43° 27.666' W72° 56.837'

30 LITTLE ROCK POND

EASY | 4.8-mile round-trip | 2.5 hours

This may be the best day hike on the A.T. in Vermont. The gentle climb from the road to the pond is a great way to get out and stretch your legs. The Trail runs alongside Little Black Brook for much of the hike, and many small waterfalls and pools are visible from the Trail.

The clear, cold water of the pond reflects Green Mountain rising above it on the opposite shore. This is a popular day hike, particularly in the fall (the foliage around the pond is breathtaking at its peak). If you want to have any solitude, try this hike during the week or leave the trailhead by 10 a.m. to beat the crowds. You can do the hike either as a round-trip or, by using the Green Mountain Trail, as a 7.5-mile loop.

Little Rock Pond is a favorite destination of locals.   *Photo: Leonard M. Adkins*

THE HIKE

From the trailhead at the parking lot on Forest Service Road (FR) 10 (Danby–Landgrove Road), hike north on the A.T. Reach the southern end of Little Rock Pond at mile 2.0. The Trail skirts the eastern shore of the pond for the next 0.4 mile. At the northern end of the pond, the Green Mountain Trail, which can be used to create a 7.5-mile loop, turns left off the A.T. Even if you don't care to follow this trail back to the parking lot, you want to follow it a short distance to reach the Little Rock Pond Loop Trail; you can follow this back to the southern end of the pond and join back up with the A.T. to reach your car.

If you decide to follow the Green Mountain Trail, climb 1.0 mile up the ridge to the summit of Green Mountain (elevation 2,500'). Continue following the Trail another 4.1 miles as it traverses and descends the ridge to FR 10, about 0.1 mile west of the parking lot at the A.T. trailhead.

TRAILHEAD DIRECTIONS

Take I-91 to Exit 8 (VT 131/US 5/Windsor/Ascutney). Turn onto VT 131 West, and drive 15.8 miles. Turn right onto VT 103 North, and drive 14.2 miles. Turn left on VT 140 West, and drive 6.5 miles; then turn left onto US 7 South. Drive 9.2 miles; then turn left onto Brooklyn Road/Mount Tabor Road/Seasonal Forestry Road, and drive 3.1 miles to the A.T. crossing.

GPS TRAILHEAD COORDINATES N43° 22.376' W72° 57.751'

31 STYLES PEAK

MODERATE | 3.2-mile round-trip | 2 hours

Because it is sandwiched between more-popular destinations (Griffith Lake and Little Rock Pond to the north, and Prospect Rock and Stratton Mountain to the south), Styles Peak is often overlooked as a day-hike destination. You have to drive 4 miles on a dirt-and-gravel road to reach the trailhead, but the ascent to the top is quick and the view worthwhile.

Looking almost due north from the summit, you will see Peru Peak nearby, with other Green Mountain summits lining

Rock steps along the trail   *Photo: Lafe Low*

up behind it. Far to the east are the mountains of southern New Hampshire, while to the south is Bromley Mountain and the ridgelines of southern Vermont.

THE HIKE

Follow the A.T. north. Volunteers with the Green Mountain Club have constructed rock steps to make the steepest sections of the climb more manageable. Continuing to ascend the forested slopes, you will reach the open summit of Styles Peak at 1.6 miles. Return via the A.T.

TRAILHEAD DIRECTIONS

From I-91 North, take Exit 6 (US 5/Rockingham) and turn left onto US 5 North; drive 0.6 mile to continue onto VT 103 North. From I-91 South, take Exit 6 (US 5/Rockingham) and turn left onto VT 103 North. Drive 9.3 miles to Chester, and continue straight onto VT 11 West. Drive 19.1 miles then take the fork on the right, onto Main Street (sign for Peru). Drive 0.3 mile, turn right onto Hapgood Pond Road, and drive 1 mile. Turn left onto North Road, drive 0.8 mile, and turn left onto Mad Tom Notch Road (Forest Service Road 21). Drive 2.1 miles to the crossing with the A.T.

GPS TRAILHEAD COORDINATES N43° 15.477' W72° 56.304'

32 PROSPECT ROCK

MODERATE | **9.8-mile round-trip** | **6 hours**

This long day hike features outstanding views of the Dorset Valley, Manchester, and Mount Equinox.

THE HIKE

From the parking area on VT 11/30, cross the road, ascend the highway bank, and enter the woods (also a boulder field). Hike nearly half a mile, and cross a stream and then the old abandoned overgrown VT 30. Hike another 0.25 mile, cross another stream, and begin to ascend steeply.

Almost 1 mile after beginning your hike, you will pass two vistas (one to the south and one to the northwest), reach a ridgetop, and descend a narrow ridge through a hardwood forest. Hike another 0.9 mile, cross an old woods road and a small brook, and ascend west and then south.

At mile 2.4, reach the junction with a side trail that leads a short distance to Spruce Peak (elevation 2,040'). At this side trail, head left along the A.T. another 0.4 mile to the side trail to Spruce Peak Shelter. Water is available from a spring just south of the shelter, which is 0.1 mile off the Trail.

Hike another 0.4 mile, cross a stream in a small gully, turn sharply left, and ascend the ridge. Reach the high point on the western flank of the ridge in 0.25 mile, continue south for slightly more than 1 mile, cross a small stream, and descend.

At mile 4.9, reach the side trail that leads a short distance to Prospect Rock (elevation 2,079'), which affords magnificent views of the Dorset Valley, Manchester, and Mount Equinox. Return to the parking area by retracing your steps north on the A.T.

TRAILHEAD DIRECTIONS

From I-91 North, take Exit 6 (US 5/Rockingham) and turn left onto US 5 North; drive 0.6 mile to continue onto VT 103 North. From I-91 South, take Exit 6 (US 5/ Rockingham) and turn left onto VT 103 North. Drive 9.3 miles to Chester, and keep straight onto VT 11 West. Drive 23.7 miles; the parking area will be to your right.

GPS TRAILHEAD COORDINATES N43° 12.423' W72° 58.189'

33 STRATTON MOUNTAIN

MODERATE | 7.6-mile round-trip | 6 hours

The summit of Stratton Mountain (elevation 3,936') is said to be the birthplace of the A.T. The views from this mountain sparked the idea of an eastern continental trail in the mind of Benton MacKaye. Sitting in a tree, admiring the panorama, MacKaye said the experience left him with the impression that he was "atop the world, with a sort of planetary feeling." MacKaye later went on to publish his concept of a continuous footpath along the Appalachian Mountains. The idea ignited interest, and by 1937 his dream was on its way to fulfillment.

The routing of the Trail over Stratton Mountain provides hikers with a beautiful climb and outstanding views of the Green Mountains and surrounding countryside. From the observation tower at the summit, you can see Somerset Reservoir and Mount Pisgah to the south, Glastenbury Mountain to the southwest, the Taconics to the west, Ascutney Mountain to the northeast, and Mount Monadnock to the southeast (the latter two in New Hampshire).

THE HIKE

From the parking area on Arlington–West Wardsboro Road (also signed as Kelley Stand Road), follow the A.T. north into the woods. After passing a beaver pond, you will begin to ascend gradually, crossing an old woods road.

At mile 1.1, pass by cellar holes and the well of an old farmstead. In another 0.25 mile, cross a dirt road and begin your ascent of the southwestern ridge of Stratton Mountain. The Trail follows switchbacks and reaches the bench below the summit of Little Stratton Mountain in another 0.75 mile. The Trail follows the bench to a col between Little Stratton and Stratton Mountains, ascending steeply by switchbacks.

At mile 3.2, pass a spring, keep an eye out for an outstanding view of Grout Pond to the south, and at mile 3.8, reach the tower at the summit. During the season (usually May–October), a caretaker with the Green Mountain Club lives in the cabin atop Stratton. The caretaker is often available to provide hikers with information about the area. Return via the A.T., heading south to the parking area.

TRAILHEAD DIRECTIONS

Take I-91 to Exit 5 (US 5/VT 123/Westminster/Bellows Falls). Turn onto Westminster Street (left from I-91 North and right from I-91 South), and drive 0.3 mile.

View from the fire tower on Stratton Mountain, looking south toward Somerset Reservoir
Photo: Nate Merrill/Flickr/CC BY 2.0 (creativecommons.org/licenses/by/2.0)

Turn right onto Back Westminster Road, and drive 2.8 miles. Turn left onto VT 121 West/Saxtons River Road, and drive 5.7 miles. Turn left onto VT 35 South, and drive 10.2 miles to Townshend. Turn right onto VT 30 North, and drive 6.0 miles; then turn left onto VT 100 South, and drive 8.8 miles. Turn right onto Stratton Arlington Road, and drive 6.9 miles to the A.T. crossing.

GPS TRAILHEAD COORDINATES N43° 03.684' W72° 58.102'

MASSACHUSETTS

Hike	Page	Length (mi)	Configuration	Time (hr)	Difficulty	Features
34. Eph's Lookout	70	6.6	round-trip	4.5	★★	scenic view
35. Mount Williams	72	1.8	round-trip	1.5	★★	mountain peak, scenic view
36. The Cobbles and Gore Pond	72	7.4	round-trip	4.5	★★	scenic view, pond or river
37. Gore Pond	74	8.4	round-trip	5.0	★★	pond or river
38. Warner Hill	75	1.4	round-trip	1.0	★	scenic view, pond or river, waterfall, historic area, bird-watching, wheelchair access
39. Finerty Pond	76	4.2	round-trip	4.0	★★	mountain peak, scenic view, pond or river
40. Upper Goose Pond	77	5.0	round-trip	3.0	★★	pond or river, bird-watching
41. Cobble Hill	78	3.2	round-trip	2.0	★	scenic view
42. Benedict Pond and The Ledges	79	3.0	round-trip	2.0	★★	scenic view, pond or river
43. Ice Gulch	80	2.2	round-trip	1.5	★★	scenic view
44. East Mountain	81	2.8	round-trip	2.0	★★	scenic view
45. Jug End	82	2.2	round-trip	2.0	★★★	scenic view
46. Jug End and Mount Everett	82	9.2	round-trip	7.0	★★★	mountain peak, scenic view, pond or river
47. Mount Everett	84	5.4	round-trip	4.0	★★★	mountain peak, scenic view, waterfall

DIFFICULTY ★★★ strenuous ★★ moderate ★ easy   CONFIGURATION round-trip

mountain peak   scenic view   pond or river   waterfall   historic area   bird-watching

wheelchair access

THE APPALACHIAN TRAIL ENTERS MASSACHUSETTS 4 miles north of a road crossing (MA 2 in North Adams), descending along the rocky ridge of East Mountain. From North Adams, the Trail continues up Prospect Mountain Ridge and over Mount Williams and Mount Fitch to the summit of Mount Greylock, the highest point in Massachusetts (elevation 3,491').

From Mount Greylock, the A.T. descends to Cheshire, heads to Dalton, and climbs the Berkshire Highlands. It traverses High Top and passes Finerty Pond before entering October Mountain State Forest. After crossing US 20 at Greenwater Pond, the A.T. continues to Upper Goose Pond and descends into the Tyringham Valley. From there, it enters Beartown State Forest, skirting Benedict Pond. These scenic ponds are perhaps the dominant feature of the A.T.'s 89 miles in Massachusetts.

The A.T. continues southwest into East Mountain State Forest, crosses Warner and June Mountains, and descends to the Housatonic River. The last miles of the Trail in the state cross the Housatonic valley to the Taconic Range, climb Mount Everett and Mount Race, pass Bear Rock Falls, and descend to the Massachusetts–Connecticut state line.

34 EPH'S LOOKOUT

MODERATE | 6.6-mile round-trip | 4.5 hours

This hike will take you to a quartzite ridge known as Eph's Lookout. Named after Colonel Ephraim Williams, the lookout has wonderful views of Williamstown, Mount Greylock, and the Berkshires. In his will, Williams changed the name of West Hoosac to Williamstown and established Williams College as a free school.

THE HIKE

From the A.T. crossing at MA 2 in North Adams, cross over the B & M Railroad and Hoosic River on a concrete and steel footbridge. At Massachusetts Avenue, turn right and follow the road about 0.25 mile. The Trail leaves the paved road, turns west along Sherman Brook, and meets a gravel driveway just before Sherman Brook goes under Massachusetts Avenue.

Follow the gravel driveway a short distance, pass over two footbridges, and follow an old spillway that releases water from a dam. At mile 0.6, a high-voltage power line

Wood sorrel is found all along the A.T.   *Photo: Leonard M. Adkins*

crosses the Trail next to the brook. For the next 0.4 mile, climb steadily through hemlocks and turn onto an old logging road, which you will follow 0.25 mile.

At mile 1.6, pass Pete's Spring to the right and reach the junction with a side trail that leads to a designated camping area. The Trail then returns to the bank of the brook, follows old logging roads 0.25 mile, and ascends a long ridge covered with patches of laurel.

At mile 2.4, turn sharply west; climb steeply through a jumble of granite, marble, and quartz; ascend a couple of steep and narrow switchbacks; and reach the top of a bluff. The bluff faces east, overlooking the Hoosic Range.

Hike 0.1 mile along a wide section of the East Mountain Ridge; pass around the north side of a fragile, mossy pond; and climb to the top of an open area with quartzite cobble. Reach the junction with the Pine Cobble Trail in 0.1 mile. There is a panoramic view a short distance south on the Pine Cobble Trail.

Continue along the A.T. and reach a dip in the ridge in 0.25 mile. In another 0.25 mile, reach the destination of the day hike—Eph's Lookout, a fine overlook with views of the Berkshires, Williamstown, Mount Greylock, the Taconic Range, and the Hoosic Valley. To return to the parking area, follow the A.T. south to MA 2.

TRAILHEAD DIRECTIONS

Take I-91 to Exit 26 (MA 2 West/Greenfield Center/North Adams). The exit ramp leads onto a traffic circle; take the exit for MA 2 West. Drive 38.1 miles, through North Adams, to the parking available at the Greylock Community Club, a short distance east of the A.T. crossing. Let someone at the club know that you are leaving your vehicle.

GPS TRAILHEAD COORDINATES   N42° 41.955' W73° 09.223'

35 MOUNT WILLIAMS

MODERATE | 1.8-mile round-trip | 1.5 hours

The view from Mount Williams takes in Williamstown, the Taconic Ridge, Eph's Lookout, and the Lower Pine Cobble. It's a great choice for a day hike if your time outdoors is limited.

THE HIKE
Follow the A.T. south from the parking area. Walk through a forest of red spruce, where, if you keep a sharp eye out, you may be able to discern the bed of the original road to the top of Mount Greylock.

You reach the summit of Mount Williams at 0.9 mile. To the west and below you is Williamstown, surrounded by open fields, while the Taconic Range in New York forms the far horizon. Eph's Lookout and Pine Cobble are visible to the north. Return via the A.T.

TRAILHEAD DIRECTIONS
Take I-91 to Exit 26 (MA 2 West/Greenfield Center/North Adams). The exit ramp leads onto a traffic circle; take the exit for MA 2 West. Drive 37.1 miles; then turn left onto Notch Road, and drive 2 miles; a day-use parking area is located about 300 feet past the trail crossing on Notch Road.

GPS TRAILHEAD COORDINATES N42° 40.232' W73° 10.077'

36 THE COBBLES AND GORE POND

MODERATE | 7.4-mile round-trip | 4.5 hours

The main attraction of this day hike is the view of Cheshire and the Hoosic River valley from the Cobbles, and scenic Gore Pond. The white quartz that makes up the Cobbles was beach sand 550 million years ago when this area was on the edge of

The view from the Cobbles takes in the small town of Cheshire.   *Photo: Leonard M. Adkins*

an ancient ocean. If you are short on time, you might want to consider hiking just to the Cobbles and back, a round-trip of 2.8 miles.

Most of this section of the A.T. was obtained from the Crane family of Dalton. The Crane Company is the manufacturer of the paper used for US currency. The company runs a currency museum in Dalton.

THE HIKE

Start at the post office on Church Street (park where you want—and can—in the town of Cheshire). On your right, you will see a replica of the press used to make Cheshire Cheese in the 1800s. Heading south on the A.T., you will cross the Ashuwillticook Rail Trail in 0.1 mile and then a bridge over the Hoosic River. After crossing the bridge, turn right at a fork in the road.

In another 0.1 mile, turn right on Furnace Hill Road, a residential street. After another 0.25 mile, turn left off Furnace Hill Road near the entrance of a private driveway.

For the next 0.75 mile, you will ascend through a hardwood forest, crossing motorcycle and logging trails; then arrive at the side trail to the north Cobble immediately after passing under a cliff. The A.T. reaches the top of the southernmost Cobble 0.25 mile later. There is a USGS bronze marker set into the rock.

Continue along the A.T. In 0.5 mile, turn east near the stone boundary marker for Dalton–Cheshire. The Trail crosses an old, grassy logging road and continues 1.3 miles, heading gradually uphill, crossing more old logging roads, and eventually reaching the summit at an overgrown pasture. From here, the Trail begins its descent to Gore Pond, reaching the outlet in about 0.5 mile. There is a logging road here that provides access to the west side of the pond, the destination of this hike. Return north to Cheshire via the A.T.

TRAILHEAD DIRECTIONS

Take I-90 West to Exit 2 (Lee/Pittsfield) and merge onto US 20 West. Drive about 1 mile; then turn right to stay on US 20 West. Drive 0.4 mile; then turn left to again stay on US 20 West. Drive 10.2 miles; then turn right onto Bank Row/MA 9 East. Drive 3.2 miles; then make a slight left onto MA 8 North/Cheshire Road, and drive 7.3 miles. Turn right onto Church Street, and drive 0.4 mile; the post office and St. Mary of the Assumption Catholic Church are along the A.T.

GPS TRAILHEAD COORDINATES N42° 33.726' W73° 09.465'

37 GORE POND

MODERATE | 8.4-mile round-trip | 5 hours

Pretty Gore Pond is the destination of this day hike, which begins in Dalton. The pond has glacial origins, but its depth fluctuates depending on the amount of beaver activity. At times, beaver dams have caused water to flood a portion of the Trail.

THE HIKE

The hike begins on Gulf Road. You will soon turn right into the woods and parallel the road. For the next 3.3 miles, the A.T. ascends and descends many ridges while skirting the wet areas between them. The A.T. follows the Dalton–Lanesboro border.

At mile 3.4 pass under a power line, and at mile 3.8 reach the junction with the side trail to the designated campsite at Crystal Mountain. Cross the brook and reach a hemlock grove with a view of the west side of Gore Pond at mile 4.2.

You may want to continue another 0.5 mile and hike around the shore of Gore Pond to its outlet, where an old logging road provides access to the west side of the pond. This will add another mile to your hike and another half hour or so to your time. To return to your vehicle, follow the A.T. south back to Gulf Road.

TRAILHEAD DIRECTIONS

Take I-90 West to Exit 2 (Lee/Pittsfield) and merge onto US 20 West. Drive about 1 mile; then turn right to stay on US 20 West. Drive 0.4 mile; then turn left to again stay on US 20 West. Drive 10.2 miles; then turn right onto Bank Row/MA 9 East. Drive 3.2 miles; then turn right onto MA 8 South/MA 9 East/Dalton Avenue. Drive 1.5 miles; then turn left onto Park Avenue, and drive 0.5 mile. Turn left onto Gulf Road, and drive 0.2 mile to the parking area.

GPS TRAILHEAD COORDINATES N42° 28.906' W73° 10.685'

38 WARNER HILL

EASY | 1.4-mile round-trip | 1 hour

In the fall, after the leaves have fallen, there are some nice views from Warner Hill, with Mount Greylock to the north being the most notable mountain. This is a pretty and leisurely day hike.

THE HIKE

From the paved Blotz Road, head south on the A.T. and climb 0.7 mile through a dense stand of evergreens to the top of Warner Hill. A cairn that sits a few feet to the left of the Trail marks the summit (elevation 2,050'). Return north via the A.T.

TRAILHEAD DIRECTIONS

Take I-90 West to Exit 2 (Lee/Pittsfield) and merge onto US 20 West. Drive about 1 mile; then turn right to stay on US 20 West. Drive 0.4 mile; then turn left to again stay on US 20 West, and drive 6.8 miles. Turn right onto Holmes Road, and drive 2.9 miles;

then turn right onto Williams Street, and drive 2.1 miles. Turn right onto Washington Mountain Road, and drive 0.1 mile. Stay left at the fork for Kirchner Road, and drive 2.5 miles (Kirchner Road becomes Blotz Road) to the parking area on the left.

GPS TRAILHEAD COORDINATES N42° 24.545' W73° 09.032'

39 FINERTY POND

MODERATE | 4.2-mile round-trip | 4 hours

The highlights of this day hike are scenic Finerty Pond and the summits of Becket and Walling Mountains, which afford nice views. You will pass through parts of October Mountain State Forest (the largest in Massachusetts, with more than 14,000 acres). This hike also features varied terrain.

THE HIKE

Beginning at the trail crossing on paved Tyne Road, head north on the A.T., climbing toward the summit of Becket Mountain (elevation 2,180'), which you will reach in just over 0.5 mile. On the summit there are concrete footings that mark the site of a former fire tower.

Continue along the ridge another 0.75 mile toward Walling Mountain. You will have a nice view to the south of the hills around the large Goose Pond. At mile 1.6, reach the overgrown summit of Walling Mountain (elevation 2,220').

From the summit, descend over a rocky trail 0.5 mile to Finerty Pond, the destination of the hike. You can skirt the pond on stepping-stones 0.25 mile or so until the A.T. turns north, away from the pond. To return to Tyne Road, follow the A.T. south.

TRAILHEAD DIRECTIONS

Take I-90 West to Exit 2 (Lee/Pittsfield) and turn left onto US 20 East. Drive 4.1 miles; then turn left onto Becket Road. Drive 0.9 mile to the A.T. crossing.

GPS TRAILHEAD COORDINATES N42° 17.809' W73° 09.007'

Upper Goose Pond   *Photo: Leonard M. Adkins*

40 UPPER GOOSE POND

MODERATE | **5-mile round-trip, with road walk on US 20** | **3 hours**

Purchased by the National Park Service for the A.T. corridor, Upper Goose Pond is one of the more outstanding features along the A.T. in Massachusetts. Arriving at this pretty New England pond, you will discover the reason for its name—it is the nesting site of many Canada geese.

THE HIKE

Walk east on US 20 (Jacob's Ladder Highway) 0.1 mile to the A.T., which you follow south. At 0.3 mile, you will cross a stream on a high bridge. This is a historic mill site as well as an outlet of Greenwater Pond.

In another 0.1 mile, cross the Massachusetts Turnpike (I-90) on twin bridges. Once off the bridge, you will enter the woods and make a steep ascent on rough trail, which eventually crosses two intermittent brooks.

At mile 1.0, reach the top of the ridge. Hike another 0.6 mile to the junction with the side trail to Upper Goose Pond Cabin, which is 0.5 mile away. There is also a camping area at the cabin; a caretaker (in season) collects fees for the cabin and tent sites.

Continue along the A.T. and pass an old chimney and a plaque marking the site of the old Mohhekennuck fishing and hunting club at mile 2.0. For the next 0.5 mile, the A.T. follows the shore of Upper Goose Pond before crossing its inlet at mile 2.5.

Follow the A.T. north back to US 20.

TRAILHEAD DIRECTIONS

Take I-90 West to Exit 2 (Lee/Pittsfield) and turn left onto US 20 East. Drive 4.6 miles to the A.T. crossing; there is a parking area just ahead.

GPS TRAILHEAD COORDINATES N42° 17.447' W73° 09.372'

41 COBBLE HILL

EASY | 3.2-mile round-trip | 2 hours

This gradual climb to the top of Cobble Hill offers fine views of the Tyringham Valley. Although there are several bog bridges, this is an otherwise easy hike and a good choice for hiking with children. It makes for a leisurely afternoon stroll along the A.T.

THE HIKE

From the trailhead on Main Road, follow the A.T. south. In 0.1 mile, cross Hop Brook on a footbridge. At mile 0.8, pass through a hemlock grove and cross a small stream. In another 0.3 mile, cross Jerusalem Road, which puts you in the Tyringham Cobble Reservation. Hike 0.5 mile from the road crossing to reach the top of Cobble Hill.

Return via the A.T.

TRAILHEAD DIRECTIONS

Take I-90 West to Exit 2 (Lee/Pittsfield) and turn left onto US 20 East; then immediately turn right onto MA 102 West. Drive 0.1 mile; then turn left onto Tyingham Road. Drive 5.1 miles to the A.T. crossing; limited parking is available along the road.

GPS TRAILHEAD COORDINATES N42° 14.081' W73° 11.658'

42 BENEDICT POND AND THE LEDGES

MODERATE | **3-mile round-trip** | **2 hours**

Rustic A.T. signage   *Photo: Lafe Low*

This hike has an unusual trailhead—a beach. From the swimming area on Benedict Pond, you will hike on a side trail along this beautiful glacial pond and then on the A.T. Your destination is The Ledges, a rocky ridge that affords fine views of Mount Everett and East Mountain. You can also see the Catskills rising in the distance.

This hike is quite steep in some places but is only rated as moderate because it is relatively short in length. You may want to save time for a swim in the pond. You can also rent canoes by the hour at the beach.

THE HIKE

From the swimming area on Benedict Pond, follow the Pond Loop Trail around the south side of the pond. At mile 0.5, reach the junction with the A.T. Turn left and follow the A.T. north. In 0.4 mile, cross the Benedict Pond outlet. The Trail begins to ascend steeply 0.6 mile as it climbs to The Ledges. To return, hike on the A.T. to the Pond Loop Trail, which you follow back to the trailhead.

TRAILHEAD DIRECTIONS

Take I-90 West to Exit 2 (Lee/Pittsfield) and turn left onto US 20 East; then immediately turn right onto MA 102 West. Drive 4.6 miles; then turn left onto US 7 South, and drive 2.7 miles. Turn left onto Monument Valley Road, drive 2 miles, and turn left onto Stony Brook Road. Drive 2.8 miles; then turn left onto Benedict Pond Road (the entrance for Beartown State Forest). Follow the signs to the swimming area at Benedict Pond.

GPS TRAILHEAD COORDINATES   N42° 12.321' W73° 17.473'

43 ICE GULCH

MODERATE | 2.2-mile round-trip | 1.5 hours

Ice Gulch. It sounds like a place where the bad guys went to hide out from the law in an old Wild West movie. Actually, it is a ravine on the south side of East Mountain so narrow and deep that its bottom rarely receives direct sunlight. As a result, ice and snow linger among the boulders until July and sometimes even into August.

The hike to the gulch is on a gradually ascending trail, with just a bit of a steep climbing near the end. A shelter nearby provides a place to rest and have lunch.

THE HIKE

Follow the A.T. south through a landscape that shows the lingering effects of a tornado that roared through the area in the mid-1990s. Look to the side of the Trail and you will see tree trunk after tree trunk that trail volunteers had to cut through to keep the Trail open.

The gradual ascent gives way to a steeper incline at 0.8 mile, but that lasts less than 0.2 mile as you descend slightly to Ice Gulch at 1.0 mile. Within the ravine lie jumbles of huge boulders, but much of the time there is not enough light to see all of the way to the bottom. However, you don't need to go any farther than the edge of the gulch to enjoy the cool breeze rising into the hot air surrounding you in midsummer.

Continue to a short side trail at 1.1 miles to take a break and enjoy the silence of the woods around the Tom Leonard Shelter.

To return, hike the A.T. back to Lake Buel Road.

TRAILHEAD DIRECTIONS

Take I-90 West to Exit 2 (Lee/Pittsfield) and turn left onto US 20 East; then immediately turn right onto MA 102 West. Drive 4.6 miles, turn left onto US 7 South, and drive 2.7 miles. Turn left onto Monument Valley Road, and drive 4.6 miles to the intersection with MA 23/MA 183. Cross MA 23 and onto Lake Buel Road; then drive about 1.2 miles. The parking area is about 300 feet before the trail crossing.

GPS TRAILHEAD COORDINATES N42° 10.458' W73° 17.628'

Watch your step on this wooden footbridge. *Photo: Lafe Low*

44 EAST MOUNTAIN

MODERATE | 2.8-mile round-trip | 2 hours

This short hike leads to East Mountain Ridge, where you will find many overlooks. The views to the south and west of Mount Everett, the Housatonic River Valley, and the distant Catskills are well worth traversing this sometimes tricky trail. On the way to the ridge, the Trail leads through glacial boulders.

THE HIKE

From Homes Road, follow the A.T. north and begin climbing, gradually at first, and then more steeply. One mile from Homes Road, you will reach the high point on the ridge. The next 0.4 mile offers several fine views. A large boulder at mile 1.4 marks the end of the hike. There is an outstanding view to the south. Return to the trailhead taking the A.T.

TRAILHEAD DIRECTIONS

Take I-90 West to Exit 2 (Lee/Pittsfield) and turn left onto US 20 East; then immediately turn right onto MA 102 West. Drive 4.6 miles; then turn left onto US 7 South, and drive 8.5 miles, through Great Barrington. Turn left onto Brookside Road, and drive 2.1 miles (during which Brookside Road becomes Home Road) to the A.T. crossing. There is limited parking along the road.

GPS TRAILHEAD COORDINATES N42° 09.288' W73° 20.472'

45 JUG END

STRENUOUS | 2.2-mile round-trip | 2 hours

This short, steep hike leads to tremendous views of the Housatonic River Valley, Mount Greylock, and the rest of the Berkshires.

THE HIKE

From Jug End Road, follow the A.T. south and ascend gradually for 0.25 mile. The climb then becomes quite steep. At mile 0.75, there is a good view from an exposed rock face. In another 0.4 mile, you will reach the summit of Jug End. To return, hike the A.T. back down to Jug End Road.

TRAILHEAD DIRECTIONS

Take I-90 West to Exit 2 (Lee/Pittsfield) and turn left onto US 20 East; then immediately turn right onto MA 102 West. Drive 4.6 miles, turn left onto US 7 South, and drive 7.6 miles. Turn right onto MA 23 West/MA 41 South, and drive 3.9 miles. Turn left to stay on MA 41 South, drive 0.1 mile, and then veer right onto Mount Washington Road. Drive 0.8 mile; then turn left onto The Avenue (which becomes Guilder Hollow Road/Jug End Road), and drive 0.9 mile to the trail crossing. There is adequate parking at the trailhead.

GPS TRAILHEAD COORDINATES N42° 08.660' W73° 25.887'

46 JUG END AND MOUNT EVERETT

STRENUOUS | 9.2-mile round-trip | 7 hours

This hike leads to tremendous views of the Housatonic River Valley, Mount Greylock, and the rest of the Berkshires from atop Jug End. It then continues to the ninth-highest peak in Massachusetts, Mount Everett, which has a panoramic view of the Taconic and Berkshire Ranges.

Exposed rock along the trail *Photo: Lafe Low*

THE HIKE

From Jug End Road, follow the A.T. south and ascend gradually 0.25 mile. The climb then becomes quite steep. At mile 0.75, there is a good view from an exposed rock face. In another 0.4 mile, reach the summit of Jug End.

Continue on the A.T., cross two unnamed peaks, and reach the summit of Mount Bushnell (elevation 1,834'). From Mount Bushnell, hike 1.1 miles to Glen Brook Shelter and another 0.1 mile to a side trail to Hemlocks Shelter. In another 0.3 mile, reach the Guilder Pond Picnic Area. The pond is on your right. There is a loop trail around the pond, which uses the A.T. to complete the loop.

From the picnic area, hike 0.7 mile to the summit of Mount Everett (elevation 2,602'). The fire tower is closed to the public, but you don't need to go to the top of it to enjoy the outstanding views from the summit.

Return via the A.T. back down to Jug End Road.

TRAILHEAD DIRECTIONS

Take I-90 West to Exit 2 (Lee/Pittsfield) and turn left onto US 20 East; then immediately turn right onto MA 102 West. Drive 4.6 miles, turn left onto US 7 South, and drive 7.6 miles. Turn right onto MA 23 West/MA 41 South, and drive 3.9 miles. Turn left to stay on MA 41 South, drive 0.1 mile, and then veer right onto Mount Washington Road. Drive 0.8 mile; then turn left onto The Avenue (which becomes Guilder Hollow Road/Jug End Road), and drive 0.9 mile to the trail crossing. There is adequate parking at the trailhead.

GPS TRAILHEAD COORDINATES N42° 08.660' W73° 25.887'

47 MOUNT EVERETT

STRENUOUS | 5.4-mile round-trip | 4 hours

The goal of this day hike is to reach the summit of Mount Everett, Massachusetts's ninth-highest mountain, where you will have a commanding view of the Taconic and Berkshire Ranges, the Housatonic River Valley, and the distant Catskills. You will pass by a number of waterfalls on the Race Brook Trail as you make your way up to the A.T. The highest one is nearly 100 feet tall.

THE HIKE

From the trailhead on MA 41, hike west on the blue-blazed Race Brook Falls Trail. In 0.25 mile, the gradual ascent will get steeper as you climb out of the valley. At mile 1.0, there is a fine view of the Housatonic Valley, and at mile 1.5, reach a designated campsite with a privy and a platform for tents. In another 0.5 mile, reach the junction with the A.T. Turn right on the A.T. and begin climbing the south side of Mount Everett. After a 0.75-mile rocky and often steep climb, you will reach the open summit of Mount Everett. Return via the Appalachian and Race Brook Falls Trails to the trailhead on MA 41.

TRAILHEAD DIRECTIONS

Take I-90 West to Exit 2 (Lee/Pittsfield), turn left onto US 20 East; then immediately turn right onto MA 102 West. Drive 4.6 miles, turn left onto US 7 South, and drive 7.6 miles. Turn right onto MA 23 West/MA 41 South, and drive 3.9 miles. Turn left to stay on MA 41 South, and drive 5.1 miles; the parking area (for the Race Brook Trail) will be on your right.

GPS TRAILHEAD COORDINATES N42° 05.390' W73° 24.675'

OPPOSITE: The hike up Mount Everett is short and steep. *Photo: Lafe Low*

CONNECTICUT

Hike	Page	Length (mi)	Configuration	Time (hr)	Difficulty	Features
48. Bear Mountain and Sages Ravine	88	8.0	round-trip	5.5	★★	mountain peak, scenic view, waterfall
49. Lions Head	89	5.6	round-trip	3.5	★★	mountain peak, scenic view
50. Lions Head and Riga Shelter	90	2.6	round-trip	1.5	★★	mountain peak, scenic view
51. Rand's View	92	6.6	round-trip	3.5	★★	scenic view
52. The River Trail	93	1.0	loop	0.5	★	waterfall, historic area, wheelchair access
53. St. Johns Ledges and Caleb's Peak	94	2.4	round-trip	1.25	★★	mountain peak, scenic view
54. Indian Rocks	96	7.4	round-trip	5.0	★★	scenic view
55. Ten Mile River and Hill	96	5.0	round-trip	2.5	★★	scenic view, pond or river, historic area, bird-watching

DIFFICULTY ★★★ strenuous ★★ moderate ★ easy   CONFIGURATION ⬈ round-trip ↻ loop

mountain peak   scenic view   pond or river   waterfall   historic area   bird-watching

wheelchair access

FROM MASSACHUSETTS, THE APPALACHIAN TRAIL climbs Bear Mountain as it enters Connecticut. The Trail follows the Taconic Range to its southern end at Lions Head, where there is an outstanding panoramic view. The A.T. then crosses a few mountains and follows along the Housatonic River. The A.T. traverses 52 miles of Connecticut.

Although the mountains in Connecticut are all less than 2,400 feet in elevation, there are many fine viewpoints in this section of the A.T. The high points—Lions Head, Rand's View, Hang Glider View, and others—offer commanding views of the countryside.

In Falls Village, the A.T. follows a portion of the River Trail, one of the first sections of the Trail to become wheelchair accessible.

The A.T. crosses into and out of New York on the side of Schaghticoke Mountain and then passes into New York for good at Hoyt Road, 7 miles farther.

48 BEAR MOUNTAIN AND SAGES RAVINE

MODERATE | 8-mile round-trip | 5.5 hours

From the ruins of a stone tower on the summit of Bear Mountain, there are fine views of the Housatonic River Valley. The marker on the summit, placed there in 1885, is incorrect, however; this is not the highest point in Connecticut. The actual high point (elevation 2,380') is on the south slope of nearby Mount Frissell, whose summit lies in Massachusetts.

The rough and rocky climb down from Bear Mountain leads to the cool, clear waters of Sages Ravine Brook, which drop through the ravine in a seemingly never-ending series of waterfalls and pools.

THE HIKE

From the parking lot on CT 41, follow the blue-blazed Undermountain Trail. Climb moderately and then more steeply 1.1 miles to the junction with the Paradise Lane Trail. Turn left, continuing to follow the Undermountain Trail, and reach Riga Junction in 0.8 mile. Turn right and follow the A.T., climbing the south slope of Bear Mountain, where there are many views along the climb. Reach the summit of Bear Mountain in 0.9 mile. The ruins of the stone tower offer a good observation platform.

Continue north on the A.T. Descend steeply over rock slabs down the north slope of Bear Mountain, passing the base of the mountain in 0.35 mile and the junction with the Paradise Lane Trail in another 0.35 mile.

Reach Sages Ravine Brook in another 0.1 mile. The A.T. follows the Brook down the ravine for the next 0.6 mile. There are many good places to picnic along the stream, particularly on the side opposite the Trail.

The return hike is via the A.T. back to near the top of the ravine. Turn left onto the blue-blazed Paradise Lane Trail and follow it 2.08 miles to its junction with the Undermountain Trail. Turn left on the Undermountain Trail and follow it 1.1 miles down the mountain to the trailhead on CT 41.

TRAILHEAD DIRECTIONS

Take I-84 to Exit 7 and merge onto US 7 North. Continue on US 7 North for 42.9 miles, veer left onto CT 112 West, and drive 1.8 miles. Turn right onto Salmon Kill Road, and drive 4.1 miles. Turn right onto US 44, and drive 0.4 mile. Veer left onto CT 41 North, and drive 3.3 miles to the parking area on the right.

GPS TRAILHEAD COORDINATES N42° 01.728' W73° 25.733'

49 LIONS HEAD

MODERATE | 5.6-mile round-trip | 3.5 hours

The summit of Lions Head offers a magnificent 360° view of the surrounding countryside. The Twin Lakes can be seen far below to the east with Mount Prospect just south of them.

THE HIKE

From CT 41, follow the A.T. north. In 0.25 mile, pass Plateau Campsite, which has a privy and tent sites. During a 1.5-mile, moderate ascent, cross and recross an old road. The climb can get steep at times. At mile 2.5, reach the junction with the Lions Head Trail. Continue following the A.T. and climb the last steep 0.2 mile to the summit of Lions Head. Hike 0.1 mile farther to the north summit of Lions Head, where you will find views to the north of Bear Mountain, and beyond that, of Mount Greylock in Massachusetts.

The return hike is via the A.T. to the parking lot on CT 41.

TRAILHEAD DIRECTIONS

Take I-84 to Exit 7 and merge onto US 7 North. Continue on US 7 North for 42.9 miles, veer left onto CT 112 West, and drive 1.8 miles. Turn right onto Salmon Kill Road, and drive 4.1 miles. Turn right onto US 44, and drive 0.4 mile. Veer left onto CT 41 North, and drive 0.8 mile to the parking area on the left, between two private residences.

GPS TRAILHEAD COORDINATES N41° 59.644' W73° 25.586'

50 LIONS HEAD AND RIGA SHELTER

MODERATE | 2.6-mile round-trip | 1.5 hours

A former route of the A.T. delivers you to the present-day A.T. and the view from Lions Head in a shorter distance than the previous hike, giving you more time and energy to go beyond it, to Riga Shelter. A shelter may seem an unusual destination for a day hike, but its grand view eastward has made it a popular attraction since being constructed by volunteers of the Appalachian Mountain Club in 1990.

The hike begins with a short, stiff climb to Lions Head, but beyond that it rises at a gentle grade to the shelter.

THE HIKE

From the parking area, ascend on the blue-blazed Lions Head Trail, which soon becomes steeper. (This trail crosses private land, so be sure to respect the owner's rights so that hikers may continue to use it.) Intersect and turn left onto the A.T. at 0.4 mile.

Ascend steeply, walking by the blue-blazed, bad-weather bypass trail at 0.5 mile. Reach Lions Head at 0.6 mile, with views south and east to Salisbury, Lakeville, and Wetauwanchu Mountain. The Twin Lakes are visible to the northeast. Continue to the north overlook at 0.7 mile and gaze northward to Mount Everett, Bear Mountain, and Mount Greylock.

View of the Twin Lakes from Lions Head *Photo: Jeriko Fox*

Stay along the ridgeline on gradually ascending trail, walking by the intersection with the bad-weather bypass trail and a blue-blazed side trail, left, that leads to private property at 1.1 miles.

At 1.3 miles, turn onto the short side trail to the Riga Shelter for the promised views. The slope you are walking on drops precipitously to a cliff face, revealing a broad valley of small towns and farm fields that is speckled with the waters of Washinee and Washining Lakes, better known as the Twin Lakes.

Retrace your steps to end up back at the trailhead.

TRAILHEAD DIRECTIONS

Take I-84 to Exit 7, and merge onto US 7 North. Continue on US 7 for 42.9 miles; then veer left onto CT 112 West, and drive 1.8 miles. Turn right onto Salmon Kill Road, and drive 4.1 miles. Turn right onto US 44, and drive 0.2 mile. Turn left onto Factory–Washinee Road, drive 0.2 mile, and make a slight right to stay on this road. Drive 0.6 mile; then stay to the right for Bunker Hill Road. Drive 0.9 mile to the parking area.

GPS TRAILHEAD COORDINATES N41° 59.924' W73° 26.280'

51 RAND'S VIEW

MODERATE | 6.6-mile round-trip | 3.5 hours

The A.T. in Connecticut offers many fine viewpoints, but the best of the best is Rand's View. This panoramic vista takes in the Twin Lakes and Housatonic Valley, as well as the entire Taconic Range. Mount Greylock, the highest peak in Massachusetts, is 50 miles away, but you can see it to the north on clear days.

If you would like a longer hike, Mount Prospect is 0.7 mile beyond Rand's View on the A.T.

Rand's View   *Photo: Tim Farrell*

THE HIKE

From the trailhead on US 44, follow the A.T. south, climbing Wetauwanchu Mountain (locally known as Barrack Matiff). Reach the high point of this mountain at mile 0.8 and a jeep road at mile 1.6. A buried cable right-of-way lies 0.25 mile past the jeep road. At mile 2.5, reach Billy's View, and in another 0.4 mile, reach Giant's Thumb, a noteworthy rock formation on the northern slope of Raccoon Hill.

Rand's View is 0.4 mile beyond Giant's Thumb. If you would like to press on to the summit of Mount Prospect (elevation 1,461'), continue following the A.T. north 0.75 mile. Mount Prospect offers fine views of the Housatonic River Valley.

The return hike, from either destination, is north on the A.T. to the trailhead on US 44.

TRAILHEAD DIRECTIONS

Take I-84 to Exit 7 and merge onto US 7 North. Continue on US 7 North for 42.9 miles, veer left onto CT 112 West, and drive 1.8 miles. Turn right onto Salmon Kill Road, and drive 4.1 miles. Turn right onto US 44, and drive 1.1 miles to the parking area.

GPS TRAILHEAD COORDINATES N41° 59.510' W73° 24.903'

Great Falls on the Housatonic River in Falls Village   Photo: Jennifer Yakey-Ault/Shutterstock

52 THE RIVER TRAIL

EASY | 1-mile loop | 30 minutes

In the 1990s, a short section of the A.T. was paved to become a portion of the River Trail, a 1-mile wheelchair-accessible pathway in Falls Village. This was done, in part, as a way to demonstrate how the A.T. could follow the spirit of the Americans with Disabilities Act.

The A.T. portion of the trip is along the Housatonic River, and signs mark sites of historic significance. The upper part of the loop follows the route of a harness racing track from the 1800s. Along the way, there are pleasant views of the rapids and small falls on the river as the Trail passes through open fields and green forests. The variety of scenery and ease of travel make this a good trip to take with the kids.

THE HIKE
From the parking area, follow the hard-packed trail to the A.T., where you will turn to travel beside the river. Bypass the first side trail to the upper portion of the River Trail before turning onto the second side trail and returning to the parking area.

TRAILHEAD DIRECTIONS
Take I-84 to Exit 7 and merge onto US 7 North. Continue on US 7 North for 43.3 miles, turn left onto Warren No. 1 Turnpike Road, and drive 1.4 miles. Turn left onto Water Street, and drive 0.1 mile to the River Trail Parking Area.

GPS TRAILHEAD COORDINATES N41° 57.367' W73° 22.061'

53 ST. JOHNS LEDGES AND CALEB'S PEAK

MODERATE | 2.4-mile round-trip | 1.25 hours

This hike has a steep ascent and a steep descent—up to and down from St. Johns Ledges—but the climb is less than 0.5 mile. Ninety rock steps installed by a trail crew from the Appalachian Mountain Club aid you. The cliffs around St. Johns Ledges are often used for rock-climbing instruction. Both St. Johns Ledges and Caleb's Peak offer wonderful views.

The trek to St. Johns Ledges is short but rocky.
Photo: Lafe Low

THE HIKE

From River Road, enter the woods heading south on the A.T. The Trail then travels toward the base of St. Johns Ledges and soon reaches the ascent of 90 stone steps. At mile 0.5, reach the top of the ledges and good views of the Housatonic Valley and the town of Kent.

Continue south along the A.T. another 0.7 mile to Caleb's Peak (elevation 1,160'). The ledge outcrop on its summit provides great views to the south. Return north to the parking area on River Road via the A.T.

TRAILHEAD DIRECTIONS

Take I-84 to Exit 7 and merge onto US 7 North. Continue on US 7 North for 25.1 miles to Kent. Turn left onto CT 341 West, and drive 0.3 mile, over the Housatonic River. Turn right onto Skiff Mountain Road, and drive 1.1 miles. At the fork, veer right onto River Road, and drive 1.7 miles (the road turns to dirt) to the trailhead.

GPS TRAILHEAD COORDINATES N41° 45.497' W73° 27.018'

54 INDIAN ROCKS

MODERATE | 7.4-mile round-trip, with road walk on CT 341 | 5 hours

This hike ascends Mount Algo and follows the ridge along Schaghticoke Mountain. At Indian Rocks, the Trail is on the Schaghticoke Indian Reservation, which is part of the last major American Indian stronghold in Connecticut. Indian settlements at the confluence of the Housatonic and Ten Mile Rivers date back to prehistory, and in 1730 more than 100 Indian families still lived in the area.

THE HIKE

From the parking area, walk east on CT 341; then follow the A.T. south, ascending through the woods. At 0.4 mile, follow a woods road to the right for a short distance before heading left into the woods and ascending gradually.

At mile 0.5, a side trail leads right to water and the Mount Algo Shelter. Continue along the A.T. and reach the height of the land at mile 1.2. Cross Thayer Brook at mile 1.5. After Thayer Brook, ascend steeply up a rocky path to the high point of Schaghticoke Mountain at mile 2.3. From here, the Trail follows ledges that offer good views to the south.

In another 0.75 mile, descend into Rattlesnake Den, a ravine with large hemlocks and tumbled boulders. After crossing a brook, you will ascend gradually. There is water here as well as a campsite with a privy on a side trail.

In another 0.25 mile, descend into Dry Gulch, a rocky ravine, and climb steeply out of it. From here, you will climb along the eastern slope of Schaghticoke and reach Indian Rocks at mile 3.7. This overlook has views to the east of the Housatonic River Valley. From here, return north to CT 341 via the A.T.

TRAILHEAD DIRECTIONS

Take I-84 to Exit 7 and merge onto US 7 North. Continue on US 7 North for 25.1 miles to Kent. Turn left onto CT 341 West, and drive 0.6 mile to the parking area, at the junction of CT 341 and Schaghticoke Road. The trail crossing is 0.2 mile farther west.

GPS TRAILHEAD COORDINATES N41° 43.854' W73° 29.436'

Bulls Bridge *Photo: Nancy Kennedy/Shutterstock*

55 TEN MILE RIVER AND HILL

MODERATE | 5-mile round-trip, including road walk | 2.5 hours

A swim in the Ten Mile River and a view of the Housatonic Valley entice you to undertake this moderate hike. You will also walk along the Housatonic River, looking at its numerous small cascades and waterfalls and enjoying the shade of the many hemlock trees.

The hike starts close to Bulls Bridge over the Housatonic River. It is one of the few remaining covered bridges in Connecticut, and one of only two that still carry traffic. It is worth taking the few extra steps over to see it, and if the water is not running high, the river just below the bridge may lure you into an after-hike swim.

THE HIKE

You could start the hike by following a side trail from the parking area. However, to stay along the A.T. throughout the hike, walk along Bulls Bridge Road for several hundred yards to turn southward on the A.T. Go over a low rise and come to the Housatonic River at 0.7 mile. The Trail follows an old road on a high bank above the river, giving you the opportunity to enjoy the stream and maybe spy a great blue heron trolling the shallow waters in search of a meal.

Walk through a break in a stone wall at 1.2 miles, a reminder of the days when this land was used for agricultural purposes. A power line right-of-way opens up a view south of Ten Mile Hill, the day's destination.

Cross Ten Mile River on the Ned Anderson Memorial Bridge at 1.3 miles. The place to take a swim is on the south side of the river, but you may want to wait until your return from the top of Ten Mile Hill. Pass through the Ten Mile River Camping Area (privy available) and begin to ascend. Pass the side trail to Ten Mile River Lean-To at 1.5 miles and the blue-blazed John Herrick Trail at 2.4 miles. Reach the summit of Ten Mile Hill at 2.5 miles and take the short side trail to the view of the Housatonic Valley. Return via the A.T.

TRAILHEAD DIRECTIONS

Take I-84 to Exit 7 and merge onto US 7 North. Continue on US 7 North for 21.2 miles. Turn left onto Bulls Bridge Road, and drive 0.4 mile, crossing the Housatonic River on the covered Bulls Bridge. The parking area will be on your left.

GPS TRAILHEAD COORDINATES N41° 40.546' W73° 30.878'

NEW YORK

Hike	Page	Length (mi)	Configuration	Time (hr)	Difficulty	Features
56. Great Swamp and Corbin Hill	100	2.8	↗	1.5	★	👀 〰️
57. West Mountain	102	2.0	↗	1.5	★★	🏔️ 👀
58. West Slope of Hosner Mountain	103	3.8	↗	2.0	★	👀
59. Canopus Hill	104	1.5	↗	< 1.0	★	👀
60. Denning Hill	104	5.2	↗	3.0	★	🏔️ H
61. Anthony's Nose	106	2.6	↗	1.5	★★★	👀
62. Buchanan Mountain	107	1.6	↗	1.0	★	🏔️ 👀
63. Fitzgerald Falls and Mombasha High Point	108	4.6	↗	3.0	★	👀 💧
64. Eastern Pinnacles and Cat Rocks	109	3.8	↗	2.5	★★	👀
65. Prospect Rock	111	3.4	↗	2.0	★	👀

DIFFICULTY ★★★ strenuous ★★ moderate ★ easy   CONFIGURATION ↗ round-trip

🏔️ mountain peak 👀 scenic view 〰️ pond or river 💧 waterfall H historic area

THE 92 MILES OF THE Appalachian Trail in New York run from Schaghticoke Mountain on the Connecticut–New York state line to the Kittatinny Range in New Jersey, passing through Clarence Fahnestock, Harriman, and Bear Mountain State Parks. Just south of the Bear Mountain Bridge, the A.T. reaches its lowest point at the Trailside Zoo in Bear Mountain State Park (elevation 124').

A portion of the Trail a short distance south of the Bear Mountain Bridge was the first section of the A.T. to be built. It was cleared in 1923 by a group from the New York–New Jersey Trail Conference. That group still maintains the Trail in New York and New Jersey.

You can see New York City's skyline on a clear day from several points along the A.T. in New York, including West Mountain Shelter and Mombasha High Point. After passing through Harriman and Bear Mountain State Parks, the A.T. travels west, then south, leaving New York near Prospect Rock.

56 GREAT SWAMP AND CORBIN HILL

EASY | 2.8-mile round-trip | 1.5 hours

You don't need a car to reach the beginning of this hike. On weekends and holidays, the Metro North commuter train from New York City stops at the Appalachian Trail Station next to NY 22. (Visit mta.info/mnr for a schedule.)

Great Swamp is the second-largest freshwater wetland in New York, encompassing thousands of acres along its 20-mile length. Muskrats and other wildlife live among nine known rare plant and animal species, including spreading globeflower and Atlantic white cedar.

The views from the open fields of Corbin Hill take in West Mountain and Cat Rocks to the west, Waldo Hill and Sharp Hills to the north, and the route of the A.T. climbing the ridge to the east.

THE HIKE

Walk southward on NY 22 from the parking area, turn right onto a dirt road at 0.1 mile, and cross the railroad tracks at the Appalachian Trail Station. Soon follow puncheon across the wet areas of Great Swamp, crossing Swamp River on a footbridge at 0.4 mile. Cattails grow in great numbers beside the trail.

Leonard M. Adkins at the Appalachian Trail Station   *Photo: Laurie Adkins*

Begin the steady but gradual climb along the side of Corbin Hill. Open meadows, dotted by summer flowers such as gentian and mullein, provide the views. It is time to turn around when the trail enters woods near the top of the rise.

TRAILHEAD DIRECTIONS

Take I-84 to Exit 17 (Ludingtonville Road). Turn east (right from I-84 West, left from I-84 East), and drive 0.6 mile. Turn left onto Mooney Hill Road, and drive 2.5 miles. Turn right onto NY 292 South, and drive 0.8 mile. Turn left onto NY 311 North, and drive 1.3 miles. Turn left onto NY 22 North, and drive 5.7 miles to the crossing; the parking area is 0.1 mile farther.

GPS TRAILHEAD COORDINATES N41° 35.575' W73° 35.247'

57 WEST MOUNTAIN

MODERATE | **2-mile round-trip** | **1.5 hours**

This short but sometimes steep climb leads to the highest of several peaks on West Mountain, which offers two fine views of the surrounding New York farmland. At the trailhead, a large oak tree on the opposite side of the road from the direction you will be hiking bears a white A.T. blaze and is known locally as the Dover Oak. At more than 100 feet tall, with a girth of more than 20 feet, the tree is believed to be the largest on the A.T.

The Dover Oak
Photo: John Hayes (gravelBoy)/Flickr

THE HIKE

From County Road 20, follow the A.T. south. In 0.25 mile, pass through a gap in an old rock wall and begin climbing the eastern slope of West Mountain. At mile 0.7, pass the 0.1-mile side trail to the Telephone Pioneers Shelter. Continue on the A.T. 0.2 mile to a short side trail to a nice view from a rock ledge. Hike another 0.1 mile south on the A.T. and reach the summit of West Mountain (elevation 1,225'), where you'll be rewarded with a fine view to the north of rural New York. The return hike is north on the A.T. back down to the trailhead on CR 20.

TRAILHEAD DIRECTIONS

Take I-84 to Exit 17 (Ludingtonville Road). Turn east (right from I-84 West, left from I-84 East), and drive 0.6 mile. Turn left onto Mooney Hill Road, and drive 2.5 miles. Turn right onto NY 292 South, and drive 0.8 mile. Turn left onto NY 311 North, and drive 1.3 miles. Turn left onto NY 22 North, and drive 4.5 miles. Turn left onto Corbin Road, and drive 0.4 mile. Turn right onto West Dover Road/CR 20, and drive 2.1 miles. Limited parking is available along the road at the trailhead.

GPS TRAILHEAD COORDINATES N41° 36.164' W73° 36.694'

58 WEST SLOPE OF HOSNER MOUNTAIN

EASY | 3.8-mile round-trip | 2 hours

This day hike is unusual because the trail never climbs to the top of the mountain you are hiking on; nevertheless, there are several fine views of the Hudson River Valley from a sidehill trail. The views are somewhat improved in the fall, when the leaves drop, but the hike is also nice in the summer. The loop part of the hike uses an old section of the A.T. (now blue blazed).

THE HIKE

From Hosner Mountain Road, hike south on the A.T. and begin climbing Hosner Mountain, passing through a hemlock grove on your way up the ridge. There is a fine view of the Hudson River Valley to the north and west. At mile 1.3, reach a blue-blazed trail (the old A.T. on which you will return), and continue following the white-blazed A.T. another 0.6 mile to reach the southern end of the blue-blazed trail.

Following the blue-blazed trail, which takes a lower route across the ridge, hike back to the A.T., and return to the trailhead on Hosner Mountain Road.

TRAILHEAD DIRECTIONS

Take I-84 to Exit 16N (Taconic State Parkway North/Albany). Merge onto Taconic State Parkway, drive 0.9 mile, and take the first exit for NY 52/Fishkill/Carmel. Turn left onto NY 52 West, and drive 0.3 mile; turn left onto Hosner Mountain Road, and drive 0.9 mile. Turn left toward the bridge, cross over the parkway, and turn right onto Hosner Mountain Road again. Drive 1.1 miles; then veer right to stay on Hosner Mountain Road and cross under the interstate. Drive 0.3 mile to the trail crossing; there is limited parking available along the road.

GPS TRAILHEAD COORDINATES N41° 32.462' W73° 45.180'

59 CANOPUS HILL

EASY | 1.5-mile round-trip | less than 1 hour

C anopus Hill is a good place to go when daily routines keep you from having much time to escape to the outdoors but the urge to be there is too strong to ignore. The hike to the top of the hill for a view of the surrounding countryside is short and easy.

THE HIKE
Follow the A.T. south, crossing a small stream in 0.1 mile and walking through a forest of evergreen and deciduous trees. The viewpoint on the top of Canopus Hill is reached only 0.75 mile from the road. Return to Canopus Hill Road by following the A.T. north.

TRAILHEAD DIRECTIONS
Take I-84 to Exit 13S (US 9 South/Peekskill). Merge (or from I-84 East, turn) onto US 9 South. Drive 11.1 miles, turn left onto Travis Corners Road, and drive 0.9 mile. Turn right onto Old Albany Post Road, and drive 0.2 mile. Turn left onto Canopus Hill Road, and drive 1.1 miles to A.T. There is parking for one car next to the trail crossing (be sure to pull far off the road).

GPS TRAILHEAD COORDINATES N41° 23.256' W73° 52.747'

60 DENNING HILL

EASY | 5.2-mile round-trip, including road walk | 3 hours

T his hike passes through an area rich in Revolutionary War history. The hills in the area, including Little Fort Hill, all bear names reminiscent of war days. The Old West Point Road once led to Benedict Arnold's headquarters at Garrison. In this area on October 9, 1777, the British moved north from Peekskill to battle with the 2,000 Continentals camped at Continental Village, which is still a small town.

The high point of the hike, Denning Hill (elevation 900'), offers great views. On clear days, you may even see the skyline of New York City.

Along the trail and into the woods   *Photo: Jeriko Fox*

THE HIKE

Walk the road back to where the A.T. crosses the intersection of US 9 and NY 403 and heads north into the woods. At 0.3 mile, you will cross a swampy area on bog bridges and then the Old Highland Turnpike, a dirt road. The A.T. continues through the woods, turning left and following a cleared strip of land in another 0.25 mile.

At mile 0.6, following a brief but steep climb, you will pass through a grassy area and turn left onto a paved road. After crossing the paved Old West Point Road (the pavement ends here), you will continue downhill on a private gravel road, turning left off that road in 0.1 mile.

The trail enters the woods, passes through an overgrown field, and begins to climb Little Fort Hill. At mile 1.4, you will come to the junction with a side trail that heads right to Graymoor Monastery. At mile 2.1, another side trail at the top of a rocky ascent leads to a viewpoint. After 0.1 mile, you will turn right onto a woods road, and after another 0.1 mile, you will turn right again, leaving the woods road. (The woods road continues left a short distance to a good view of the Hudson River.) At mile 2.6, after a short but steep climb, you reach the ridge of Denning Hill. After turning right, follow the ridge a short distance to a viewpoint in a clearing. From here, follow the A.T. south back to US 9 and NY 403.

TRAILHEAD DIRECTIONS

Take I-84 to Exit 13S (US 9 South/Peekskill). Merge (or from I-84 East, turn) onto US 9 South. Drive 13.4 miles to the junction with NY 403, which is also the A.T. crossing. Parking is available on a short road between US 9 and NY 403, about 0.1 mile on the right before the trail crossing.

GPS TRAILHEAD COORDINATES N41° 21.044' W73° 55.559'

61 ANTHONY'S NOSE

STRENUOUS | 2.6-mile round-trip | 1.5 hours

Without a doubt, Anthony's Nose has one of the most inspiring and spectacular views in this part of New York. The rocky formation, composed of erosion-resistant granite and gneiss, sits 900 feet above the Hudson River and looks directly down onto the Bear Mountain Bridge. In a sweeping south–north vista, your gaze can take in Iona Island jutting out into the river, Bear Mountain rising high from the opposite bank with Hessian Lake in front of it, and the houses and roadways of Fort Montgomery. On clear days, you can see the skyline of New York City, about 50 miles south.

Because of its position, Anthony's Nose has been an important military site since before the Revolutionary War. In fact, the A.T. used to pass over it until it was closed to hikers in World War II. It wasn't until 1993 that the state once again opened it to the public.

THE HIKE

Use caution as you walk northward from the parking area on busy NY 9D. At about 0.2 mile, cross the highway and follow the A.T. into the woods. The climb is steep, gaining 500 feet in the next 0.5 mile.

Intersect a dirt road at 0.7 mile and turn right onto blue-blazed Camp Smith Trail, gaining more elevation before coming to Anthony's Nose and its Olympian aerie at 1.3 miles. Retrace your steps to return to NY 9D.

TRAILHEAD DIRECTIONS

From I-87, take Exit 16 (NY 17 West/US 6/Harriman). Continue onto NY 17 West; then take the first exit for Woodbury Outlets Boulevard/Central Valley/US 6 East. Turn left onto NY 32 South, drive 0.3 mile, and turn left to merge onto US 6 East. Drive 6.5 miles; at the traffic circle, take the third exit to stay on US 6 East, and drive 3 miles. At the next traffic circle, take the second exit (toward the Bear Mountain Bridge) to stay on US 6 East, and drive 0.6 mile. Just on the other side of the bridge, turn left onto NY 9D North, and drive 0.3 mile to the small parking area and trail crossing.

GPS TRAILHEAD COORDINATES N41° 19.348' W73° 58.563'

Little Dam Lake *Photo: TheTurducken/Flickr*

62 BUCHANAN MOUNTAIN

EASY | 1.6-mile round-trip | 1 hour

Highlights of this short day hike include views from the first and second summits of Buchanan Mountain (elevation 1,142').

THE HIKE

From the A.T. crossing at East Mombasha Road, enter the woods heading south and climb steadily. In 0.25 mile, you will reach the first viewpoint on the secondary summit of Buchanan Mountain. Enjoy views to the east over Little Dam Lake.

Descend steeply to a rocky, hemlock-covered slope and continue along the footpath. In 0.1 mile, cross a stream, and in another 0.1 mile, cross a second stream. At mile 0.5, you will cross the third stream in your descent before climbing the final 0.25 mile to the primary summit of Buchanan Mountain. After enjoying the view, turn around and head back to the parking area on East Mombasha Road.

TRAILHEAD DIRECTIONS

From I-87, take Exit 16 (NY 17 West/US 6/Harriman). Continue onto NY 17 West; then take the first exit for Woodbury Outlets Boulevard/Central Valley/US 6 East. Turn left onto NY 17 South, and drive 5.9 miles. Turn right onto Orange Turnpike, and drive 0.9 mile. Turn left onto Bramertown Road/West Mombasha Road, and drive 0.8 mile. Turn right onto East Mombasha Road, and drive 0.5 mile to the trail crossing. Only day parking is permitted at the trail crossing.

GPS TRAILHEAD COORDINATES N41° 15.970' W74° 11.642'

The A.T. ascends beside Fitzgerald Falls. *Photo: Leonard M. Adkins*

63 FITZGERALD FALLS AND MOMBASHA HIGH POINT

EASY | 4.6-mile round-trip | 3 hours

This day hike will take you to the beautiful Fitzgerald Falls and Mombasha High Point, where there are good views. On especially clear days, you can see New York City from the High Point.

THE HIKE

From the A.T. crossing at Lakes Road (Monroe Road), the footpath descends and crosses a wood truss bridge over Trout Brook. In 0.25 mile you will cross another brook; turn left and follow the brook through a hemlock grove. Because this area is frequently flooded, there is a blue-blazed bypass trail to avoid the crossing of two more brooks in wet weather. The side trail ascends to the right through hemlocks and rejoins the A.T. after 0.1 mile (at Fitzgerald Falls).

Fitzgerald Falls flows 25 feet through a rocky cleft. Crossing the stream just below the falls, climb steeply up rock steps alongside the falls. After 0.1 mile, cross a stream and a tributary before passing through a hemlock grove, and in another 0.1 mile, cross another tributary stream and a dirt road as you continue to ascend. At mile 0.75, pass some stone walls to the left. These are the remains of an abandoned settlement.

Just over 0.5 mile later, make a left before climbing steadily 0.1 mile later. At mile 1.5, at the top of a rise, the blue-blazed Allis Trail heads right. A viewpoint is located a short distance north on the Allis Trail, which was named for an early treasurer of the Appalachian Trail Conservancy. From the viewpoint, High Point Monument in New Jersey and Mount Tammany at the Pennsylvania–New Jersey state line are visible to the west.

The trail levels off here and reaches Mombasha High Point (elevation 1,280') in another 0.75 mile. The view to the left is of Mombasha Lake with Shunemunk Mountain behind it to the northeast. Kloiber's Pond is straight ahead along West Mombasha Road; Harriman State Park is to the east. You can see New York City on the southern horizon on clear days, and Bellvale Mountain is to the west. Return to the parking area on Lakes Road by heading south on the A.T.

TRAILHEAD DIRECTIONS

From I-87, take Exit 16 (NY 17 West/US 6/Harriman). Continue onto NY 17 West; then, in 1.1 mile, continue onto US 6 West, and drive 3.1 miles to Exit 130 (NY 208/ Monroe/Washingtonville). Turn left onto NY 208 South, and drive 0.7 mile; then turn right onto Schunemunk Road, and drive 0.3 mile. Turn left onto NY 17M East, and drive 0.5 mile. Turn right onto Lakes Road, and drive 5.3 miles to the trail crossing.

GPS TRAILHEAD COORDINATES N41° 16.411' W74° 15.2516'

64 EASTERN PINNACLES AND CAT ROCKS

MODERATE
3.8-mile round-trip, with road walk on Continental Road and NY 17a
2.5 hours

The many rock formations along the ridgeline of Bellvale Mountain provide a number of views to the south and east. Two of the best vistas are seen from Eastern Pinnacles and Cat Rocks.

THE HIKE

From the parking area, walk back toward NY 17A, turn right onto it, make a left into the woods on the A.T. about 100 yards later, and rise at a gradual rate. Within

Stepladders enable hikers to reach Cat Rocks.   *Photo: Leonard M. Adkins*

a few hundred feet, pass by a blue-blazed side trail that leads to a platform used by hawk-watchers during the raptors' annual fall migration.

Join a woods road at 0.5 mile and cross a utility right-of-way at 0.8 mile. Make a short, steep climb to the top of Eastern Pinnacles at 1.4 miles. A blue-blazed trail bypasses this steep climb but also misses the view. This red, pudding stone rock, shaped by moving glaciers, rises above the vegetation and provides views south of Greenwood Lake and north and east across the forested lands of Sterling Forest.

This vista would have been much different if, in the 1990s, a coalition of organizations, including the Appalachian Trail Conservancy, had not been able to protect the forest from planned development. Instead of woodland, you would have been gazing upon 14,000 homes and scores of office buildings, commercial businesses, and golf courses.

Continue along the A.T., climbing up and over small bumps on the ridgeline, and going over occasional open areas. Cross a small stream at 1.7 miles, and climb to the top of Cat Rocks (a blue-blazed trail bypasses it) at 1.9 miles for additional views. Return by following the A.T. south.

TRAILHEAD DIRECTIONS

From I-87, take Exit 16 (NY 17 West/US 6/Harriman). Continue onto NY 17 West; then, in 1.1 mile, continue onto US 6 West, and drive 3.1 miles to Exit 130 (NY 208/ Monroe/Washingtonville). Turn left onto NY 208 South, and drive 0.7 mile; then turn right onto Schunemunk Road, and drive 0.3 mile. Turn left onto NY 17M East, and drive 0.5 mile. Turn right onto Lakes Road, and drive 8.7 miles. Turn right onto Mountain Lakes Lane, and drive 0.1 mile; then turn right onto NY 17A West, and drive 1.5 miles to the trail crossing. The parking area is just ahead on the left.

GPS TRAILHEAD COORDINATES   N41° 14.677' W74° 17.181'

65 PROSPECT ROCK

EASY | 3.4-mile round-trip | 2 hours

Prospect Rock, with its magnificent views of Greenwood Lake and the Taylor Mountains, is the destination of this hike. You will walk the State Line Trail, which runs along the New York–New Jersey state line, to access the A.T.

THE HIKE

Begin hiking on the State Line Trail and ascend 0.25 mile before turning right (houses are still in view here). For the next 0.25 mile, the trail uses log steps to prevent erosion.

At mile 0.75, the Ernest Walter Trail (yellow blazes) heads left. This trail makes a loop around Surprise Lake and West Pond. After 0.1 mile, the State Line Trail turns sharply left and then right. For the next 0.4 mile, the trail heads west, crossing over the ridge of Bellvale Mountain with several short ascents and descents.

At mile 1.2, the State Line Trail joins the A.T. at the New York–New Jersey state line, heading north on the A.T. 0.1 mile to good western views from open rocks. After 0.25 mile, there is a trail register on a pine tree to the right of the trail, and 0.5 mile after joining the A.T. (following a short climb), you will reach Prospect Rock (elevation 1,433').

Return by following the A.T. south 0.5 mile, pick up the State Line Trail, and descend to Greenwood Lake.

TRAILHEAD DIRECTIONS

From I-87, take Exit 16 (NY 17 West/US 6/Harriman). Continue onto NY 17 West; then take the first exit for Woodbury Outlets Boulevard/Central Valley/US 6 East. Turn left onto NY 17 South, and drive 6.9 miles. Turn right toward NY 17A, and at the top of the ramp turn right onto NY 17A West. Drive 7.3 miles to Greenwood Lake; then stay left at the fork, onto Windermere Avenue, and drive 0.5 mile. Turn right onto NY 210 South/Jersey Avenue, and drive 3.4 miles to the state line and parking area. The State Line Trail begins opposite the Greenwood Lake Marina.

GPS TRAILHEAD COORDINATES N41° 11.217' W74° 19.880'

NEW JERSEY

Hike	Page	Length (mi)	Configuration	Time (hr)	Difficulty	Features
66. Pinwheel's Vista	114	8.6	↗	5.0	★	👀
67. Pochuck Crossing	115	2.0	↗	1.0	★	〰️ 💧
68. High Point Monument	117	3.0	↗	2.0	★★	⛰️ 👀
69. Sunrise Mountain and Culver Fire Tower	118	7.2	↗	4.0	★★	👀
70. Rattlesnake Mountain	119	9.6	↗	5.5	★★	⛰️ 👀
71. Sunfish Pond	120	8.9	↗	5.0	★★	〰️

DIFFICULTY ★★★ strenuous ★★ moderate ★ easy   CONFIGURATION ↗ round-trip

⛰️ mountain peak   👀 scenic view   〰️ pond or river   💧 waterfall

PASSING THROUGH ABRAM S. HEWITT STATE FOREST, the beginning of New Jersey's portion of the A.T. parallels the New York–New Jersey state line, which runs along Bearfort Mountain above Greenwood Lake. It passes through Wawayanda State Park before descending to Vernon.

Crossing the Vernon Valley, a former glacial lake, the A.T. ascends Pochuck Mountain and descends to the Kittatinny Valley. It continues across the valley to High Point State Park after passing close to Unionville, New York.

High Point is, as the name indicates, the highest point in the state. Although the A.T. doesn't reach the summit, a short side trail does. From High Point State Park, the A.T. traces Kittatinny Ridge to Stokes State Forest, moving along a rocky footpath through hickory and scrub oak forests.

From the Forest, the Trail continues along Kittatinny Ridge through Worthington State Forest to the Delaware Water Gap National Recreation Area. The highlight of the southern end of the A.T. in New Jersey is Sunfish Pond, a beautiful glacial pool.

66 PINWHEEL'S VISTA

EASY | 8.6-mile round-trip | 5 hours

A nice stroll, often along old woods roads, leads to Pinwheel's Vista, a viewpoint with a magnificent view of Vernon Valley and the Kittatinny Ridge. New York's Catskills and Shawangunks can be seen to the north. There are a few steep ascents and descents. Wawayanda, which means "water on the mountain," was the name the Lenape Indians gave to a nearby creek.

THE HIKE

From the Wawayanda State Park headquarters, follow the 0.3-mile blue-blazed trail, which leads to the A.T. Turn left and follow the white-blazed A.T. south. In 0.1 mile, reach the 0.1-mile side trail to Wawayanda Shelter and continue hiking along the A.T. as it follows several other woods roads. The iron bridge over a stream is 0.8 mile from the shelter side trail. As you walk along the mountain, the Trail continues to follow and cross roads and in and out of the forest.

At 1.9 miles beyond the iron bridge, walk alongside a stream and then cross another stream near a waterfall. In 0.5 mile, cross a stone wall, descend and climb again, and reach the junction with the blue-blazed Wawayanda Ridge Trail at mile 4.1.

View of Vernon Valley and the Kittatinny Ridge   *Photo: Michelle Herman*

Continue following the A.T. and, in 0.1 mile, reach a second blue-blazed trail, which leads to the right 0.1 mile to Pinwheel's Vista. To return, hike back on the A.T. and pick up the blue-blazed trail to the Wawayanda State Park headquarters.

TRAILHEAD DIRECTIONS

From I-287, take Exit 57 (Skyline Drive/Ringwood). From I-287 South, merge onto Skyline Drive; from I-287 North, turn left onto West Oakland Avenue, which quickly becomes Skyline Drive. Drive 5.1 miles; then turn right onto Greenwood Lake Turnpike, and drive 8.3 miles. At the fork, veer right onto Warwick Turnpike. Drive 4.6 miles to the headquarters for Wawayanda State Park.

GPS TRAILHEAD COORDINATES N41° 12.083' W74° 23.491'

67 POCHUCK CROSSING

EASY | 2-mile round-trip | 1 hour

It took 24 years of discussions, planning, and hard work among a coalition of many organizations and hundreds of volunteers to enable you to cross what was once known as the "Pochuck Quagmire." A boardwalk—completed in 2002 and nearly a mile in length, with a 100-foot suspension bridge in the middle of it—allows you to

The Pochuck Crossing boardwalk is nearly a mile long.   *Photo: Leonard M. Adkins*

cross the fields, swamps, and marshes of Pochuck Creek without getting wet. In dry weather, the creek is not much more than a trickle. In wet weather, it easily overflows its channel, flooding the land and turning it into a half-mile-wide lake.

Handicap accessible, the boardwalk takes visitors into a land rich with cardinal flowers, goldenrod, thistle, cattails, marsh hawks, black bears, and limestone formations rising dozens of feet above the floodplain. The open views from the boardwalk include Pochuck Mountain to the west and Wawayanda Mountain to the east.

THE HIKE

The boardwalk starts shortly after following the A.T. south from the parking area. Depending on when you visit, you could be traveling over dry-to-moist land or across a vast and shallow lake. When you reach the suspension bridge you are about halfway through the route.

The end of the boardwalk marks the place to turn around and return to your car.

TRAILHEAD DIRECTIONS

From I-287, take Exit 52A-52B (NJ 23 North/Riverdale), following signs for NJ 23 North. Merge onto NJ 23 North; then drive 13.8 miles. Stay right, following signs for Stockholm Vernon Road; turn right onto Stockholm Vernon Road, and drive 10 miles (during which Stockholm Vernon Road becomes CR 515). Turn left onto Maple Grange Road, and drive 1 mile; then turn right onto Canal Road, and drive 0.5 mile; parking is available at the trail crossing.

GPS TRAILHEAD COORDINATES   N41° 13.671' W74° 28.046'

68 HIGH POINT MONUMENT

MODERATE | 3-mile round-trip | 2 hours

A moderate climb with only one short, steep section will take you to the highest point in the state. From both the wooden observation platform on the A.T. and from High Point Monument, you will be treated to a magnificent 360° view into three states: New Jersey, New York, and Pennsylvania.

THE HIKE

From the parking lot at the park headquarters, follow the A.T. north, cross NJ 23, and reenter the woods. In 0.75 mile, there is a short, steep

High Point Monument   *Photo: Matt Willen*

ascent. In another 0.25 mile, you will reach the observation tower with its commanding view of the area. From the platform, hike 0.25 mile to the blue-blazed side trail, and follow it 0.25 mile to the summit (elevation 1,803') and High Point Monument. To the west is Lake Marcia, just below the mountain in the park; in the distance are the Pocono Mountains in Pennsylvania. To the southwest is Delaware Water Gap, and to the east are Kittatinny Valley and Pochuck and Wawayanda Mountains.

To return, hike on the blue-blazed trail, pick up the A.T., and head south to the parking lot at the park headquarters.

TRAILHEAD DIRECTIONS

From I-84 in New York, take Exit 1 (NJ 23/US 6/Port Jervis/Sussex). From I-84 East, turn left onto NJ 23 South; from I-84 West, turn left onto US 6 West, and then turn left onto NJ 23 South. Drive about 4.6 miles to the High Point State Park headquarters. Turn right into the parking lot, and look for the trail crossing on the driveway near the road.

GPS TRAILHEAD COORDINATES N41° 18.322' W74° 40.208'

69 SUNRISE MOUNTAIN AND CULVER FIRE TOWER

MODERATE | 7.2-mile round-trip | 4 hours

There are several excellent views along this moderate day hike, and one of them is located just a few feet from the trailhead parking area. The walking is easy, and the only thing that classifies the outing as moderate is its length and the many small ascents and descents.

Views from Sunrise Mountain include farmlands and small settlements of the Wallkill Valley to the east and the Pocono Mountains of Pennsylvania across the Delaware River to the west. A 360° view from the fire tower offers the added bonus of looking onto Lakes Owassa and Kittatinny to the south.

THE HIKE

Follow a short side trail from the parking area, coming to the views from the Sunrise Mountain Pavilion at 0.1 mile. The shelter was built in the 1930s and, true to its name, is the place to be as dawn puts an end to darkness.

Continuing south on the A.T., a ledge provides an additional viewpoint before you enter woods and walk the broad crest of Kittatinny Mountain. Pass by Tinsley Trail to the right at 1.1 miles, a slight view to the west at 1.2 miles, and the Stony Brook Trail (leading to Gren Anderson Shelter) at 2.5 miles.

Cross Stony Brook at 2.6 miles, pass the Tower Trail at 3.5 miles, and come to Culver Fire Tower at 3.6 miles. The clearing around the tower will provide excellent views if you don't want to climb its steps for the 360° vista. Return to the Sunrise Mountain parking area by heading north on the A.T.

TRAILHEAD DIRECTIONS

From I-84 in Pennsylvania, take Exit 46 (US 6/Milford). Turn onto US 6 East, and drive 2.3 miles into Milford; continue straight onto US 209 South, and drive 0.9 mile. Turn left onto US 206 South, and drive 9.9 miles. Turn left onto Upper North Shore Road, and drive 0.2 mile; then turn left onto Sunrise Mountain Road, and drive 4.8 miles to the parking area at the road's end.

GPS TRAILHEAD COORDINATES N41° 13.163' W74° 43.072'

Buttermilk Falls   *Photo: Andrew F. Kazmierski/Shutterstock*

70 RATTLESNAKE MOUNTAIN

MODERATE | 9.6-mile round-trip | 5.5 hours

A pleasant walk over gravel roads and trail takes you to the rocky summit of Rattlesnake Mountain. From the summit, overlooking the Poconos in Pennsylvania, there is a fine but limited view of the valley below.

THE HIKE

From Blue Mountain Lakes Road, which the A.T. follows about 30 yards, hike north on the A.T. and cross a dirt road in 0.25 mile. In another 1.4 miles, cross a gravel road and descend a short, steep section before reaching a second gravel road at mile 1.8. A short, blue-blazed side trail leads from this gravel road to a view of Crater Lake. Hike along gravel roads for the next 1.4 miles. At mile 3, a steep, 1.5-mile side trail leads to the base of Buttermilk Falls, which is 1,000 feet downhill.

Continuing on the A.T., you will leave the gravel roads behind in 0.25 mile. In 0.75 mile, a short side trail leads to a viewpoint, and in 0.5 mile, after a stream crossing, a blue-blazed side trail leads to water. Begin climbing 0.25 mile and reach the rocky summit of Rattlesnake Mountain (elevation 1,492'), where you'll find views to the west. Return on the A.T. to the trailhead on Flatbrookville Road.

TRAILHEAD DIRECTIONS

From I-80, take Exit 12 (CR 521/Hope Blairstown). From I-80 West, stay right to merge onto Hope Blairstown Road; from I-80 East, turn left onto Hope Blairstown Road. Drive about 5.1 miles; then turn left onto NJ 94 South. Drive 0.3 mile; then turn right onto Stillwater Road; immediately veer left at the fork onto Bridge Street, and drive 0.2 mile. Turn right onto High Street; then almost immediately veer left onto Millbrook Road, and drive 7.2 miles. Turn right onto Old Mine Road, and drive 1.5 miles. Turn right onto Flatbrookville Stillwater Road, and drive about 2.9 miles. Parking is available along the side of the road about 50 yards beyond the trail crossing.

GPS TRAILHEAD COORDINATES N41° 05.419' W74° 54.671'

71 SUNFISH POND

MODERATE | 8.9-mile round-trip | 5 hours

This hike starts alongside Dunnfield Creek in Delaware Water Gap and climbs Kittatinny Mountain to reach the cool, clear waters of Sunfish Pond (elevation 1,382'). The pond is a glacial lake high on the mountain. Because this trip is a favorite with day hikers, the area can get crowded. If you want to avoid the crowds, try hiking during the week if possible, or early in the day. By starting at the parking lot before 9 a.m., you may find some solitude at the pond.

THE HIKE

From the parking lot of the Dunnfield Creek Natural Area, hike north on the A.T. and cross a bridge over Dunnfield Creek. In 0.4 mile, reach the junction with a blue-blazed trail leading to Mount Tammany, where there is a spectacular view of Delaware Water Gap. Continuing north on the A.T., hike 1.1 miles to reach the junction with the

Sunfish Pond is the A.T.'s southernmost glacial pond. *Photo: Leonard M. Adkins*

yellow-blazed Beulahland Trail, and another 1.6 miles to the junction with the blue-blazed Douglas Trail. Reach the southwest corner of the pond in 0.6 mile (mile 3.7).

The A.T. follows the edge of the pond for the next 0.75 mile. The return hike is south on the A.T. to the parking lot at the trailhead.

TRAILHEAD DIRECTIONS

From I-80 East in Pennsylvania, cross into New Jersey and take the first exit ramp for the Dunnfield Creek Natural Area/Delaware Water Gap National Recreational Area. From I-80 West, take the exit about 3.5 miles past the interchange with NJ 94, following signs for Dunnfield Creek/Appalachian Trail. You will see the white-blazed A.T. as you pass by the information center. Follow the blazes as you drive to the parking lot at the trailhead, which is 0.5 mile beyond the information center.

GPS TRAILHEAD COORDINATES N40° 58.292' W75° 07.533'

PENNSYLVANIA

Hike	Page	Length (mi)	Configuration	Time (hr)	Difficulty	Features
72. Winona Cliff, Lookout Rock, and Mount Minsi	125	4.6	↗	5.0	★★	🏔️ 🔭
73. Wolf Rocks	126	3.2	↗	2.0	★★	🔭
74. Lookout Rock and Hahn's Lookout	127	2.0	↗	1.5	★★	🔭
75. Weathering Knob	128	2.0	↗	1.5	★★	🔭
76. Blue Mountain	129	6.3	↻	4.0	★★	🔭
77. Bake Oven Knob	130	0.8	↗	0.5	★	🔭 🗡️
78. The Cliffs and Bear Rocks	131	7.0	↗	4.0	★★	🔭
79. Windsor Furnace, Pulpit Rock, and The Pinnacle	132	10.2	↗	5.5	★★	🔭 🏛️
80. Auburn Lookout	134	5.0	↗	3.0	★★	🔭
81. Table Rock	135	4.2	↗	2.0	★	🔭
82. Hawk Rock	136	3.0	↗	2.0	★★★	🔭
83. Boiling Springs	137	0.6	↗	0.3	★	🔭 〰️ 🏛️
84. Chimney Rocks	138	3.0	↗	2.0	★★★	🔭

DIFFICULTY ★★★ strenuous ★★ moderate ★ easy   CONFIGURATION ↗ round-trip ↻ loop

🏔️ mountain peak   🔭 scenic view   〰️ pond or river   🏛️ historic area   🗡️ bird-watching

WITH CLOSE TO 230 MILES TO TRAVERSE, the Appalachian Trail in Pennsylvania is one of the easiest and one of the hardest to hike. The Trail is often characterized by a tough climb up a ridge, followed by a level but rocky walk.

The Trail in Pennsylvania begins at Delaware Water Gap in the Kittatinny Mountains, where it climbs more than 1,000 feet to the summit of Mount Minsi. This rough and rocky trail traverses the ridge from gap to gap: Totts, Fox, Wind, Smith, Little, and finally the rocky face of Lehigh Gap.

For the next 30 miles (after you climb out of Lehigh Gap), the Trail once again follows the ridge, passing Bake Oven Knob, the Cliffs, and Blue Mountain Summit before reaching Hawk Mountain Sanctuary near Eckville.

From here, the Trail climbs once again to the ridge, passing The Pinnacle, an outstanding viewpoint over the Pennsylvania countryside.

From The Pinnacle, the A.T. drops down to Windsor Furnace, the site of an old iron-stove plant; glassy slag can still be seen along the Trail. The A.T. continues to Port Clinton, where it regains the ridge and follows it more than 30 miles.

From Swatara Gap, the Trail leaves Blue Mountain, crosses St. Anthony's Wilderness, and passes the sites of Rausch Gap and Yellow Gap villages. After ascending Second Mountain, Sharp Mountain, and Stony Mountain, the Trail climbs to the ridge of Peters Mountain and follows it 15 miles before descending to the Susquehanna River at Duncannon.

The A.T. heads southwest at the Susquehanna, crossing Cove and Blue Mountains and falling to the Cumberland Valley. This area of the Trail was once famous for its long road walk, but the Trail has now been rerouted from roads to woods and rolling farmland. At the end of the valley, the Trail climbs South Mountain, which it follows all the way through Maryland.

Before it reaches the Pennsylvania–Maryland state line, the southern section of Trail passes through the village of Boiling Springs, with its beautiful Children's Lake; Pine Grove Furnace State Park, with its model furnace and Ironmaster's Mansion; and Caledonia State Park, with the Thaddeus Stevens Museum.

View into the Delaware Water Gap from Lookout Rock   *Photo: Matt Willen*

72 WINONA CLIFF, LOOKOUT ROCK, AND MOUNT MINSI

MODERATE | **4.6-mile round-trip** | **5 hours**

There are a few steep climbs on this hike, but the Trail has much to offer. As you climb up from Delaware Water Gap, you will pass several outstanding views of the gap with Mount Tammany rising over the Delaware River. On the way to Mount Minsi, there are good views from Council Rock, Winona Cliff, and Lookout Rock.

THE HIKE

From Mountain Road in Delaware Water Gap (elevation 300'), hike south on the A.T. As you hike a paved road, pass by Lake Lenape on the right at mile 0.2. Beyond the lake, the Trail gradually climbs a ridge, which parallels the river below.

At mile 0.7, reach Council Rock and a view of the gap and the Delaware River. Soon, reach Winona Cliff. This is the best viewpoint of Chief Tammany—look for the profile in the mountain across the river. Cross a stream in 0.1 mile, and reach Lookout Rock at 1.3 miles. From Lookout Rock, hike 1.0 mile to the summit of Mount Minsi (elevation 1,461'), which you cross on a gravel road. The return hike is north on the A.T. to the trailhead.

TRAILHEAD DIRECTIONS

From I-80 West, take Exit 310 (PA 611/Delaware Water Gap). Continue onto Foxtown Hill Road, and drive 0.3 mile. Turn left onto PA 611 South, and drive 0.7 mile; then turn right onto Mountain Road and look for the hiker's parking lot.

From I-80 East, take Exit 310 (PA 611/Delaware Water Gap). Continue onto Broad Street, and drive 0.4 mile. Turn left onto Main Street, and drive 0.3 mile. Turn right onto Mountain Road and look for the hiker's parking lot.

GPS TRAILHEAD COORDINATES N40° 58.790' W75° 08.529'

73 WOLF ROCKS

MODERATE | 3.2-mile round-trip | 2 hours

The A.T. in Pennsylvania is said to be where old boots go to die, because the rocky trail is so tough on them (and feet). Wolf Rocks, which offers a view of Cherry Valley below, is one of the rockiest spots on the A.T. However, the worst of the rocks are west of the section you will be hiking. Be careful following the blazes at Wolf Rocks. If you wander off the Trail, all of the rocks start to look alike, and it can be difficult to find the Trail again.

THE HIKE

From PA 191 in Fox Gap, hike south on the A.T. and cross under a telephone line in 0.25 mile. Hike another 0.5 mile to where the Trail joins a woods road, and follow it 0.6 mile. After leaving the woods road, hike 0.25 mile to Wolf Rocks. The return hike is back down the A.T. to Fox Gap on PA 91.

TRAILHEAD DIRECTIONS

From I-80 East, take Exit 307 (PA 611/Park Avenue). Turn right onto PA 611 South, and drive 0.3 mile; then turn right onto PA 191 South, and drive 3.8 miles to Fox Gap; there is a small parking area.

From I-80 West, take Exit 307 (PA 611/Park Avenue). Turn left onto PA 191, and drive 4.3 miles to Fox Gap; there is a small parking area.

GPS TRAILHEAD COORDINATES N40° 56.124' W75° 11.803'

Pleasant Valley, Pennsylvania, from the A.T. west of Wind Gap
Photo: Nicholas A. Tonelli/Flickr/CC BY 2.0 (creativecommons.org/licenses/by/2.0)

74 LOOKOUT ROCK AND HAHN'S LOOKOUT

MODERATE | 2-mile round-trip | 1.5 hours

It is a short, sometimes steep, climb up out of Wind Gap to Lookout Rock and Hahn's Lookout. These two viewpoints offer fine views of the gap and the Poconos.

THE HIKE

From the parking lot in Wind Gap, follow the A.T. south along the road, go under PA 33, and follow the Trail as it turns left and begins climbing. It is a 0.75-mile ascent along switchbacks to Lookout Rock, where you will find views to the north. From Lookout Rock, climb another 0.25 mile to Hahn's Lookout, where there is a view to the south of the town of Wind Gap and beyond. Return back down the A.T. to the trailhead.

TRAILHEAD DIRECTIONS

From I-80 East, take Exit 302A and merge onto PA 33 South. Drive 10.8 miles; then take the exit toward Wind Gap. Turn left onto PA 115, and drive 0.1 mile to the parking area on your left.

From I-80 West, take Exit 302 (PA 611/Bartonsville). Follow signs for PA 611 North and get in the far left lane; when safe, make a U-turn at the light onto PA 33 South. Drive 10.7 miles; then take the exit toward Wind Gap. Turn left onto PA 115, and drive 0.1 mile to the parking area on your left.

GPS TRAILHEAD COORDINATES N40° 51.641' W75° 17.561'

75 WEATHERING KNOB

MODERATE | 2-mile round-trip | 1.5 hours

A stiff but short climb of 0.3 mile leads to a viewpoint on Weathering Knob. After that, it is a relatively easy walk to another view atop a second knob.

THE HIKE

Follow the A.T. north, first passing through an area that, except in the driest of years, is wet and boggy. From here, it is a steep climb over rocks and boulders (made easier by stone steps built by volunteers) to the top of Weathering Knob at 0.3 mile. The view to the north looks onto the valley carved by Aquashicola Creek and framed by Stony and Chestnut Ridges.

Northwest view of the Mahoning Valley from Weathering Knob
Photo: Nicholas A. Tonelli/Flickr/CC BY 2.0 (creativecommons.org/licenses/by/2.0)

You have gained about all of the elevation you need to, so the hiking will be quite easy as you continue along the crest of Blue Mountain to a second knob at 1 mile. Agricultural fields and small settlements are visible to the south. Return via the A.T.

TRAILHEAD DIRECTIONS

From I-476, take Exit 74 (Mahoning Valley) and follow signs for US 209 North. Merge onto US 209 North, and drive 2.1 miles. Turn right onto Hemlock Street, and drive 1.3 miles. Turn left onto Boyer Farm Road, and drive 1 mile; then turn right onto Forest Inn Road, and drive 1.2 mile. Turn left onto Little Gap Road, and drive 3.4 miles. Turn right onto Lower Smith Gap Road, and drive 0.8 mile; then veer right onto Blue Mountain Drive and go 1.8 miles to the A.T. crossing.

GPS TRAILHEAD COORDINATES N40° 48.465' W75° 32.080'

76 BLUE MOUNTAIN

MODERATE | 6.3-mile loop | 4 hours

This section of Blue Mountain is one of the best areas along the entire A.T. to collect blueberries during the summer. Some bushes are so full that you can gather a handful within moments of picking. The ascent of the mountain is gradual, and the use of a side trail enables you to loop around to a grand view of the Lehigh Valley. Additional views are scattered throughout the hike.

THE HIKE

Ascend south over rocky terrain on the A.T. Pass a reliable spring at 0.6 mile, soon walking by the George W. Outerbridge Shelter and reaching an intersection at 0.8 mile.

Bear right onto blue-blazed North Trail, crossing over the main ridgeline of Blue Mountain and coming to another pathway at 1.1 miles. Bear right to descend to Devil's Pulpit overlooking a major bend of the Lehigh River at 1.5 miles. Return to North Trail and bear right, enjoying the traverse of the main crest of the mountain. During late June and into July, your forward progress may be retarded by the urge to gather the abundant blueberries.

Intersect the A.T. at 3.9 miles, turn left, and begin a gradual descent back to the Outerbridge Shelter at 5.6 miles. The area around the shelter is evidence of nature's own healing power. In the 1970s and early 1980s, there was almost no vegetation here due to pollution from now-closed nearby zinc factories. Today, plant life is so lush that views are quite limited. Continue to descend, and return to the parking area at 6.3 miles.

TRAILHEAD DIRECTIONS

From I-476, take Exit 74 (Mahoning Valley) and follow signs for US 209 South. Merge onto US 209 South, and drive 1.6 miles. Turn left onto PA 248 East, and drive 6.8 miles. Turn right onto PA 873 South (signs for Slatington), and drive 0.3 mile to the A.T. crossing. Limited parking is on the right.

GPS TRAILHEAD COORDINATES N40° 46.874' W75° 36.522'

The Lehigh Valley from the A.T. at Bake Oven Knob
Photo: Nicholas A. Tonelli/Flickr/CC BY 2.0 (creativecommons.org/licenses/by/2.0)

77 BAKE OVEN KNOB

EASY | 0.8-mile round-trip | 30 minutes

This is really just a leg stretcher. The goal is a magnificent view of Pennsylvania farmland from Bake Oven Knob. This area is also a popular spot for hawk-watching during the fall migrations.

THE HIKE

From Bake Oven Knob Road, hike north on the A.T. and reach the summit of Bake Oven Knob (elevation 1,560') at mile 0.4. There are a couple of vantage points. The first offers a view to the north, the second, to the south. Return to the parking lot by hiking south on the A.T.

TRAILHEAD DIRECTIONS

From I-78, take Exit 45 (Lynnport/New Smithville). Turn left onto PA 863 North, and drive 1.3 miles. Turn right onto Lyon Valley Road, and drive 3.2 miles. Turn left onto PA 100 North, and drive 4.1 miles. Turn right onto PA 309 South, and drive 0.3 mile; then turn left onto Bake Oven Road, and drive 4.2 miles. Turn left to stay on Bake Oven Road, and drive 0.6 mile; then turn right to stay on Bake Oven Road again. Drive 1.1 miles to the parking area on the left.

GPS TRAILHEAD COORDINATES N40° 44.660' W75° 44.304'

78 THE CLIFFS AND BEAR ROCKS

MODERATE | 7-mile round-trip | 4 hours

This hike travels through one of the most scenic sections of the A.T. in Pennsylvania. The Trail features a knife-edge walk along the Cliffs and panoramic views from Bear Rocks.

THE HIKE

Follow the blue-blazed trail from the parking lot and hike north along the A.T. At mile 1.0, reach the ridge and hike along an old woods road. Hike another 0.75 mile to a power line right-of-way and beyond to a rocky footpath. Reach the junction with a blue-blazed trail that heads left 0.25 mile to the base of the val-

Snow begins to fall on Bear Rocks.
Photo: Matt Willen

ley and, a short distance farther, to New Tripoli Campsite and spring.

Continue along the A.T., turn left at mile 2.6, follow the rocky knife edge known as the Cliffs, and look ahead to Bear Rocks. Reach the side trail to Bear Rocks at mile 3.5. It is a short hike along the blue-blazed side trail to the 360° view overlooking the Pennsylvania countryside. From here, return south to PA 309 via the A.T.

TRAILHEAD DIRECTIONS

From I-78, take Exit 40 (Kutstown/Krumsville). Turn onto PA 737 North, and drive 3.5 miles. Turn right onto Wessnersville Road, and drive 1.1 miles. Turn right onto Kistler Valley Road, and drive 0.9 mile; then turn left onto PA 863 North, and drive 2.3 miles. Turn right to stay on PA 863 North, and drive 1 mile. Turn right onto PA 143 North, and drive 1.8 miles. Turn left onto Gun Club Road, and drive 2.4 miles. Turn left onto PA 309 North, and drive 0.6 mile; the parking area will be on your left.

GPS TRAILHEAD COORDINATES N40° 42.447' W75° 48.479'

79 WINDSOR FURNACE, PULPIT ROCK, AND THE PINNACLE

MODERATE | 10.2-mile round-trip with walk along dirt road | 5.5 hours

From the site of Windsor Furnace, an early pig-iron works, to the wonderful views from Pulpit Rock and The Pinnacle, this hike is full of interesting sights. Keep an eye out for the glassy slag in the footpath in the vicinity of Windsor Furnace. You can also see the remains of the old engine foundation in the undergrowth. Iron stoves were once manufactured here, as was, more interestingly, an iron replica of *The Last Supper.* Also, be on the lookout for charcoal hearths, which were used to hold fuel for the furnace. These flat, round burning sites are 30–50 feet in diameter.

Pulpit Rock (elevation 1,582') offers excellent views of The Pinnacle to the left and Blue Rocks in the foreground. Blue Rocks, a 40,000-year-old stretch of tumbled boulders left by the last glacial period, is a mile long. The rocks get their name from the quartzite and other minerals that give them a bluish hue early in the morning and on moonlit evenings. The tumbled rocks at The Pinnacle (elevation 1,635') offer outstanding views of Pennsylvania farmland.

THE HIKE

From the parking area, hike north along the dirt road until you reach the A.T. crossing. Turn right onto the Trail at the site of Windsor Furnace, follow a dirt road as it crosses Furnace Creek, and head right along a woods road.

Turn right again in 0.25 mile at the junction with a blue-blazed side trail that heads left a short distance to the Windsor Furnace Shelter. From here, the A.T. ascends Blue Mountain, first moderately and then a bit more steeply.

At mile 2.5, pass the Astronomical Park of the Lehigh Valley Amateur Astronomical Society, and reach Pulpit Rock in another 0.1 mile. There are views of The Pinnacle to the left and Blue Rocks in the foreground.

Continue along the A.T., pass a tower to your left in 0.1 mile and an excellent view from a rock outcrop in another 0.1 mile. Pass a rock field to your left with good views to the north in 0.25 mile, pass through a cleft in a rock formation in another 0.1 mile, and soon thereafter pass through another rock field. Reach a yellow-blazed side trail at mile 4.3. The side trail heads downhill 1.3 miles to Blue Rocks, and 0.25 mile beyond to Blue Rocks Campground (privately owned).

Patchwork farmland spreads out beyond The Pinnacle.   *Photo: Leonard M. Adkins*

From the side trail, hike the A.T. less than 0.5 mile to the blue-blazed side trail leading to The Pinnacle, which is a short distance off the A.T. Below The Pinnacle, there are a couple of caves and some sheer cliffs to explore, but watch out for copperhead snakes. From here, return to the parking area by retracing your steps south along the A.T. and the dirt road to the parking area.

TRAILHEAD DIRECTIONS

From I-78, take Exit 35 (PA 143/Lenhartsville). Turn left onto PA 143 North; drive about 0.8 mile. Turn left onto Mountain Road, and drive 2.9 miles. Turn right onto Reservoir Road, and drive 0.5 mile to the parking area; it is a 0.4-mile hike to the A.T. crossing.

GPS TRAILHEAD COORDINATES   N40° 35.104' W75° 56.533'

80 AUBURN LOOKOUT

MODERATE | 5-mile round-trip | 3 hours

There is a steep climb of almost 1,000 feet at the beginning of this hike, but once you gain that elevation, the walking is easy (if you don't mind thousands of rocks underfoot) along the nearly level crest of Blue Mountain. Two viewpoints, one from a pipeline right-of-way and the other from a rock outcrop, are the destinations for the day's hike.

Charming signage near the train tracks
Photo: Nicholas A. Tonelli/Flickr/CC BY 2.0
(creativecommons.org/licenses/by/2.0)

THE HIKE

Follow the A.T. south as it makes use of a railroad bridge to cross the Schuylkill River. Turn left across railroad tracks still actively used by the Blue Mountain and Reading Railroad. A few feet later climb a steep embankment to an old railbed. Turn left and follow it for close to 50 yards before turning right and ascending steeply via switchbacks.

The view from the first pipeline right-of-way at 1.0 mile is of the long valley to the south, with I-78 snaking through the middle of it. Cross a second pipeline at 1.4 miles, and cross Dynamite Road (a blue-blazed trail) at 1.5 miles. Cross a Pennsylvania State Game Lands road at 2.0 miles and another at 2.4 miles.

Come to Auburn Lookout at 2.5 miles for a view north across the green slopes of Weiser State Forest and the small town of Auburn Village, located next to the Schuylkill River. Return to the parking area by taking the A.T. north.

TRAILHEAD DIRECTIONS

From I-78 East, take Exit 29 (PA 61 North/Pottsville) and turn left onto PA 61 North; from I-78 West, take Exit 29B and merge onto PA 61 North. Drive 2.3 miles; then turn left onto Broad Street, and drive 0.2 mile; after crossing over the Schuylkill River and some railroad tracks, turn left, and drive 0.2 mile to the parking area.

GPS TRAILHEAD COORDINATES N40° 34.664' W76° 01.580'

81 TABLE ROCK

EASY | 4.2-mile round-trip | 2 hours

Great views from Table Rock are the highlight of this day hike. A power line right-of-way along the route offers good views of the Susquehanna River. At 444 miles long, it is one of the longest rivers the A.T. crosses.

THE HIKE

From the trailhead parking area, follow the A.T. north. Pass a radio facility for the Pennsylvania Fish Commission on your right in 0.25 mile, and cross a power line right-of-way in 0.5 mile, with excellent views to the east of the Susquehanna River and Valley. A short side trail to the right at mile 1.6 leads to a good view to the south. At mile 1.7, you will pass over Fumitory Rocks, and reach the junction with the short side trail to Table

Looking across Clark Creek Valley to Third Mountain *Photo: Matt Willen*

Rock Outlook 0.3 mile ahead. The side trail heads right to the outcrop. Bring a picnic lunch and enjoy the view. Return to the parking area by retracing your steps south along the A.T.

TRAILHEAD DIRECTIONS

From I-81, take Exit 67, following signs for US 22 West. Merge onto US 22 West, and drive about 5.8 miles. Take the exit for PA 225/Halifax and continue onto PA 225 North. Drive 3.8 miles to the trailhead parking area, on your right at the crest of Peters Mountain.

GPS TRAILHEAD COORDINATES N40° 24.718' W76° 55.809'

This is just a portion of the view from Hawk Rock.   *Photo: Leonard M. Adkins*

82 HAWK ROCK

STRENUOUS | **3-mile round-trip** | **2 hours**

This steep and strenuous climb leads to outstanding views from Hawk Rock, which overlooks the Susquehanna and Juniata Rivers. There are also good views of Peters Mountain.

THE HIKE

After crossing the Shermans Creek Bridge in Duncannon, find a parking space. The A.T. follows this paved road 0.25 mile after crossing the bridge—park anywhere in this area and follow the A.T. along the road.

Turning off the road, the Trail steeply ascends Cove Mountain 0.5 mile to an old mountain road. Climb the road along the north side of the ridge, and cross a rockslide at mile 1.2. The Trail becomes a footpath again and reaches Hawk Rock at mile 1.5. From here, return to Duncannon by following the A.T. north.

TRAILHEAD DIRECTIONS

From I-81, take Exit 65, following signs for US 15 North. Merge onto US 15 North, and drive 10.3 miles. Take the exit for PA 274 West/Duncannon and turn left onto South Main Street. Drive 0.4 mile to the trail crossing.

GPS TRAILHEAD COORDINATES N40° 22.887' W77° 01.771'

Children's Lake in Boiling Springs *Photo: Leonard M. Adkins*

83 BOILING SPRINGS

EASY | 0.6-mile round-trip | 20 minutes

This short hike is centered on Children's Lake in Boiling Springs. The town was established in the 1700s around the iron industry and in the 19th century developed into a vacation spot and recreation area. Today, listed on the National Register of Historic Places, Boiling Springs is mostly residential. The springs that fill Children's Lake are the highlight of this hike (although *stroll* would probably be a more accurate description). More than 24,000 gallons bubble up through the ground each day. Parts of the lake are crystal clear, and ducks and geese add to the bucolic setting. The Trail also passes a township park with a restored iron furnace.

THE HIKE

The hike begins at the Appalachian Trail Conservancy's Mid-Atlantic Regional Headquarters in Boiling Springs. Following the blazes from the parking area, the Trail leads you beside Children's Lake, past a township park with a restored iron furnace, and to a stone-arch highway bridge over Yellow Breeches Creek.

Take some time to explore the area, especially some of the springs to the right of the conservancy headquarters. Bring a picnic lunch and enjoy the scenery.

TRAILHEAD DIRECTIONS

From I-81 North, take Exit 48 (PA 74/York Road). Turn right onto PA 74 South, and drive 0.2 mile; then turn right onto Westminster Drive and go 0.1 mile. Turn left onto Forge Road, and drive 3.3 miles; then turn left onto East First Street, and drive 0.1 mile to the ATC headquarters on the right. Limited parking is available.

From I-81 South, take Exit 49 (PA 641/High Street). Turn right onto PA 641 West; immediately turn left onto Fairfield Street, and drive 0.4 mile. Turn left onto PA 74 South, and drive 0.3 mile; then turn right onto Westminster Drive, and drive 0.1 mile. Turn left onto Forge Road, and drive 3.3 miles; then turn left onto East First Street, and drive 0.1 mile to the ATC headquarters on the right. Limited parking is available.

GPS TRAILHEAD COORDINATES N40° 08.998' W77° 07.617'

84 CHIMNEY ROCKS

STRENUOUS | 3-mile round-trip | 2 hours

Chimney Rocks (elevation 1,940') is the destination of this short but strenuous hike. There are outstanding views of Greenridge and the Waynesboro Reservoir from this magnificent outcrop.

THE HIKE

From the Trail crossing at Antietam (Old Forge) Road, cross Tumbling Run on a bridge. The Trail turns right off the road in 0.1 mile and begins to climb moderately, then steeply.

Reach the junction with the blue-blazed trail that leads a short distance to Tumbling Run Shelter and continues another 0.5 mile to Hermitage Cabin, which is run by the Potomac Appalachian Trail Club. The cabin is locked, and reservations must be made to rent it. From Hermitage Cabin, the blue-blazed trail rejoins the A.T. in another 0.9 mile.

Continue along the A.T. 1.2 miles to the junction with the blue-blazed side trail that leads right 0.1 mile to Chimney Rocks. To the left, the blue-blazed trail continues to Hermitage Cabin.

From here, you can either retrace your steps south on the A.T. back to Antietam Road or make a loop by taking the side trail to Hermitage Cabin and Tumbling Run Shelter. The side trail adds only 0.25 mile or so to the total mileage of the trip.

Along the side trail to Hermitage Cabin   *Photo: Matt Willen*

TRAILHEAD DIRECTIONS

Take I-81 to Exit 10 (PA 914/Marion). Turn onto PA 914 East, and drive 0.9 mile; turn left to stay on PA 914 East, and drive 2.5 miles. Turn right onto PA 316 South, and drive 4 miles. Turn left onto Manheim Road, and drive 1.7 miles. Turn right onto PA 997 South, and drive 1.4 miles. Turn left onto Mentzer Gap Road, and drive 1.6 miles. Stay left to stay on Mentzer Gap Road; then drive 3.1 miles. Turn left onto Old Forge Road, and drive 3.8 miles to the trail crossing.

GPS TRAILHEAD COORDINATES   N39° 48.093' W77° 28.616'

MARYLAND

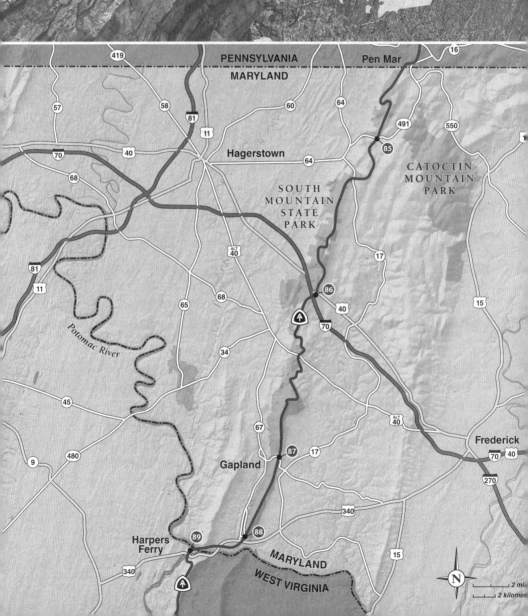

PENNSYLVANIA
MARYLAND

Pen Mar

419 · 16

57 · 58 · 81 · 11 · 60 · 64 · 491 · 550

70 · 40 · Hagerstown · 64 · 85

CATOCTIN
MOUNTAIN
PARK

68

SOUTH
MOUNTAIN
STATE
PARK

81 · 11

ALT 40

17

15

Potomac River

65 · 68 · 86 · 40 · 70

34

45

67 · ALT 40

9 · 480 · 87 · 17

Gapland

Frederick

70 · 40

270

340

15

Harpers
Ferry · 89 · 88

340

MARYLAND

WEST VIRGINIA

N

2 mi.

2 kilometers

Hike	Page	Length (mi)	Configuration	Time (hr)	Difficulty	Features
85. Raven Rock, Devils Racecourse, and High Rock	142	7.2	⤢	4.5	★★	👀
86. Annapolis Rock and Black Rock Cliffs	144	7.0	⤢	4.0	★★	👀
87. White Rocks	145	7.0	⤢	3.5	★★	👀 🏰
88. Weverton Cliffs	147	2.0	⤢	1.5	★★★	👀
89. C&O Canal Towpath	148	5.4	⤢	2.5	★	👀 〰️ 🏰

DIFFICULTY ★★★ strenuous ★★ moderate ★ easy CONFIGURATION ⤢ round-trip

👀 scenic view   〰️ pond or river   🏰 historic area

THE A.T. FOLLOWS THE RIDGE of South Mountain through Maryland for close to 40 miles and descends to the Potomac River at Harpers Ferry, West Virginia. From Pen Mar Park in the north to Weverton Cliffs in the south, the Trail in Maryland is steeped in history, particularly concerning the Civil War era.

The A.T. passes by High Rock, Buzzard Knob, Black Rock Cliffs, Annapolis Rock, Monument Knob, White Rocks, Crampton Gap, and Weverton Cliffs. Of particular historical note are Washington Monument State Park, Turners Gap and South Mountain Inn, Crampton Gap and Gathland State Park, and the town of Weverton.

85 RAVEN ROCK, DEVILS RACECOURSE, AND HIGH ROCK

MODERATE | 7.2-mile round-trip | 4.5 hours

Two vistas and an interesting geological phenomenon await those willing to undertake this moderate hike. You reach the view from Raven Rock after just 0.2 mile of hiking, while High Rock is at the end of the northbound leg of the journey. In between these two is side trip to Devils Racecourse, described by some as a "river of rock." Although glaciers did not reach this far south, the expansion of freezing water that had seeped into small cracks in the rocks on the hillside caused them to break apart into small pieces and flow into the valley below.

THE HIKE

Take the A.T. north to ascend through a forest of deciduous and evergreen trees. The side trail to the right at 0.2 mile will take you about 100 feet to Raven Rock, a prominent cliff with views of the hollow you just ascended.

Continue on the A.T. and gain the crest of South Mountain. Come to a three-way intersection and turn left onto the blue-blazed trail to Raven Rock Shelter at 1.0 mile. Reach the structure at 1.1 miles. To see the rocks and boulders of the Devils Racecourse that fill the valley floor, turn right at the intersection and follow blue blazes to a spring in 200 feet, and continue approximately another 0.2 mile to the beginning of the racecourse.

The Great Valley as seen from High Rock   *Photo: Leonard M. Adkins*

Return to the A.T. and continue northward, passing the highest point of the Trail in Maryland (1,890') on the southern slope of Quirak Mountain at 2.4 miles. A right turn onto the blue-blazed trail at 3.5 miles takes you 0.1 mile to High Rock and its broad and sweeping view of the Great Valley to the west. This is the same valley that the A.T. parallels and crosses numerous times from southern Virginia all the way to eastern Pennsylvania. Retrace your steps to return to the starting point.

TRAILHEAD DIRECTIONS

From I-70, take Exit 35 (MD 66/Boonsboro/Smithsburg). Turn onto MD 66 North, and drive about 1.4 miles; at the traffic circle, take the second exit to stay on MD 66, and drive 3.5 miles. Turn right onto MD 64 East, and drive 1.6 miles; then turn right onto MD 491, and drive 1.9 miles to the trail crossing in Raven Rock Hollow.

GPS TRAILHEAD COORDINATES N39° 39.859' W77° 32.134'

86 ANNAPOLIS ROCK AND BLACK ROCK CLIFFS

MODERATE | 7-mile round-trip | 4 hours

The two destinations of this day hike, Annapolis Rock and Black Rock Cliffs, offer spectacular western views of the Maryland countryside as well as southwestern views of Greenbrier Lake.

THE HIKE

From the parking area off US 40, hike 0.1 mile to the trailhead. Pick up the A.T. at the US 40 overpass, and follow a dirt road that climbs into the woods to the right. Turn left in 0.1 mile and, shortly thereafter, pass a road leading to a farmhouse on the right.

The flowers begin to bloom in April.
Photo: Matt Willen

At mile 0.4, cross a telephone line right-of-way, bear right at a fork, and reach the junction with the side trail that leads to Pine Knob Shelter, just over 0.1 mile to your left. Water is available from a spring at the shelter.

Continue along the A.T. and reach the junction with two paths to the left. Soon thereafter, head right at the junction with an old road and keep left of the "island" just ahead. At mile 0.75, bear right at the fork and begin to climb steeply through a laurel grove.

Reach a level crest just below Pine Knob, pass an old road that intersects the Trail from the right, and pass another old road that intersects the Trail from the left. From here, begin to descend steeply.

At mile 1.0, go around another "island," continue straight past an old road that intersects the Trail to the right, and begin to climb again very gradually in 0.25 mile. At mile 1.8, go left at the fork and reach the side trail to Annapolis Rock in another 0.5 mile. The blue-blazed trail leads 0.2 mile to the overhanging rocks that make up this cliff. The views from here are outstanding. There is a spring nearby here as well.

When you return to the A.T., continue ahead and begin to descend in just over 0.5 mile. At mile 3.7, reach the side trail that leads a short distance to Black Rock Cliffs. The 180° view from this lookout point is outstanding, and you may want to note the considerable amount of broken rock, or scree, at the bottom of the cliff. From here, return to the parking area off US 40 by following the A.T. south.

TRAILHEAD DIRECTIONS

From I-70 West, take Exit 42 and merge onto MD 17 North. Drive 0.9 mile; then turn right to stay on MD 17 North, and drive 0.4 mile. Turn left onto US 40 West, and drive 3 miles to the parking area on your left. A blue-blazed trail leads to the A.T. from the parking area.

From I-70 East, take Exit 32A and merge onto US 40 East. Drive 6.5 miles to the parking area on your right (just after crossing the bridge where US 40 passes back over I-70). A blue-blazed trail leads to the A.T. from the parking area.

GPS TRAILHEAD COORDINATES N39° 32.127' W77° 36.241'

87 WHITE ROCKS

MODERATE | **7-mile round-trip** | **3.5 hours**

The highlight of this hike is a small quartzite cliff known as White Rocks. The views offered from this overlook are poor in the summer but excellent in the late fall and winter. This hike begins at Crampton Gap in Gathland State Park, where a memorial arch honors Civil War correspondents and artists. A battle was also fought in the vicinity, and the ruins of Gathland can still be seen.

Civil War correspondent George Alfred Townsend, who used the pen name Gath, built his estate on South Mountain in 1884 with the proceeds from his war fiction and newspaper articles. He built a home, a hall, a library, a lodge, a guesthouse, a house for his wife, servants' quarters, a stable, and a tomb for himself (although he was not buried in it). He named the estate Gathland after his pseudonym. Since 1884, all the buildings, though built of stone, have been vandalized to such a degree that only a wing of Gath Hall has been restored. This building now houses a museum. Restrooms, water, and picnic tables are available in the park.

The arch also remains intact. Framing the Catoctin Valley, the 50-foot-tall structure faces the battlefields of Winchester and Gettysburg. Inscriptions cover the arch, and mythological figures are carved into its stonework. It remains a mystery as to whether it is a combination of a Moorish arch and the old Frederick fire company station, or a reproduction of the front of the former Antietam Fire Company building. It was designed by Gath and is now administered by the National Park Service, whereas the Maryland Department of Natural Resources maintains the 135-acre park.

THE HIKE

From Gapland Road (MD 572)—also called Crampton Gap, in Gathland State Park—pass through a gap in a stone fence and follow the A.T. north across a field. Heavy fighting occurred in this field during the Battle of Crampton's Gap on September 14, 1862. Soon, pass the ruins of a large stone barn built in 1887. Climb an old road and turn left off the road onto a path in 0.1 mile.

Join the old road in 0.25 mile, and in another 0.1 mile, reach the junction with a blue-blazed side trail that heads right 0.25 mile to Crampton Gap Shelter. At mile 1.7, reach an interesting knoll where, to your right, there is a pile of evenly fractured boulders. This is an excellent viewpoint in the winter.

From here, hike nearly 0.5 mile to another viewpoint from a large rock pile, which offers limited views of Elk Ridge and Pleasant Valley. The footing becomes rocky as you come to another winter view to your right at mile 2.3. Continue through woods with heavy undergrowth and, at about mile 3.0, turn left at a trail junction and begin to climb. The blue-blazed side trail here leads 0.25 mile to Bear Spring and another 0.5 mile to the locked Bear Spring Cabin.

Continue along the A.T., head straight at the fork in 0.1 mile, and soon thereafter pass a rock outcrop to your right. Turn left at a trail junction in another 0.25 mile. Note the azaleas, red maples, and chestnuts here.

A short distance later, reach the junction with the side trail that leads to White Rocks. Hike a very short distance along the blue-blazed trail to the quartzite cliffs, which offer excellent views in the winter. From here, return south to Crampton Gap via the A.T.

TRAILHEAD DIRECTIONS

From I-70, take Exit 42 (MD 17/Myersville). Turn onto MD 17 South, and drive about 11.3 miles. Turn right onto Gapland Road/W Main Street, and drive 1.1 miles. Turn left onto Arnoldtown Road, and drive 0.1 mile to the parking lot in Gathland State Park.

GPS TRAILHEAD COORDINATES N39° 24.308' W77° 38.415'

Weverton Cliffs rise high above the Potomac River.   *Photo: Leonard M. Adkins*

88 WEVERTON CLIFFS

STRENUOUS | 2-mile round-trip | 1.5 hours

This hike is steep, but it rewards you with a spectacular view of the Potomac River Gorge from the rock outcrop at Weverton Cliffs. This is the most popular section of the Trail in Maryland, with the possible exception of a 0.1-mile piece in Washington Monument Park. Weverton Cliffs can get crowded on pleasant summer days, but the walk is just as pretty in the off-season if you are interested in some solitude. The plaque at Weverton Cliffs remembers Congressman Goodloe E. Byron, a longtime supporter of the A.T.

THE HIKE
From the trailhead, follow the A.T. north. The climb is steep and involves switch-backs. Reach the short side trail to the cliffs at mile 1.0.

TRAILHEAD DIRECTIONS
From I-70, take Exit 52 and merge onto US 15 South/US 340 West. Drive 14.7 miles; then take the exit toward MD 67/Boonsboro and turn right onto MD 67 North. Drive just 0.2 mile; then turn right onto Weverton Cliff Road, and drive 0.3 mile to the parking area on the right. The trail crossing is a little farther down Weverton Road.

GPS TRAILHEAD COORDINATES N39° 19.981' W77° 41.001'

89 C&O CANAL TOWPATH

EASY | 5.4-mile round-trip | 2.5 hours

A leisurely stroll will take you from historic Harpers Ferry, West Virginia, over the Potomac River into Maryland for a nice walk along the Chesapeake and Ohio Canal Towpath. The canal once provided a means to bypass the rapids on the Potomac River, which had blocked the flow of goods. The towpath served as a vital link connecting towns along the Potomac with Washington, D.C. Built in the late 1700s and early 1800s, it ran 185 miles from Cumberland, Maryland, to Georgetown, on the edge of the nation's capital.

The hike is listed as a 5.4-mile round-trip, but that takes you to the A.T.'s other junction with the towpath. It is only 0.25 mile from Harpers Ferry to the towpath itself, and round-trip hikes as short as 0.5 mile are possible. This is a good area to stretch your legs and enjoy a walk along the river. Hike as much of the towpath as you like, leaving time for the return trip.

THE HIKE

From John Brown's Fort in Harpers Ferry, West Virginia, follow the white blazes that lead to the Goodloe E. Byron Memorial Footbridge over the Potomac River. On the Maryland side of the Potomac River, descend stairs to the C&O Towpath. Turn east and follow the A.T./C&O Towpath, which share the same footpath for the next 2.6 miles. Hike out as far along the A.T./C&O Towpath as you like. Retrace your steps to return to Harpers Ferry.

TRAILHEAD DIRECTIONS

From I-70 in Maryland, take Exit 52 and merge onto US 15 South/US 340 West. Drive about 19.7 miles, passing briefly through Virginia and into West Virginia. Turn left onto Shoreline Drive, and park at the visitor center for Harpers Ferry National Historical Park. There is a parking fee; shuttle buses will bring you to the historic town. The hike begins from the small National Park Service parking lot on Shenandoah Street just east of US 340.

GPS TRAILHEAD COORDINATES N39° 19.299' W77° 44.597'

This historical structure was once a home and store along the C&O Canal.
Photo: Jon Bilous/Shutterstock

WEST VIRGINIA & VIRGINIA

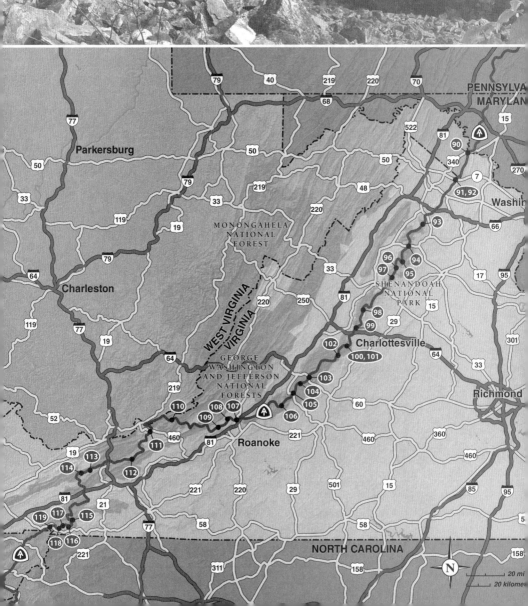

PENNSYLVA
MARYLAN

Parkersburg

MONONGAHELA
NATIONAL
FOREST

SHENANDOAH
NATIONAL
PARK

Charlottesville

Charleston

WEST VIRGINIA
VIRGINIA

GEORGE
WASHINGTON
AND JEFFERSON
NATIONAL
FORESTS

Richmond

Roanoke

Washir

NORTH CAROLINA

20 mi
20 kilome

N

Hike	Page	Length (mi)	Configuration	Time (hr)	Difficulty	Features
90. Harpers Ferry and Split Rock	153	5.5	round-trip	3.5	★★	scenic view, pond or river, historic area
91. Devils Racecourse	155	6.6	round-trip	3.5	★★	scenic view
92. Bears Den Rocks and Lookout Point	156	6.5	round-trip	3.5	★★	scenic view
93. Compton Gap to Compton Peak	157	2.4	round-trip	1.25	★★	scenic view
94. Marys Rock	158	4.0	round-trip	2.5	★★	mountain peak, scenic view, bird-watching
95. Hawksbill Loop	160	2.8	round-trip	1.75	★★	scenic view
96. Lewis Spring Falls and Blackrock	161	3.3	round-trip	2.0	★★	scenic view, waterfall
97. Bearfence Mountain Loop	162	1.5	round-trip	1.0	★★	mountain peak, scenic view
98. Blackrock	164	2.0	round-trip	1.0	★★	scenic view
99. Bear Den Mountain	165	2.2	round-trip	1.25	★★	mountain peak, scenic view, bird-watching
100. Mill Creek	166	5.8	round-trip	3.5	★★	waterfall
101. Humpback Rocks	167	7.2	round-trip	4.0	★★	scenic view, historic area
102. Hanging Rock	168	7.4	round-trip	4.5	★★	mountain peak, scenic view
103. Brown Mountain Creek	170	5.6	round-trip	3.0	★	waterfall, historic area
104. Bluff Mountain	171	4.0	round-trip	3.0	★★	mountain peak, scenic view, pond or river
105. Fullers Rocks and Big Rocky Row	172	9.4	loop	5.5	★★★	scenic view
106. Apple Orchard Mountain and The Guillotine	173	4.0	round-trip	2.0	★	mountain peak, scenic view
107. Hay Rock	174	7.8	round-trip	4.5	★★	scenic view
108. Tinker Cliffs	176	8.2	round-trip	5.5	★★★	scenic view, pond or river
109. McAfee Knob	177	7.4	round-trip	4.0	★★	scenic view
110. Wind Rock	178	0.5	round-trip	0.5	★	scenic view
111. Angels Rest and Pearls Mountain	179	9.4	round-trip	5.5	★★★	scenic view
112. Dismal Creek Falls	180	4.3	round-trip	2.5	★★	waterfall
113. Garden Mountain	181	3.8	round-trip	2.5	★★	mountain peak, scenic view
114. Chestnut Knob	182	2.8	round-trip	2.0	★★	mountain peak, scenic view
115. Comers Creek Falls	182	2.4	round-trip	1.5	★	waterfall
116. Rhododendron Gap	183	5.2	round-trip	3.0	★★	scenic view
117. Mount Rogers	184	9.0	round-trip	5.5	★★★	mountain peak, scenic view
118. Buzzard Rock	186	1.8	round-trip	1.0	★	scenic view
119. Straight Mountain and the Virginia Creeper Trail	186	10.0	round-trip	5.75	★★	scenic view, waterfall

DIFFICULTY ★★★ strenuous ★★ moderate ★ easy CONFIGURATION ◢ round-trip ↻ loop

⛰ mountain peak 👓 scenic view 〰 pond or river ⛲ waterfall 🏰 historic area ✈ bird-watching

THE PORTION OF THE APPALACHIAN TRAIL that lies solely in West Virginia is 2.4 miles long, but the Trail also follows the Virginia–West Virginia state line for another 20-plus miles in two places: on Peters Mountain north of Pearisburg, Virginia, and for about 15 miles south of Harpers Ferry, West Virginia, home to the Appalachian Trail Conservancy.

The longest stretch of the A.T., more than a quarter of its total length, is in Virginia. From the Potomac River near Harpers Ferry, the A.T. ridge runs along the Blue Ridge into Shenandoah National Park. It traverses the park for more than 100 miles, leaving the park behind at Rockfish Gap and picking up the Blue Ridge Parkway, which it more or less parallels for 100 miles to the Roanoke area. Along the parkway, it traverses Humpback Mountain, Three Ridges, The Priest, Spy Rock, Punchbowl, and Bluff Mountains, and then descends to the James River. From the James River, the Trail climbs to Apple Orchard Mountain, the highest point on the Blue Ridge Parkway in Virginia.

At Troutville, the A.T. heads west toward the border of West Virginia. As it crosses this area, it passes by the remarkable features of Tinker Cliffs and McAfee Knob. The crest of Peters Mountain forms the Virginia–West Virginia state line. From here, the A.T. descends to Pearisburg, Virginia, climbs Angels Rest on Pearis Mountain, and slowly winds its way back toward I-81, though not before crossing I-77 near Bastian.

From Atkins, Virginia, the A.T. heads south into the Mount Rogers National Recreation Area, passing through Grayson Highlands and within 0.5 mile of the summit of Mount Rogers, 5,729 feet above sea level, Virginia's highest point. From Mount Rogers, it is less than 30 miles to the Virginia–Tennessee state line. In this southern section of Virginia, the Trail traverses Whitetop Mountain, Buzzard Rock, and Straight Mountain before descending into the hiker-friendly town of Damascus. The town holds an annual Trail Days festival each May. The state line is approximately 3 miles south of Damascus.

About 100 miles of the A.T. in Virginia pass through Shenandoah National Park. The park is one of the most popular areas to hike along the Trail. Established by President Calvin Coolidge in 1926, Shenandoah National Park took 10 years to complete. President Franklin Roosevelt's Civilian Conservation Corps (CCC) did most of the work. Roosevelt officially dedicated the park in 1936. Skyline Drive was a part of the original concept and took eight years to complete. Construction of the southern, central, and northern sections began in 1931; they opened as they were completed (in 1939, 1934, and 1936, respectively).

Although the A.T. was first constructed in this area in the 1920s and opened in 1929, much of the Trail was relocated as Skyline Drive was built. The CCC was also put to work rebuilding the A.T., and you will note the laborious rockwork that shores up much of the Trail in the park.

The history of the Shenandoah—natural, geological, and cultural—can and does fill books. For additional information on the park, look for books sold at the park's visitor centers.

The fauna of the park is varied and includes everything from black bear and white-tailed deer (the latter extremely prevalent) to the less often seen bobcats. The areas of intense defoliation you will see have been caused by the gypsy moth. Deer ticks are also present in Shenandoah, so search your body carefully for this carrier of Lyme disease. As for flora, everything from hemlock and other hardwood forests to boreal forests can be found. Flowers and flowering shrubs also abound, making the park a fairyland walk from late spring through midsummer.

90 HARPERS FERRY AND SPLIT ROCK

MODERATELY STRENUOUS | 5.5-mile round-trip | 3.5 hours

At one time, the A.T. did not drop off Loudoun Heights to cross the Shenandoah River and pass through Harpers Ferry, West Virginia. Rather, it stayed on the ridgeline, passing remnants of Civil War fortifications and a grandstand view onto the confluence of the Shenandoah and Potomac Rivers from Split Rock. It then crossed the Potomac River, and hikers could make a loop hike by turning west onto the C&O Canal Towpath. Recrossing the river, they would pass through Harpers Ferry and return to the starting point.

When the A.T. was rerouted into Harpers Ferry, the old route was maintained and it was still possible to accomplish the loop hike. Unfortunately, it is now no longer possible because of a landowner who prohibits hikers from passing through just a short section of private property.

Thankfully, though, it is still possible to hike to Split Rock on a round-trip hike that begins in Harpers Ferry and uses the A.T., a side trail, and the Loudoun Heights Trail to reach the overlook.

During your visit to Harpers Ferry, drop by the Appalachian Trail Conservancy, located at the corner of Washington and Jackson Streets, just up the hill from the A.T.

THE HIKE

Walk toward US 340 and follow the A.T.'s white blazes across the bridge over the Shenandoah River. Cross to the other side of the road when there is a break in the heavy traffic speeding by.

Follow the A.T. as it ascends stone steps into the forest. At 0.6 mile, cross paved Chestnut Hill Road; the trail becomes a bit steeper with a few switchbacks to help ease the climb. An orange-blazed trail comes in from the left at 1.0 mile, but continue right, ascending on the A.T. (You will use the other pathway on the way back.)

Attain the ridgeline and an intersection at 1.3 miles. The A.T. turns right on its way to Georgia; this hike bears left onto blue-blazed Loudoun Heights Trail. The stone foundations you pass at 1.6 miles are the remains of fortifications built by Union forces during the Civil War.

The orange-blazed trail comes in from the left at 1.9 miles. Stay right on the Loudoun Heights Trail, but turn left onto a side trail at 2.2 miles that leads, in just a few yards, to a view of Harpers Ferry and the confluence of the Shenandoah and Potomac Rivers. A second short side trail at 2.4 miles goes to another view, this one with an increased range of where the A.T. ascends Weverton Cliffs in Maryland.

The day's objective is reached when you turn left onto the 50-foot-long side trail leading to Split Rock at 2.9 miles. Far below, shimmering ripples and bits of white-water in the Shenandoah and Potomac Rivers reflect the light of bright, sunny days. Spanning the Potomac River upstream from where the two rivers meet is the B&O Railroad bridge. The attached footbridge is the route of the A.T. All of Harpers Ferry is spread out before you.

Retrace your steps back to the orange-blazed trail at 3.9 miles and turn right to follow its descending route to intersect the A.T. at 4.5 miles. Continue the descent by turning right to retrace your steps along that white-blazed pathway and return to the hike's starting point at 5.5 miles.

TRAILHEAD DIRECTIONS

From I-70 in Maryland, take Exit 52 and merge onto US 15 South/US 340 West. Drive about 19.7 miles, passing briefly through Virginia and then into West Virginia. Turn left onto Shoreline Drive and park at the visitor center for Harpers Ferry National Historical Park. There is a parking fee; shuttle buses will bring you to the historic town. The hike begins from the small Park Service parking lot on Shenandoah Street just east of US 340.

GPS TRAILHEAD COORDINATES N39° 19.299' W77° 44.598'

View from Crescent Rock   *Photo: Potomac Appalachian Trail Club GPS Rangers*

91 DEVILS RACECOURSE

MODERATE | 6.6-mile round-trip | 3.5 hours

Devils Racecourse, the destination of this hike, is an ancient streambed with only the boulders remaining. While day hiking along the Blue Ridge in northern Virginia, you will find excellent views of the Shenandoah Valley from Crescent Rock, 0.5 mile before reaching Devils Racecourse. Although this hike begins in Virginia, about half of this section of the A.T. is located in Jefferson County, West Virginia.

THE HIKE

Walk north on the A.T. from the parking lot and climb into a forest of laurel, pine, and chestnut oak. Reach a rock outcrop at mile 0.6, where you will find good views of the valley, and then descend through rocks (sometimes steeply and on switchbacks) 0.25 mile to a stream crossing at Pigeon Hollow. Climb steeply and continue when you reach the junction with an old path. At mile 1.1, hike through a forest of old pines mixed with oaks.

Begin to climb steeply, then more moderately, through the woods, and reach a good view of the Shenandoah Valley at a quartzite rock outcrop to your left at mile 1.7. Soon thereafter, begin to descend gradually, then more steeply through rocks. This particular area is notorious for its poison ivy. Watch out!

Just past mile 2.0, head left and continue to descend through a forest. Shortly thereafter, bear left again, cross a rocky creekbed, and pass a path to your right. Turn right at the next fork and reach the junction with a blue-blazed side trail to the left that heads to a reliable spring (first passing a poor spring).

Continue along the A.T. and begin a short ascent that can be slippery in wet or icy weather. At mile 2.6, reach Crescent Rock, where there are views of the Shenandoah Valley and Massanutten Mountain in the distance.

If you have the time, you may want to take the side trail that leads a short distance to a point where the cliff can be descended. If you walk back along the base of Crescent Rock, you can see the geological folds that give the rock its name. The core of the fold has been removed by the action of ice in the crevices, and a 6-foot-deep arch has been formed in the cliff. About 150 feet west of Crescent Rock is another geological formation, called Pulpit Rock (Pinnacle). This column of rock is separated from the cliff by about 10 feet. Watch out for snakes that enjoy sunning themselves on the exposed rocks.

Continue along the A.T., climb through woods, and head left at a junction with an old road, which heads right 0.5 mile to parking at VA 601. The A.T. descends steeply ahead, bears right at a fork, leaves the old road, and arrives at Devils Racecourse. Listen carefully for the small stream that still runs beneath this ancient deposit of boulders.

From here, return to the parking area by heading south on the A.T.

TRAILHEAD DIRECTIONS

From I-81, take Exit 315 (VA 7/Winchester/Berryville). Turn left onto VA 7 East, and drive about 16.6 miles. Turn left onto VA 679; the parking area is immediately on your right.

GPS TRAILHEAD COORDINATES N39° 06.998' W77° 51.152'

92 BEARS DEN ROCKS AND LOOKOUT POINT

MODERATE | 6.5-mile round-trip | 3.5 hours

Excellent views of the Shenandoah Valley from Bears Den Rocks and Lookout Point are the highlights of this day hike. If your time is limited, you could hike out just to Bears Den Rocks and back, a round-trip journey that will take about 1 hour to cover the 1.7 miles.

THE HIKE

Follow the blue-blazed trail from the parking lot 0.25 mile to intersect and turn south on the A.T. The footpath immediately climbs 0.5 mile to Bears Den Rocks. A side trail to the left heads 0.25 mile to Bears Den Hostel.

Continue along the A.T., descend through pines, and at mile 1.5 cross a creek on a footbridge. Shortly thereafter, cross another stream where the pines end.

Next cross an old road, continue through woods, and descend steeply at mile 2.25. The descent soon becomes more gradual and you will cross Spout Run in a narrow, steep ravine at mile 2.5. After crossing the run, step over a badly eroded old road, begin to climb steeply, and reach the ridge crest at mile 3.0.

The sparsely wooded crest has a dense undergrowth of weeds, briars, and poison ivy. Watch your step. You will reach the peak of the ridge at mile 3.25, and Lookout Point shortly thereafter. Lookout Point boasts excellent views of the mountains to the south. From here, return to the parking lot by retracing your steps.

TRAILHEAD DIRECTIONS

From I-81, take Exit 315 (VA 7/Winchester/Berryville). Turn left onto VA 7 East, and drive about 16.9 miles. Turn right into the commuter parking lot; a blue-blazed trail runs from the parking lot to the A.T.

GPS TRAILHEAD COORDINATES N39° 06.925' W77° 50.835'

93 COMPTON GAP TO COMPTON PEAK

MODERATE | 2.4-mile round-trip | 1.25 hours

The highlights of this hike to Compton Peak include good views and an interesting formation of columnar basalt.

THE HIKE

From Compton Gap at Skyline Drive milepost 10.4 (elevation 2,415'), head south on the A.T. and climb via switchbacks. In mid-May, you may see yellow lady's slippers blooming; in early June, white clintonia and speckled wood lily. At mile 0.8, reach a signpost at the junction of a blue-blazed trail that heads left and right to viewpoints (these trails are ungraded and rough but are worth the short trips to the viewpoints).

Follow the blue-blazed trail on the left 0.2 mile to an interesting rock formation composed of columnar basalt. To see this structure, you must climb below the rocks. At the top of the rock outcrop, you will find spectacular views west and north of Page Valley and the Shenandoah River.

Return to the A.T. and follow the blue-blazed trail right to the summit of Compton Peak (elevation 2,909'). You can continue another 0.2 mile beyond the peak to a rocky ledge with more good views to the west and north. Return to Compton Gap by retracing your steps north on the A.T.

TRAILHEAD DIRECTIONS

From I-66, take Exit 6 (US 340/US 522/Front Royal). Turn onto US 340 South, and drive 2 miles. Turn left onto West 14th Street to stay on US 340 South, and drive 0.2 mile; then turn right onto North Royal Avenue to stay on US 340 South, and drive 2.1 miles. Turn left onto Skyline Drive, and drive 10.4 miles. Turn left into the Compton Gap parking area.

GPS TRAILHEAD COORDINATES N38° 49.424' W78° 10.233'

94 MARYS ROCK

MODERATE | 4-mile round-trip | 2.5 hours

The trek to Marys Rock is a good introduction to the trails of Shenandoah National Park. The elevation it gains is on a well-graded, switchbacked pathway leading to one of the most easily reached 360° views in the park. Along the way, you will pass through tunnels of mountain laurel and, except for the coldest months of the year, a grand array of wildflowers.

THE HIKE

Enter the woods on a wide trail from the turnaround circle at the end of the parking lot, intersect the A.T. in a few feet, and turn left.

A break in the vegetation at 0.6 mile provides a view of Thornton Gap and some of the mountains of the park to the north. At 0.9 mile, cushiony moss growing on boulders along the Trail helps soften the look and feel of a rock field you walk through. The rock walls at 1.2 miles that were built by the Civilian Conservation Corps during the Great Depression to shore up this sidehill trail are still performing their duty. Make a right onto a side trail at 1.9 miles and ascend 0.1 mile to Marys Rock.

Marys Rock is a good place to watch the fall hawk migration.   *Photo: Leonard M. Adkins*

The large outcrop is a favorite perch where birders watch the fall hawk migration. Obtain the 360° view by scrambling 80 feet to its summit. To the north is the road intersection from which you began the hike. Pass Mountain forms the ridgeline closest to you, and behind it are the Three Sisters and Neighbor, Knob, and Hogback Mountains. Scanning to the east you may be able to make out the gorge of Little Devils Stairs between Little Hogback and Mount Marshall. The Piedmont is clearly visible beyond Oventop and Jenkins Mountain. Southward are The Pinnacle and Stony Man, while to the west is Massanutten Mountain, rising up to bisect the Shenandoah Valley. Return by following the A.T. north.

TRAILHEAD DIRECTIONS

From I-81, take Exit 264 (US 211/New Market/Timberville/Luray). Turn onto US 211 East, and drive 0.2 mile; then turn left onto North Congress Street, and drive 0.3 mile. Turn right onto US 211 East, and drive 22.8 miles; then turn right into the Panorama parking area.

GPS TRAILHEAD COORDINATES   N38° 39.587' W78° 19.256'

Dramatic views abound from Hawksbill. *Photo: Johnny Molloy*

95 HAWKSBILL LOOP

MODERATE | 2.8-mile round-trip | 1.75 hours

Hawksbill is not the tallest mountain in the Old Dominion (Mount Rogers has that honor), but it does have the distinction of being the loftiest peak within the boundaries of Shenandoah National Park. Unlike the long and involved climbs you must undertake to attain many other paramount pinnacles, Hawksbill is reached in a moderately easy ascent of less than 700 feet in elevation.

THE HIKE

Take the Hawksbill Trail from the parking lot and ascend through balsam fir and red spruce. At 0.7 mile make a right at a trail intersection to come to Byrds Nest Shelter 2 and Hawksbill's summit at 0.8 mile.

Continue to the stone-walled outlook for the almost-360° panorama. Beneath you are Timber and Buracker Hollows, which funnel East Hawksbill Creek to the town of Luray, some 3,000 feet below. The view west is of Page Valley and Massanutten Mountain. To the north is Stony Man, to the east is Old Rag, and to the south are Spitler Hill and Naked Top.

Return to the shelter, walking past it to turn right off of the dirt road and onto the blue-blazed trail. A few yards down this pathway is another fine view to the west and a new perspective on the southwest. At 1.1 miles you switchback away from the road and intersect the A.T. at 1.7 miles. Turn right on the fern-lined, white-blazed pathway. At 2.2 miles, swing around a large rock promontory to cross a series of talus slopes, whose openings in the forest canopy provide limited views of Stony Man.

Begin a quick switchbacking descent to arrive at an intersection at 2.7 miles. Turn right and go 500 feet to the parking area in Hawksbill Gap.

TRAILHEAD DIRECTIONS

From I-81, take Exit 264 (US 211/New Market/Timberville/Luray). Turn onto US 211 East, and drive 0.2 mile; then turn left onto North Congress Street, and drive 0.3 mile. Turn right onto US 211 East, and drive 23 miles. Turn left onto Skyline Drive at the sign for Shenandoah National Park, and stay left on the ramp to merge onto Skyline Drive going south. Drive 14.2 miles, to the Hawksbill Gap Parking Area (at Skyline Drive milepost 45.6).

GPS TRAILHEAD COORDINATES N38° 33.372' W78° 23.209'

96 LEWIS SPRING FALLS AND BLACKROCK

MODERATE | 3.3-mile round-trip | 2 hours

Lewis Spring Falls and the grand view across Shenandoah Valley to West Virginia's Allegheny Mountains are reason enough to pay the park's entrance fee. Savoring a meal while enjoying the scenery from Big Meadows Lodge is further enticement.

THE HIKE

Follow the pathway between the amphitheater parking and the lodge to cross over the A.T.; then continue along blue-blazed Lewis Spring Falls Trail as it gradually drops through the forest. Turn right and steeply descend along a side trail at 1.2 miles to enjoy the falls near the base.

Return to the main pathway; then turn right onto another short side route at 1.7 miles to enjoy the head of the falls. Upon rejoining the main pathway, ascend the steep slope to come onto the Lewis Spring service road at 2.3 miles and turn left onto the A.T.

Ascend steadily along the western side of a ridgeline to intersect a pathway (at 2.7 miles) leading right 0.1 mile to Blackrock Viewpoint. While it is almost always worthwhile to take such short side routes, you'll be just as rewarded if you continue along the A.T. several more yards for basically the same extraordinary view westward. On clear days you can gaze out across the width of the Shenandoah Valley, up and over Massanutten Mountain, and all of the way to the distant Great North and Allegheny Mountains along the Virginia–West Virginia state line.

Proceeding along the A.T., skirt the cliffs of Blackrock and return to the initial intersection of this hike. Bear right to return to the parking area at 3.3 miles.

TRAILHEAD DIRECTIONS

From I-81, take Exit 247A (US 33 East/Market Street) and merge onto US 33 East. Drive about 21.7 miles; then turn left onto the exit for Skyline Drive/Shenandoah National Park. Turn left onto Skyline Drive and go 14.3 miles. Turn left into Big Meadows; drive a little over a mile to the Big Meadows Lodge amphitheater parking.

GPS TRAILHEAD COORDINATES N38° 31.841' W78° 26.369'

97 BEARFENCE MOUNTAIN LOOP

MODERATE | 1.5-mile round-trip | 1 hour

This short hike is not a true loop but rather a figure eight. You will hike over a very rough section of trail to the rocky top of Bearfence Mountain, which offers fine views of Skyline Drive, the surrounding mountains, and the valley. The Bearfence Mountain Loop is listed as a moderate hike because it is short, but the climbs involve using your hands, as well as your feet, to scramble over the rocks. In the summer, naturalist-led hikes leave from the parking area. If you are interested in going on one, check with the park for times and dates.

THE HIKE

From the Bearfence Mountain Parking Area, follow the blue-blazed trail across the road from the parking area. In 0.1 mile, reach a junction with the A.T., but continue following the blue-blazed trail (you will return on the A.T.). In the next 0.25 mile, the Trail will climb over a rough and rocky ridge on the north slope of Bearfence Mountain, where there are fine views from the ridgetop.

The view from atop Bearfence Mountain   *Photo: Johnny Molloy*

The blue-blazed trail joins the Bearfence Mountain Loop Trail at its junction with the A.T. Continue following the blue-blazed trail and climb to the summit of Bearfence Mountain (elevation 3,500'). The Bearfence Trail then descends to its second junction with the A.T. Turn right on the white-blazed A.T., and in 0.25 mile reach the junction with the Bearfence Mountain Loop Trail. Continue following the A.T., and in another 0.25 mile reach the junction with the blue-blazed trail leading right 0.1 mile to the parking area at the trailhead.

TRAILHEAD DIRECTIONS
From I-81, take Exit 247A (US 33 East/Market Street) and merge onto US 33 East. Drive about 21.7 miles; then turn left onto the exit for Skyline Drive/Shenandoah National Park. Turn left onto Skyline Drive and go 9.1 miles to the Bearfence Mountain Parking Area on your left (Skyline Drive milepost 56.4).

GPS TRAILHEAD COORDINATES N38° 27.148' W78° 28.020'

Trail builders have cleared the way through the boulders on Blackrock.   *Photo: Leonard M. Adkins*

98 BLACKROCK

MODERATE | 2-mile round-trip | 1 hour

This short hike leads to outstanding views from Blackrock. The Trail nearly circles the mountain as it passes around its north, west, and south sides.

THE HIKE

From the parking area at the trailhead, hike a short distance of the Jones Run Trail to the junction with the A.T. Turn right on the A.T. and hike south 0.25 mile to Skyline Drive. Cross Skyline Drive and continue following the A.T., climbing gradually.

Pass most of the way around the summit of Blackrock (elevation 3,100'). There are several fine views from this section of trail. The return hike is back north on the A.T. to the Jones Run Trail, which leads to the parking area.

TRAILHEAD DIRECTIONS

From I-64, take Exit 99 (US 250/Afton/Waynesboro). Turn right onto US 250 East, and drive 0.3 mile; then turn left onto the small road toward Skyline Drive and go 0.1 mile. Turn right onto Skyline Drive, and drive 21.3 miles to the Jones Run Parking Area on your right (Skyline Drive milepost 83.8).

GPS TRAILHEAD COORDINATES N38° 13.800' W78° 43.573'

99 BEAR DEN MOUNTAIN

MODERATE | 2.2-mile round-trip | 1.25 hours

It is a moderate, almost easy, walk to the open crestline of Bear Den Mountain for a superb 360° view. Like Calf Mountain to the north, Bear Den Mountain offers a great seat from which to watch the thousands of hawks that glide along the Blue Ridge Mountains during the annual fall migration.

THE HIKE

You don't have to hike anywhere to enjoy the views from the open meadows of Beagle Gap, which look eastward into the folded recesses of Tuckedaway Branch and Greenwood Hol-low. To begin the hike, cross Skyline Drive

View from Beagle Gap Overlook
Photo: Kevin Borland

and follow the A.T. south, snacking on wild strawberries in June and turning around every once in a while to look onto the fields of Calf Mountain to the north.

Communication towers at 0.5 mile mark your arrival on the summit. Continue a bit beyond this to the rock outcrops of green shale for a break. To the west is Waynes-boro, with US 250 running through the Shenandoah Valley. Turn around and you can see the same road descending into the piedmont to the east. To enjoy the views a little longer, continue along the open mountainside and turn around when the A.T. enters the woods at 1.1 miles.

The return hike is north on the A.T. to Beagle Gap.

TRAILHEAD DIRECTIONS

From I-64, take Exit 99 (US 250/Afton/Waynesboro). Turn right onto US 250 East, and drive 0.3 mile; then turn left onto the small road toward Skyline Drive and go 0.1 mile. Turn right onto Skyline Drive, and drive 5.8 miles to the dirt parking lot on the right (Skyline Drive milepost 99.5).

GPS TRAILHEAD COORDINATES N38° 04.375' W78° 47.585'

100 MILL CREEK

MODERATE | 5.8-mile round-trip | 3.5 hours

Save this outing, with a descent (and then ascent on the return) of 500 feet, for midsummer. By then, hot temperatures will have warmed the waters of Mill Creek enough so that you will not hesitate to wade in and cool off in the pool at the base of a scenic waterfall.

THE HIKE

Follow the (possibly) unmarked trail as it descends from the middle of the parking area. (It is the only one that descends. The other two ascend.) Come to the A.T. at 0.25 mile and turn left, reaching a short side trail to the left at 1.0 mile that leads 0.2 mile to a view of Glass Hollow.

Continue on the A.T., staying to the right at another intersection at 1.8 miles, and pass by a viewpoint of Rockfish Valley and Southwest Mountain as you descend via switchbacks. Cross Mill Creek and come to the Paul C. Wolfe Shelter at 2.8 miles. Walk downstream for about 0.1 mile to the waterfall and swimming hole.

Return by retracing your steps along the A.T. and the side trail to return to your car at 5.8 miles.

TRAILHEAD DIRECTIONS

From I-64, take Exit 99 (US 250/Afton/Waynesboro). Turn right onto US 250 East, and drive 0.3 mile; then turn left onto the small road toward Skyline Drive, and drive 0.1 mile. Turn left onto Skyline Drive, which quickly becomes the Blue Ridge Parkway. Drive 6 miles; then turn left into the Humpback Gap Parking Area (Blue Ridge Parkway milepost 6).

GPS TRAILHEAD COORDINATES N37° 58.112' W78° 53.770'

The view from Humpback Rocks attracts many hikers to the summit.   *Photo: Leonard M. Adkins*

101 HUMPBACK ROCKS

MODERATE | 7.2-mile round-trip | 4 hours

This hike will take you from the Blue Ridge Parkway to the top of Humpback Rocks. The destination is a jagged rock outcrop with fine views to the west. Due to its location on the Blue Ridge Parkway, this is a popular place and may be very crowded on nice weekends throughout the year.

Humpback Rocks was an important landmark on the Old Howardsville Turnpike, which was a major trade road that connected the Rockfish and Shenandoah valleys in the 1800s. The A.T. was moved onto a portion of this route near the turn of the twenty-first century, and part of this historic roadbed is still discernible as it winds its way through the forest.

THE HIKE

Follow the (possibly) unmarked trail as it descends from the middle of the parking area. It is the only one that descends; the other two ascend. Come to the A.T.

at 0.25 mile, turn right, and soon ascend switchbacks to pass by Bear Spring at 1.7 miles and a second spring at 2.5 miles.

Turn right onto the side trail at 3.3 miles and follow it for 0.2 mile to another right turn to reach Humpback Rocks at 3.6 miles. If you are feeling energetic, you can return to the A.T. and follow it to the south for 1.0 mile to the summit of Humpback Mountain for additional views to the north and east. This will add 2.0 miles to the overall length of the hike.

Retrace your steps to return to the parking area.

TRAILHEAD DIRECTIONS

From I-64, take Exit 99 (US 250/Afton/Waynesboro). Turn right onto US 250 East, and drive 0.3 mile. Turn left onto the small road toward Skyline Drive and go 0.1 mile. Turn left onto Skyline Drive, which quickly becomes the Blue Ridge Parkway. Drive 6 miles; then turn left into the Humpback Gap Parking Area (Blue Ridge Parkway milepost 6).

GPS TRAILHEAD COORDINATES N37° 58.112' W78° 53.770'

102 HANGING ROCK

MODERATE | 7.4-mile round-trip | 4.5 hours

A long this hike you will pass over the summit of Meadow Mountain (elevation 3,100'), where a rocky outcrop on the west side of the Trail provides a view across the valley toward Torrey Ridge. You will also walk over the top of Bee Mountain (elevation 3,000'), which offers views when the leaves are off the trees. At Hanging Rock, the destination of this trip, you will be treated to a view of the peak of Three Ridges (elevation 3,970') and out across rural Tye River Valley (elevation 900') to the hulking mass of The Priest (elevation 4,063').

THE HIKE

From Reids Gap, hike south on the A.T. At mile 0.8, cross the summit of Meadow Mountain. At mile 1.7, reach Maupin Field and a trail junction. The Maupin Field Shelter is 300 feet to the right along the Mau-Har Trail.

Continue following the A.T. south from the trail junction for 0.4 mile to the summit of Bee Mountain. The Trail then descends to a gap and begins climbing along the

Hanging Rock juts above the crest of Peters Mountain. *Photo: Johnny Molloy*

northern slope of Three Ridges. At mile 3.7, where white blazes on rocks mark the route, Hanging Rock (elevation 3,400') is located 50 feet to the west of the A.T.

The return hike is back north on the A.T. to Reids Gap.

TRAILHEAD DIRECTIONS

From I-64, take Exit 99 (US 250/Afton/Waynesboro). Turn right onto US 250 East, and drive 0.3 mile; then turn left onto the small road toward Skyline Drive, and drive 0.1 mile. Turn left onto Skyline Drive, which quickly becomes the Blue Ridge Parkway. Drive 13.6 miles to Reids Gap, where a parking area is located at the intersection with VA 664 (Blue Ridge Parkway milepost 13.6).

GPS TRAILHEAD COORDINATES N37° 54.082' W78° 59.131'

The A.T. follows Brown Mountain Creek for more than a mile.   *Photo: Leonard M. Adkins*

103 BROWN MOUNTAIN CREEK

EASY | 5.6-mile round-trip | 3 hours

Along the banks of Brown Mountain Creek, you will find old chimneys, rock walls, and building foundations that recall a time in the 1800s when this creek was at the heart of a busy community. The little valley is now known for its tremendous wildflower display, which includes rhododendron, mountain laurel, showy orchids, and a variety of ferns.

THE HIKE

From Long Mountain Wayside on US 60, hike south on the A.T. and descend into Brown Mountain Creek Valley. Hike 1.0 mile, and cross the creek for the first time. The Trail follows alongside the creek for the remainder of the hike, and it passes by old walls and foundations. Pass by the Brown Mountain Creek Shelter at mile 1.8. Water is available from two small springs. At mile 2.8, there is a footbridge over the creek. On the far side, the Trail begins to climb again.

To return, climb north on the A.T. back to the highway.

TRAILHEAD DIRECTIONS

From I-81, take Exit 188A and merge onto US 60 East. Drive 13.4 miles to a small parking area on the right at the trailhead.

GPS TRAILHEAD COORDINATES N37° 43.399' W79° 14.980'

Laurie Adkins looks out at the Shenandoah Valley from Bluff Mountain.   *Photo: Leonard M. Adkins*

104 BLUFF MOUNTAIN

MODERATE | 4-mile round-trip | 3 hours

Bluff Mountain offers more views today than it did in the past. Sadly, most of the spruce trees that covered much of the summit have died, but this has opened up a wonderful vista onto the mountains framing the Shenandoah Valley. Also on the mountaintop is a plaque in memory of Ottie Cline Powell, a youth who wandered away from school and died in the mountains. The plaque tells his sad tale.

You can also make a 0.4-mile side trip to Punchbowl Shelter, which has an idyllic setting on the side of a small pond. This relatively short hike takes you up a steady climb of more than 1,100 feet. The ascent could be listed as strenuous, but the Trail is graded well and the climb is short.

THE HIKE

From the small parking area, diagonally cross the Blue Ridge Parkway, hike south on the A.T., and begin climbing the northeast slope of Punchbowl Mountain. At mile 0.4, reach the junction with the blue-blazed side trail, which leads 0.2 mile to Punchbowl Shelter. Continue on the A.T., and in 0.5 mile reach the tree-covered summit of Punchbowl Mountain (elevation 2,868').

Descend 0.25 mile to a gap and begin climbing Bluff Mountain. At mile 2.0, reach the summit of Bluff Mountain (elevation 3,372'). Note the plaque in memory of Ottie Cline Powell just a few feet to the south along the Trail. Having just climbed to the summit yourself, you can appreciate the troubles the small child must have encountered.

The return hike is north on the A.T. to the parking area.

TRAILHEAD DIRECTIONS

From I-81, take Exit 188A and merge onto US 60 East. Drive 8.1 miles; then turn left onto the small road toward the Blue Ridge Parkway. Turn left onto Blue Ridge Parkway, and drive 6.2 miles to the parking area on the left (Blue Ridge Parkway milepost 51.7).

GPS TRAILHEAD COORDINATES N37° 40.452' W79° 20.063'

105 FULLERS ROCKS AND BIG ROCKY ROW

STRENUOUS | 9.4-mile loop | 5.5 hours

Fullers Rocks and Big Rocky Row provide what can only be described as Olympian views. From overlooks close to 2,000 feet above the James River, you can watch the stream course its way through the gap that was created for it ages ago, when rocks on both sides where uplifted during a geological event. It is Virginia's longest river, stretching 450 miles from the West Virginia–Virginia state line to Chesapeake Bay.

The hike has an historic aspect, too. Saddle Gap Trail, which you use during this loop, was part of an original A.T. segment, built here in 1930.

THE HIKE

Take the A.T. to the north and begin the long, 1,630-foot climb to Fullers Rocks. Cross Johns Creek at 0.4 mile, and pass by the side trail to Johns Hollow Shelter at 0.6 mile. Reach the first of 21 switchbacks at 1.4 miles and begin the final ascent of 1,000 feet.

Come to the first viewpoint and pass by blue-blazed Rocky Row Trail to the left at 2.6 miles. Reach Fullers Rocks at 2.7 miles, where three side trails, one right after the other, lead to spectacular views from the rock. In the center of the vista is the James River, flanked by the dramatically steep slopes of the James River Face

Wilderness. To the south are High Cock Knob and Apple Orchard Mountain (with a radar dome on its summit) along the Blue Ridge Parkway. Big Piney and Peavine Mountains are north of the river.

Continue north on the A.T., dropping into a sag before rising to a side trail at 3.3 miles that leads to a view westward, and passing by another view to the west at 3.6 miles. About 0.1 mile beyond the summit of Big Rocky Row is a side trail to the right, with another grandstand view of the James River and mountain summits.

Gradually drop to Saddle Gap at 5.2 miles and turn right to descend along blue-blazed Saddle Gap Trail. Turn right onto Forest Service Road (FR) 36 (Hercules Road) at 7.7 miles and parallel Rocky Row Run as you go downhill to your car at 9.4 miles.

TRAILHEAD DIRECTIONS

From I-81, take Exit 175 (US 11 North/Natural Bridge). Turn onto US 11 North, and drive about 1.6 miles. Turn right onto VA 130 East, and drive 6.3 miles. Turn right onto US 501 South, and drive 5.7 miles. Turn left onto VA 812, and drive 0.9 mile to the A.T. crossing.

GPS TRAILHEAD COORDINATES N37° 36.295' W79° 23.302'

106 APPLE ORCHARD MOUNTAIN AND THE GUILLOTINE

EASY | 4-mile round-trip | 2 hours

This unusual day hike takes you to the summit of Apple Orchard Mountain, which has a large Federal Aviation Administration antenna on the top. The antenna is the only working remnant of Bedford Air Force Base, which operated on the summit from 1954 to 1974. As many as 120 airmen were stationed on the mountain during those 20 years.

Just 0.3 mile beyond the summit of Apple Orchard Mountain, you will reach another highlight of this day hike—110 rock steps built by the Natural Bridge Appalachian Trail Club with help from the ATC's volunteer trail crew. The steps take the Trail in and around several interesting rock formations, including The Guillotine, a large boulder that hangs over the Trail, trapped in a cleft of another rock.

THE HIKE

From Sunset Field, follow the blue-blazed Apple Orchard Falls Trail as it descends 0.25 mile to the junction with the A.T. Turn right and follow the A.T. north, climbing up to Forest Service Road 812 on steps. Cross the gravel road and again ascend on steps. The A.T. winds up the wooded side of Apple Orchard Mountain—with trillium and other wildflowers abounding in the spring—for a little more than a mile, where it enters the field on the summit of the mountain. Views of mountain peaks more than 40 miles away are visible from rocks just a few feet off the Trail. Continue north on the A.T. to rock steps that descend around rock formations and pass under The Guillotine at 2.0 miles.

The return hike is south on the A.T. to the Apple Orchard Falls Trail, which you follow back to Sunset Field.

TRAILHEAD DIRECTIONS

From I-81, take Exit 168 (VA 614/Arcadia). Turn onto VA 614 (right from I-81 South, left from I-81 North); then immediately turn left onto the I-81 Frontage Road, and drive 1 mile. Then continue onto US 11 South, and drive 1.3 miles. Turn left onto VA 43 South, and drive 4.7 miles; then turn left onto the short ramp (sign for Bedford). Turn left onto VA 43 South, and drive 4.9 miles; then continue onto the Blue Ridge Parkway as you pass the visitor center on your left. Drive 7.5 miles to the Sunset Field parking area on your left (Blue Ridge Parkway milepost 78.4).

GPS TRAILHEAD COORDINATES   N37° 30.461' W79° 31.448'

107 HAY ROCK

MODERATE | 7.8-mile round-trip | 4.5 hours

Hay Rock is an exposed and upturned portion of the sandstone spine of Tinker Mountain. A climb to the top of its sloping west face provides soaring views of McAfee Knob and Carvin Cove, the reservoir that supplies water to the city of Roanoke.

The climb of approximately 1,000 feet is made easier by a series of switchbacks. Additional views are passed along the way.

Hay Rock sits directly on the A.T. *Photo: Johnny Molloy*

THE HIKE

Follow the unmarked trail (actually an old road) from the back of the parking lot, intersect the A.T. in 0.2 mile, turn left to follow it to the south, and descend to cross Tinker Creek on a concrete bridge. Step over railroad tracks at 0.4 mile and rise to the first of numerous switchbacks at 1.5 miles.

Soon after passing close to a private dirt road, the Trail climbs steeply to the top of Tinker Ridge at 2.0 miles for a view of I-81 passing through the Great Valley of Virginia, which is bordered on the east by Fullhardt Knob and other Blue Ridge Mountain summits.

Continue along the rough and rocky ridgeline to a view of Carvin Cove and surrounding slopes at 2.6 miles. A power line right-of-way provides another lookout point at 2.7 miles before you reach Hay Rock at 3.9 miles. Obtain views by climbing the back side of the rock.

Follow the A.T. north to return to the parking lot.

TRAILHEAD DIRECTIONS

From I-81 North, take Exit 150B (US 11 North/Troutville/Fincastle). Turn right onto US 11, and drive 0.2 mile; then turn right onto US 220 North, and drive 0.4 mile. Turn left onto VA 816/Tinker Mountain Road; the commuter parking lot will be immediately in front of you.

From I-81 South, take Exit 150B (US 220 North/Daleville/Fincastle). Merge onto US 220 North, and immediately turn left onto VA 816/Tinker Mountain Road. The commuter parking lot will be immediately in front of you.

GPS TRAILHEAD COORDINATES N37° 23.470' W79° 54.389'

108 TINKER CLIFFS

STRENUOUS | 8.2-mile round-trip | 5.5 hours

The destination of this strenuous hike is Tinker Cliffs, a dramatic rock wall that stretches for 0.5 mile near the crest of Tinker Mountain. With inspiring views, the cliffs look down onto bucolic Catawba Valley and out to McAfee Knob, Dragons Tooth, North Mountain, and other ridgelines to the west. A walk beside two streams and through open pasturelands adds to the beauty of the hike.

This journey follows the A.T. for only 2.0 miles, but it lives up to the spirit of this book because the other 6.2 miles are along a former route of the A.T.

THE HIKE

The hike begins by following the Andy Layne Trail from the parking lot. This former route of the A.T. is named in memory of one of the hardest working, and jovial, volunteer trail workers in the history of the Appalachian Trail Conservancy. Cross a low knob and descend to parallel Little Catawba Creek before using a footbridge to cross it at 0.6 mile. Walk through a meadowland, cross Catawba Creek at 0.9 mile, and begin the long climb to the A.T. in Scorched Earth Gap at 3.1 miles.

According to Roanoke Appalachian Trail Club lore, a group of volunteers were on a scouting trip and had just climbed Tinker Mountain, via what is now the Andy Layne Trail. A female participant, known to be quite religious, surprised everyone with her anger at the steepness of the route. She let loose such a volatile succession of expletives that the hike leader proclaimed she had "scorched the earth."

Turn right onto the A.T. and, at 3.6 miles, come to the Well, a natural hole in the rocks that marks the northern end of Tinker Cliffs. Follow the cliffs for the next 0.5 mile, enjoying the views and taking care to watch your footing along the precipitous edge.

Retrace your steps to return to the parking lot.

TRAILHEAD DIRECTIONS

From I-81 North, take Exit 150B, turn right onto US 11, and drive 0.2 mile; turn right onto US 220 North. From I-81 South, take Exit 150B and merge onto US 220 North. Drive 1.8 miles; then turn left onto VA 779/Catawba Road, and drive 8.4 miles to the parking lot on the left.

GPS TRAILHEAD COORDINATES N37° 27.459' W80° 01.040'

109 McAFEE KNOB

MODERATE | 7.4-mile round-trip | 4 hours

McAfee Knob, an overhanging rock ledge with outstanding views, is the destination of this day hike. From the ledges, you can see both the Catawba and Roanoke Valleys, as well as the mountain ridges to the north and the west. To the right, view Tinker Cliffs; to the left, across the valley, view North Mountain, the former site of the A.T.

THE HIKE

From the parking area at VA 311, head north on the A.T. by crossing the road (carefully, because southbound traffic has limited visibility), and pass under two power lines. Turn left and begin to climb the ridge along switchbacks.

Hike 0.25 mile to the crest of the ridge, bear right, and climb along an old woods road for 0.1 mile; follow the rocky crest of the ridge to your right. Begin to descend, heading right, and rejoin the old woods road. Turn right, leave the road, and arrive at a bulletin board (to your left).

A sharp left turn will bring you parallel to the crest of the ridge, and for the next 1.5 miles, follow the ridge with minor ups and downs. In the fall and winter, Fort Lewis Mountain can be seen on the right. At mile 1.0, pass a trailside shelter to your right.

At mile 1.9, merge onto another old road, begin to descend, and shortly thereafter, pass by a spring to your left. After crossing a small water run, pass a couple of blue-blazed trails on your right that lead to the Catawba Mountain Shelter.

Shortly thereafter, begin to climb, cross a dirt road, pass through an area of thick laurel growth, and then head toward McAfee Knob. At about mile 3.4, turn left onto an old road and continue to climb past large boulders. Many trails crisscross this area, so keep an eye out for the white blazes marking the A.T. At a small clearing at the end of the road, a side trail heads left to the cliffs at McAfee Knob.

Return to the parking area by retracing your steps south on the A.T.

TRAILHEAD DIRECTIONS

From I-81, take Exit 141 (VA 419/Salem/Newcastle). Turn onto VA 419 North, and drive 0.4 mile; then turn right onto VA 311 North, and drive 5.6 miles to the parking area on your left.

GPS TRAILHEAD COORDINATES N37° 22.805' W80° 05.384'

It is only a 0.25-mile walk to Wind Rock.   *Photo: Leonard M. Adkins*

110 WIND ROCK

EASY | 0.5-mile round-trip | 30 minutes

A short hike on the Trail will bring you to Wind Rock, a fine viewpoint. This easy leg-stretcher is a good way to introduce your nonhiker friends to the A.T.

THE HIKE

From Salt Sulphur Turnpike, hike north on the A.T. Follow an old woods road up the mountain for 0.25 mile to Wind Rock (elevation 4,100'). Look to the north for a nice view of Stony Creek Valley.

The return hike is back down the A.T. to the turnpike.

TRAILHEAD DIRECTIONS

From I-81, take Exit 118 C-B-A and merge onto US 460 West. Drive 20.7 miles; then turn right onto VA 700, and drive 12 miles, during which VA 700 becomes VA 613. You'll reach a high point between Big Mountain and Potts Mountain, and the A.T. crossing.

GPS TRAILHEAD COORDINATES N37° 24.722' W80° 31.386'

111 ANGELS REST AND PEARIS MOUNTAIN

STRENUOUS | 9.4-mile round-trip | 5.5 hours

Excellent viewpoints reward you for climbing close to 1,500 feet from the New River Valley to the top of Pearis Mountain. Long, gradually rising switchbacks, constructed by volunteers of the Roanoke Appalachian Trail Club, ease the huff-and-puff factor.

Dutchman's breeches   *Photo: Leonard M. Adkins*

THE HIKE

Follow the A.T. south as it gains elevation following a ravine to cross VA 634 in 1.1 miles. Continue to ascend within a mixed hardwood forest and cross a boulder field at 1.0 mile. Dutchman's breeches grow well and are quite abundant along the trail during early spring.

Rock formations mark your arrival at Angels Rest at 3.6 miles. Take the short blue-blazed side trail to the right and walk onto the large rock for excellent views of the New River winding through the valley it has created for itself through thousands of years of erosive action. Peters Mountain rises from the far side of the river.

Return to the A.T., continue to ascend, and pass a side trail to a spring and campsite at 4.1 miles. The rock ledge to the left at 4.7 miles overlooks the New River, wide Wilburn Valley dotted by farmlands and small settlements, and Sugar Run and Salt Pond Mountains to the east.

Follow the A.T. north to return to the trailhead.

TRAILHEAD DIRECTIONS

From I-81, take Exit 118 C-B-A and merge onto US 460 West. Drive 33.4 miles; then turn left onto Thomas Drive and go 0.3 mile to the A.T. parking area on the right.

GPS TRAILHEAD COORDINATES N37° 20.063' W80° 45.378'

The pool below Dismal Falls beckons on hot days.   *Photo: Leonard M. Adkins*

112 DISMAL CREEK FALLS

MODERATE | 4.3-mile round-trip | 2.5 hours

On this hike to the broad cascade of Dismal Falls, you will pass through thick groves of rhododendron. This day hike is a good choice for mid-June because the rhododendron bloom is at its peak. Dismal Creek is a popular trout stream.

THE HIKE

From the trailhead on VA 606, hike north on the A.T. and begin climbing Brushy Mountain. At mile 1.9, reach the junction with the blue-blazed side trail to Dismal Creek Falls. Turn left on the side trail and hike another 0.25 mile to the falls overlook.

To return, hike back to the A.T. on the side trail, turn right on the A.T., and hike south to VA 606.

TRAILHEAD DIRECTIONS

From I-77, take Exit 52 (US 52/VA 42). Turn onto US 52 North, and drive 0.6 mile; then turn left to stay on US 52 North, and drive 0.1 mile. Turn right onto VA 42 East, and drive 13.2 miles. Turn left onto VA 606, and drive 0.3 mile to the trail crossing.

GPS TRAILHEAD COORDINATES   N37° 10.212' W80° 54.117'

113 GARDEN MOUNTAIN

MODERATE | 3.8-mile round-trip | 2.5 hours

Burkes Garden is an oval-shaped bowl of more than 20,000 acres that looks like a volcanic crater. It was actually carved by water eroding the underlying layer of limestone rock. The porous quality and mineral composition make this some of the most fertile land in Virginia, producing high crop yields. Spared the disturbances of modern development, it remains one of the state's largest rural, and scenic, areas. With the circular ridgeline of Garden Mountain surrounding this indentation in the landscape, it is easy to see why some people refer to it as God's thumbprint.

This round-trip hike along Garden Mountain provides a chance to descend to the edge of the garden for a view across its open farmlands and to hike to another view that looks southward to Walker Mountain—where the A.T. was once located. There is very little change of elevation along the route of the A.T., but be aware that the descent to the garden view is quite steep. You could shorten the hike by 0.8 mile if you decide not to go there.

THE HIKE

Hike north on the A.T., which uses stone steps to negotiate a rock formation. Come to an intersection at 1.0 mile and turn left to descend steeply for 0.4 mile to the Davis Farm Campsite and the view of Burkes Garden. Return to the A.T., turn left, and arrive at a rock outcrop in another 0.5 mile. The view from the top of the rocks takes in the undisturbed landscape of Hunting Creek Valley and the wider expanse of Walker Creek Valley framed by Walker Mountain's long ridgeline.

Retrace your steps along the A.T. to return to your automobile.

TRAILHEAD DIRECTIONS

From I-77, take Exit 52 (US 52/VA 42). Turn onto US 52 South, and drive 4.1 miles; then turn right onto VA 42 West, and drive 6.3 miles. Turn right onto VA 623, and drive 7.3 miles to the crest of Garden Mountain.

GPS TRAILHEAD COORDINATES N37° 04.627' W81° 18.427'

114 CHESTNUT KNOB

MODERATE | 2.8-mile round-trip | 2 hours

The open summit of Chestnut Knob offers a commanding view of Burkes Garden and the surrounding countryside. The knob is at the southwest corner of the garden.

THE HIKE

From the parking area in Walker Gap, hike south on the A.T. and begin climbing Chestnut Knob. You will cross an old woods road and a gravel road on the climb up the knob. At mile 1.4, reach the open summit of Chestnut Knob (elevation 4,409').

The return hike is back north on the A.T. to the gravel road in Walker Gap.

TRAILHEAD DIRECTIONS

From I-77, take Exit 52 (US 52/VA 42). Turn onto US 52 South, and drive 4.1 miles; then turn right onto VA 42 West, and drive 6.3 miles. Turn right onto VA 623, and drive 11.7 miles; then turn left onto VA 727. Drive about 5 miles to where the gravel road dead-ends at Walker Gap. This can be a very rough road.

GPS TRAILHEAD COORDINATES N37° 03.270' W81° 22.719'

115 COMERS CREEK FALLS

EASY | 2.4-mile round-trip | 1.5 hours

This easy hike leads to Comers Creek Falls, where there is a nice swimming hole at the base of this small waterfall. In response to statements of opposition during a series of public meetings, and hundreds of letters of protest by Virginia residents and other A.T. supporters, the Virginia Department of Transportation in 1996 canceled plans to build a four-lane highway across the Trail. The road would have split the Mount Rogers National Recreation area in two and turned Comers Creek and Comers Creek Falls into a concrete culvert.

THE HIKE

From the trailhead at Dickey Gap, follow the A.T. south. The Trail from the gap to the falls is along the side of Iron Mountain, which is actually more of a ridge than a mountain. At mile 1.2, cross Comers Creek at the base of the 10-foot falls.

The return hike is back north to the trailhead at Dickey Gap.

TRAILHEAD DIRECTIONS

From I-81, take Exit 45 (VA 16/Marion). Turn onto VA 16 South, and drive 14.7 miles. Turn right onto Comers Creek Road/VA 650; the trailhead is immediately on your right.

GPS TRAILHEAD COORDINATES N36° 43.224' W81° 27.698'

116 RHODODENDRON GAP

MODERATE | 5.2-mile round-trip | 3 hours

This hike takes you through the heart of the Virginia Highlands, an area of breathtaking beauty. You will climb to Wilburn Ridge and follow a loop trail along the ridge to Rhododendron Gap. Wilburn Ridge has rock outcrops that afford many magnificent views, and Rhododendron Gap surrounds the Trail with hundreds of acres of rhododendrons. The rhododendrons are usually at peak bloom between the third week in June and the first week in July. The vast garden in bloom is an awesome sight to see. This is not a secret spot, however, and the Trail can be crowded during peak bloom, particularly on weekends. Rhododendron Gap is also a great place to pick blueberries in late August.

Grayson Highlands State Park is home to free-ranging ponies, which are frequently seen along the A.T. The ponies are not really wild, but they should not be approached or attempted to ride. Some of the ponies are sold at auction during the park's fall festival to raise money to care for the herd.

THE HIKE

From the main park road at Massie Gap, hike 0.5 mile on the blue-blazed Rhododendron Trail to the A.T. Turn left and follow the A.T. south. Hike another 0.5 mile and cross a fence, leaving Grayson Highlands State Park behind and entering the Jefferson

National Forest. Reach the junction with a blue-blazed side trail in 0.25 mile. Follow this trail, which leads straight up and over Wilburn Ridge to rejoin the A.T. on the other side of the two high points on the ridge. After rejoining the A.T., continue south and descend to Rhododendron Gap. After exploring the gap (there is a nice view from the rocks), hike back north on the A.T., which bears left around the high points on Wilburn Ridge. At the junction with the Rhododendron Trail, turn right and return to the parking area on the Grayson Highlands State Park road at Massie Gap.

TRAILHEAD DIRECTIONS
From I-81, take Exit 45 (VA 16/Marion). Turn onto VA 16 South, and drive 23.9 miles. Turn right onto US 58 West, and drive 7.7 miles. Turn right onto VA 362 North and into Grayson Highlands State Park; drive 3.5 miles on the main park road, and then turn right to get to the Massey Gap parking area and the trailhead.

GPS TRAILHEAD COORDINATES N36° 38.039' W81° 30.575'

117 MOUNT ROGERS

STRENUOUS | 9-mile round-trip | 5.5 hours

Mount Rogers, at 5,729 feet, is the highest point in Virginia. Named for William Barton Rogers, the first state geologist of Virginia, Mount Rogers was once known as Balsam Mountain. Its summit supports the northernmost natural stand of Fraser fir, and boasts an annual rainfall average of 60 inches and a snowfall average of 57 inches.

Although there are many views along the way, there is no vista from the summit of Mount Rogers. However, the fir-covered peak makes a wonderful picnic spot.

THE HIKE
From the parking area at VA 600 (elevation 4,434'), cross the road, pass through the gate, head left, and climb through a field toward Mount Rogers. Keep an eye out for blazes here.

At mile 0.25, reach the crest of the ridge, where you'll find good views. Hike another 0.25 mile, cross a fence on a stile, and enter the Lewis Fork Wilderness. The A.T. continues to climb toward Mount Rogers through woods.

One of Grayson Highlands' wild ponies   *Photo: Johnny Molloy*

At mile 1.8, reach the former site of the Deep Gap Shelter (elevation 4,900'). A spring is located just south of the shelter site; the Virginia Highlands Horse Trail also passes through here. The shelter is now on display at a park in Damascus, Virginia.

Hike another 0.25 mile, cross the Virginia Highlands Horse Trail, and turn right uphill. Here, the blue-blazed Elk Garden Trail heads left 4.0 miles to the U.S. Forest Service's Grindstone Campground at VA 603.

Descend briefly and turn left. To your right, enjoy views from a fence surrounding an open meadow. Climb the southern slope of Mount Rogers, cross several streams, enter an overgrown field, and continue to climb. At mile 4.8, turn left onto the blue-blazed side trail that leads 0.5 mile to the summit of Mount Rogers (elevation 5,729').

From the summit, return to the A.T. and follow the Trail south to the parking area at VA 600.

TRAILHEAD DIRECTIONS
From I-81, take Exit 35 (VA 107/Chilhowie). Turn right onto Whitetop Road, and drive 11.3 miles. Turn left onto County Road 600/Whitetop Road, and drive 5.2 miles to the Elk Garden parking area on the right.

GPS TRAILHEAD COORDINATES N36° 38.748' W81° 34.991'

118 BUZZARD ROCK

EASY | 1.8-mile round-trip | 1 hour

This short and relatively easy day hike takes you to stupendous views from Buzzard Rock atop Whitetop Mountain.

THE HIKE

From the parking area on Whitetop Mountain Road, walk back to the A.T. and turn south onto it to head forward. As you descend through the open field, you will see your destination—a prominent rock peak. From Buzzard Rock, enjoy excellent views to the south and west. Return to the parking area by climbing back up the A.T., north.

TRAILHEAD DIRECTIONS

From I-81, take Exit 35 (VA 107/Chilhowie). Turn right onto Whitetop Road, and drive 11.3 miles. Turn left onto County Road 600/Whitetop Road, and drive 6.5 miles. Turn right onto Mud Creek Lane, and drive 2.8 miles to the trailhead. Parking is at the picnic area just ahead.

GPS TRAILHEAD COORDINATES N36° 38.198' W81° 36.501'

119 STRAIGHT MOUNTAIN AND THE VIRGINIA CREEPER TRAIL

MODERATE | 10-mile round-trip | 5.75 hours

At 9.4 miles, this is one of the longer day hikes in this book, yet the walking is relatively easy, and the ascents are gradual with just a few short, steep climbs. The rewards are a number of views from Straight Mountain and a walk of several miles beside Whitetop Laurel Creek on the Virginia Creeper Trail. Many consider it the best and most scenic rail-trail in the state.

THE HIKE

Descend from US 58 on the purple-blazed Beartree Gap Trail, and turn right onto the A.T. at 0.5 mile. One of the day's best vistas comes into view at 1.4 miles. To the east are Whitetop Mountain and Mount Rogers. Continuing along the ridgeline, there are several views of Beartree Lake and the crest of Iron Mountain to the northwest.

The Trail dips for a bit before resuming the ascent to pass a side trail to Saunders Shelter at 2.8 miles. Come to the crest of Straight Mountain less than 600 feet later. Receding to the southeast, and getting progressively higher, you will see a succession of ridgelines—Laurel, Chestnut, Beech, and Whitetop Mountains. Within a few hundred feet of this overlook, the A.T. begins a long descent on a series of switchbacks constructed by the Civilian Conservation Corps in the 1930s. Another pathway to the shelter is passed at 3.2 miles.

Turn left onto the blue-blazed trail at 4.6 miles and make a short descent to turn left onto the Virginia Creeper Trail at 4.8 miles. You will be walking upstream beside scenic Whitetop Laurel Creek. Break out of the woods as you walk by fields in the small community of Taylors Valley, where public restrooms are available at the parking lot near one end of town.

Continue back into the woods, passing by campsites about 7.8 miles into the hike. Come to an intersection with the A.T. at 8.8 miles and turn left to leave the creek and follow white blazes on an ascent across the slope of Straight Mountain. Pass by a small pond at 9.4 miles, turn right onto purple-blazed Beartree Gap Trail at 9.5 miles, and return to US 58 at 10 miles.

TRAILHEAD DIRECTIONS

From I-81, take Exit 19 (US 11/US 58/Abingdon/Damascus). Turn onto US 58 East, and drive 10.7 miles to Damascus. Turn right on Douglas Drive to stay on US 58 East. Drive 0.9 mile; then turn left to stay on US 58 East. Drive 7.1 miles, just past the Beartree Recreation Area entrance, to limited parking at the trailhead of the Beartree Gap Trail.

GPS TRAILHEAD COORDINATES N36° 39.258' W81° 41.336'

TENNESSEE & NORTH CAROLINA

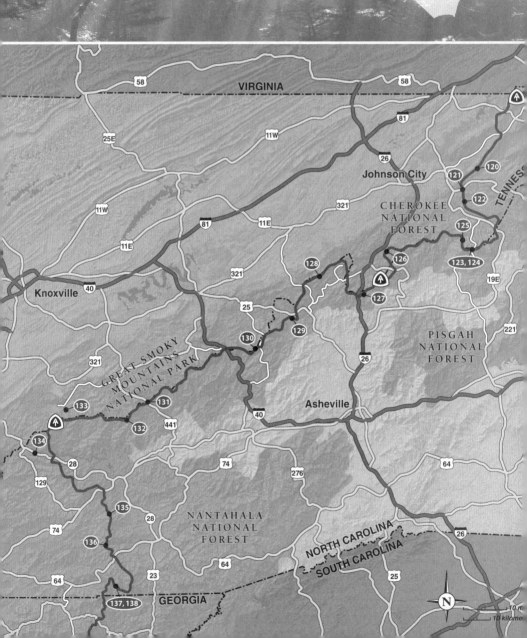

Hike	Page	Length (mi.)	Configuration	Time (hr.)	Difficulty*	Features
120. Iron Mountain	191	9.4	round-trip	4.5	★★	scenic view, pond or river
121. Laurel Fork Gorge and Falls	192	5.0	round-trip	2.5	★	mountain peak, waterfall
122. Dennis Cove Loop	193	3.6	loop	3.0	★★	scenic view, waterfall, historic area, bird-watching, wheelchair access
123. Grassy Ridge	194	4.8	round-trip	3.5	★	mountain peak, scenic view
124. Roan Mountain	196	3.8	round-trip	2.0	★★	mountain peak, scenic view, historic area
125. Little Rock Knob	197	4.6	round-trip	2.5	★	scenic view
126. Cliff Ridge	198	3.6	round-trip	2.5	★★	scenic view
127. Big Bald	199	8.4	round-trip	5.0	★★	mountain peak, scenic view
128. White Rocks Cliffs, Blackstack Cliffs, and Big Firescald Knob	200	6.4	round-trip	3.0	★	scenic view
129. Lovers Leap Rock	202	2.8	round-trip	2.0	★★★	scenic view
130. Max Patch	203	1.6	round-trip	1.5	★★	mountain peak, scenic view
131. Charlies Bunion	204	8.0	round-trip	5.0	★★★	scenic view
132. Clingmans Dome and Mount Collins	205	7.0	round-trip	3.5	★★	mountain peak, scenic view
133. Rocky Top	207	11.6	round-trip	7.0	★★★	mountain peak, scenic view
134. Shuckstack	208	11.0	round-trip	6.0	★★	scenic view, waterfall
135. Wesser Bald	209	2.8	round-trip	2.0	★★★	mountain peak, scenic view
136. Siler Bald	210	3.8	round-trip	2.5	★★★	mountain peak, scenic view
137. Standing Indian Mountain	211	4.8	round-trip	3.0	★★★	mountain peak, scenic view
138. Ravenrock Ridge	212	9.0	round-trip	5.0	★★★	scenic view

DIFFICULTY ★★★ strenuous ★★ moderate ★ easy   CONFIGURATION round-trip loop

mountain peak   scenic view   pond or river   waterfall   historic area   bird-watching

 wheelchair access

BECAUSE SO MANY MILES OF THE APPALACHIAN TRAIL traverse the Tennessee–North Carolina state line, these two states are usually placed together in trail guides. Combined, the two states offer more than 370 miles of trail. Heading south, the Trail begins in Tennessee (heading north, in North Carolina).

For the first 37 miles, the Trail traverses the ridgeline as it makes its way to Wautaga Lake near Hampton, Tennessee. From Hampton, the Trail heads through Laurel Fork Gorge with its spectacular waterfalls, and continues up White Rocks Mountain before it descends to Elk Park, North Carolina.

From Elk Park, a strenuous climb to the Hump Mountains brings you to Grassy Ridge (a 6,000-foot grassy bald), Roan Highlands, Roan High Knob, and Roan High Bluff. Roan High Bluff, more than 6,000 feet in elevation, is known for its spectacular rhododendron gardens that bloom profusely each June. From Roan, the Trail continues along the Tennessee–North Carolina state line for nearly 100 miles as it makes its way to Hot Springs, North Carolina, and heads into Great Smoky Mountains National Park. In this section, the Trail passes Little Rock Knob, Unaka Mountain, and Beauty Spot. It descends to Erwin, Tennessee, and continues to Hot Springs.

From Hot Springs, it is just over 30 miles to Davenport Gap, the northern entrance of the A.T. into the Smoky Mountains. In the Smokies, the Trail traverses Mount Cammerer, the Sawteeth, and Charlies Bunion; reaches Newfound Gap; and proceeds to Clingmans Dome, the highest point on the entire A.T. (elevation 6,643').

The A.T. continues across Silers Bald (which is different from Siler Bald; see below) to Thunderhead and Rocky Top, and down to grassy Spence and Russell Fields. It then continues along to Shuckstack and descends to Fontana Dam at the Little Tennessee River, the southern boundary of Great Smoky Mountains National Park.

From the Smokies, the A.T. ascends into the Nantahalas, where there are peaks from 4,000–5,000 feet in elevation. The area between Fontana and Wesser is said to be one of the toughest sections on the A.T. From the Nantahala Outdoor Center at Wesser, the A.T. climbs up to Wesser Bald, Wayah Bald, and Siler Bald before heading up the ridge to Standing Indian Mountain. Albert Mountain is also a notable climb in this section. From Albert, it is not far to the North Carolina–Georgia state line at Bly Gap.

120 IRON MOUNTAIN

MODERATE | 9.4-mile round-trip | 4.5 hours

This hike will take you from the shore of Watauga Lake to two viewpoints high above the lake at rock outcrops on Iron Mountain, and it involves a 1,000-foot gain in elevation. The entire hike lies within the Big Laurel Branch Wilderness.

THE HIKE

From Wilbur Dam Road, hike north on the A.T. and begin climbing Iron Mountain in the Big Laurel Branch Wilderness. As you climb along the ridge, the Trail skirts high points, keeping a

Watauga Lake   *Photo: Johnny Molloy*

moderate grade, crossing summits at 2.4 and 2.6 miles. Continue following the A.T. to reach a rock outcrop on the right at 4.0 miles with superior views of the Watauga Valley. Hike another 0.7 mile to Vandeventer Shelter. The rock outcrop behind the shelter offers a fine view of Watauga Lake about 600 feet below.

To return, hike south on the A.T. to the trailhead on Wilbur Dam Road.

TRAILHEAD DIRECTIONS

From I-26 in Tennessee, take Exit 24 (US 321/TN 67/Elizabethton). Turn right onto US 321, and drive 8.5 miles. Turn left onto US 19E North, and drive 0.2 mile; then take the exit for TN 91 North/Stoney Creek/Shady Valley, and merge onto TN 91 North. Drive 2.9 miles; then turn right onto Blue Springs Road, and drive 0.9 mile. Continue straight onto Steel Bridge Road, which quickly becomes Wilbur Dam Road, and drive 3.8 miles. Turn left to stay on Wilbur Dam Road, and drive 1.5 miles to the trailhead.

GPS TRAILHEAD COORDINATES N36° 19.762' W82° 06.694'

Laurel Fork Falls cascades 40 feet into the pool below. *Photo: Victoria and Frank Logue*

121 LAUREL FORK GORGE AND FALLS

EASY | 5-mile round-trip | 2.5 hours

This leisurely hike will take you into the heart of rugged Laurel Fork Gorge. The vertical walls of the gorge rise more than 100 feet above the stream in some places. Pond and Black Mountains also tower over the gorge, rising well over 1,000 feet above Laurel Fork. The destination of this hike is the 40-foot-tall Laurel Fork Falls. There are many wildflowers and flowering shrubs that bloom, in season, in the gorge. The best known include the Catawba and Carolina rhododendrons and mountain laurel, which usually bloom by late May. Because the A.T. is the only trail to these popular falls, the area can be quite crowded on spring and summer weekends.

THE HIKE

From the trailhead, follow the blue-blazed trail into the Gorge. At mile 0.4, pass Buckled Rock, a rock wall across the stream from the Trail. Hike another 0.6 mile to the junction with the A.T., and follow the A.T. south, hiking upstream along Laurel Fork for 0.2 mile, and cross the stream on a footbridge, crossing another bridge in another 0.2 mile. The Trail beyond the bridge climbs and briefly follows a ridge where there are good views of the gorge. Reach the junction with the side trail to Laurel Fork Shelter, and the high-water bypass trail at 1.8 miles. The A.T. then drops down off the low ridge and at mile 2.3 skirts the base of a cliff on a built-up section of trail. Hike another 0.2 mile to the base of Laurel Fork Falls.

To return, hike north on the A.T. to the blue-blazed trail leading back to the trailhead.

TRAILHEAD DIRECTIONS

From I-26 in Tennessee, take Exit 32 (TN 173/Unicoi Road). Turn onto TN 173 (from I-26 West, a right turn; from I-26 East, a left turn), and drive 1 mile. Turn left onto TN 107 East, and drive 0.7 mile; then turn left onto Sciota Road, and drive 5.9 miles. Turn right onto TN 361 East, and drive 2.5 miles; then turn right to stay on TN 361 East, and drive 2.4 miles. Turn left onto US 19E North, and drive 2 miles; then turn right onto US 321 South, and drive 1.3 miles. Just across the bridge, there is a parking area at the trailhead on the right.

GPS TRAILHEAD COORDINATES N36° 17.133' W82° 09.128'

122 DENNIS COVE LOOP

MODERATE | 3.6-mile loop | 3 hours

This Dennis Cove loop crosses through a white pine forest, takes in a nice viewpoint, and passes Coon Den Falls, which cascades 80 feet down a rock face.

THE HIKE

From the parking area at Forest Service Road (FR) 50 at Dennis Cove, cross the road and head south along the A.T. for 0.2 mile before following an old road alongside a pond and field.

At 1.2 miles into the hike, you will reach a cliff at the end of a spur that affords good views both to the north and west. Turn right, and climb the ridge, heading through rhododendron.

At 1.6 miles, reach another cliff on the right that offers good views to the west and north. Hike another 0.1 mile, and reach the blue-blazed FR 37, which was the former route of the A.T. Follow the blue-blazed trail descending 0.8 mile to Coon Den Falls.

From the falls, hike 0.5 mile farther to the paved road. Turn left. This portion of the paved road is blue blazed for the 0.6 mile back to the trailhead and the end of this loop.

TRAILHEAD DIRECTIONS

From I-26 in Tennessee, take Exit 32 (TN 173/Unicoi Road). Turn onto TN 173 (from I-26 West, a right turn; from I-26 East, a left turn), and drive 1 mile. Turn left onto TN 107 East, and drive 0.7 mile; then turn left onto Sciota Road, and drive 5.9 miles. Turn right onto TN 361 East, and drive 2.5 miles; then turn right to stay on TN 361 East, and drive 2.4 miles. Turn left onto US 19E North, and drive 2 miles; then turn right onto US 321 South, and drive 0.8 mile. Turn right onto Dennis Cove Road, and drive 3.9 miles to the parking area on your left.

GPS TRAILHEAD COORDINATES N36° 15.845' W82° 07.398'

123 GRASSY RIDGE

EASY | 4.8-mile round-trip | 3.5 hours

The destination of this day hike is Grassy Ridge, a southern Appalachian bald that is more than 6,000 feet in elevation and offers a 360° view. All other peaks of this elevation near the A.T. are either covered with trees or are topped with artificial structures (such as Clingmans Dome).

From Grassy Ridge, there are views of Grandfather Mountain, Beech Mountain, and White Rocks Mountain. Rhododendron, flame azalea, and Gray's lily can all be found blooming in this area in late June.

THE HIKE

From the parking area at Carvers Gap (elevation 5,512'), head north on the A.T. Climb stone steps and pass through a V zig-zag in a fence. The A.T. has been rerouted to lessen damage to the open slope of Round Bald. You will climb along a gravel trail with log steps as you pass through a forest, and as you near the summit, you will pass a stand of spruce at 0.6 mile. These were planted a long time ago to see if spruce would grow on a bald.

At mile 0.7, pass to the left of Round Bald summit (elevation 5,826') and begin to descend along a gravel path (hardened to protect the fragile soil). Hike another 0.25 mile to Engine Gap, named for an abandoned sawmill engine. From here, begin

Hiking through the forest on the climb to Grassy Ridge   *Photo: Victoria and Frank Logue*

to climb, passing a rock formation where there are good views at mile 1.3. As you hike you will continue to pass rock formations. The exposed rocks here are 1.1 billion-year-old gneiss, which have been intruded upon by 740 million-year-old plutonic rock dikes (these black bands are called the Bakersfield gabbro). These are some of the oldest rocks along the Appalachian Trail.

Reach the summit of Jane Bald (elevation 5,807') in another 0.1 mile. This is a favorite rest or lunch spot for hikers. From Jane Bald, descend for 0.5 mile until the Trail narrows and leaves the main crest of the ridge. Head right (east) onto a trail that passes through alder brush. The narrow trail straight ahead leads 0.5 mile to the flat summit of Grassy Bald.

If you take this side trail, turn right near the summit through an open field scattered with alder brush, and reach a gap (elevation 6,050') that is surrounded by Catawba rhododendron. This gap is 0.25 mile from the summit. There is a spring a short distance down the eastern side of the gap, and a rock outcrop with excellent views 0.25 mile south of the gap.

To return to the parking area at Carvers Gap, follow the A.T. south.

TRAILHEAD DIRECTIONS
From I-26 in Tennessee, take Exit 32 (TN 173/Unicoi Road). Turn onto TN 173 (from I-26 West, a right turn; from I-26 East, a left turn), and drive 1 mile. Turn left onto TN 107 East, and drive 10.1 miles. Continue onto NC 226 South, and drive 7.7 miles. Turn left onto Fork Mountain Road, and drive 4.2 miles. Turn left onto NC 261, and drive 9.2 miles to the Carvers Gap parking area on the left at the North Carolina–Tennessee state line.

GPS TRAILHEAD COORDINATES N36° 06.390' W82° 06.624'

The trail winds through spruce–fir forest.   *Photo: Victoria and Frank Logue*

124 ROAN MOUNTAIN

MODERATE | 3.8-mile round-trip | 2 hours

Roan Mountain, with its spruce-and-fir-covered summits, is the destination of this day hike. Roan High Bluff, a summit of Roan Mountain, has an elevation of 6,267 feet; Roan High Knob has an elevation of 6,285 feet. In late June, when the rhododendrons are blooming, the nearby Cloudland Rhododendron Garden is definitely worth the short side trip. Here you will find Catawba rhododendrons growing in such profusion that it seems as if surely they must have been planted on purpose. But many balds in the southern Appalachians—such as Craggy Gardens on the Blue Ridge Parkway and Grayson Highlands near Mount Rogers in Virginia—also boast magnificent concentrations of rhododendrons.

THE HIKE

From the parking area at Carvers Gap (elevation 5,512'), head west on TN 143 for 175 feet to the A.T. trailhead. Enter balsam forest.

At mile 0.4, reach the former Hack Line Road, the old carriage route from Roan Mountain Village to the former Cloudland Hotel near the summit of Roan High Knob. Turn right, and follow the road through balsam and rhododendron. Climb along switchbacks and reach the junction with a blue-blazed trail at mile 1.5. The side trail heads left 0.1 mile to the summit of Roan High Knob, where a shelter (an old fire warden's cabin) is located. This is the highest shelter on the entire A.T. A spring is located a short distance behind the cabin.

The A.T. continues along the old road and reaches a gap in another 0.5 mile. The Trail continues, and, a short distance later, passes through rhododendron.

At mile 2.2, reach an old cabin site, and shortly thereafter, enter the woods and continue to climb. You will soon leave the woods and climb through a grassy area with spruce trees. Here, you are at the left front corner of the site of the old Cloudland Hotel (elevation 6,150'), which was open from the late 1800s until 1910. Interpretive signs can be found just to the east, and to the left is a large parking lot built in 1952. The road beyond the parking lot leads to the rhododendron gardens. You can obtain water at drinking fountains here. Just beyond this area is Roan High Bluff. Return to the parking area at Carvers Gap by backtracking, following the A.T. north.

TRAILHEAD DIRECTIONS

From I-26 in Tennessee, take Exit 32 (TN 173/Unicoi Road). Turn onto TN 173 (from I-26 West, a right turn; from I-26 East, a left turn), and drive 1 mile. Turn left onto TN 107 East, and drive 10.1 miles. Continue onto NC 226 South, and drive 7.7 miles. Turn left onto Fork Mountain Road, and drive 4.2 miles. Turn left onto NC 261, and drive 9.2 miles to the Carvers Gap parking area on the left at the North Carolina–Tennessee state line.

GPS TRAILHEAD COORDINATES N36° 06.390' W82° 06.624'

125 LITTLE ROCK KNOB

EASY | 4.6-mile round-trip | 2.5 hours

Relocations of the A.T. have transformed this once difficult hike into something manageable. The elevation changes 900 feet in the 2.2 miles from Hughes Gap to Little Rock Knob. However, the knob will richly reward you for your efforts, offering a magnificent view of the valley below. This hike is not as popular as the nearby Roan Mountain, and it is a better choice for weekend hikers looking for a nice hike without the crowds attracted to Roan on pretty spring and summer days.

THE HIKE

The hike starts on the same side of the gap as the small dirt parking area. Follow the A.T. south as it gradually ascends to a high point on the ridge in 0.25 mile. At mile 0.6, pass through a gap. The Trail climbs sharply from the gap and never reaches the summit of the knob. At mile 2.2, reach Little Rock Knob high point (elevation 4,918'); then descend slightly for 0.1 mile to a rock outcrop. There are excellent 180° views from this lookout. Look north to view White Rocks Mountain, which the A.T. passes over.

To return, hike north on the A.T. to the trailhead at Hughes Gap.

TRAILHEAD DIRECTIONS

From I-26 in Tennessee, take Exit 32 (TN 173/Unicoi Road). Turn onto TN 173 (from I-26 West, a right turn; from I-26 East, a left turn), and drive 1 mile. Turn left onto TN 107 East, and drive 5.6 miles; then turn left onto TN 173 East, and drive 6.5 miles. Turn right onto US 19 East, and drive 7.7 miles. Turn right onto TN 143 South, and drive 5.3 miles. Turn right onto Cove Creek Road/Hughes Gap Road, and drive 3 miles; parking is on the right side of the road in a small dirt parking area.

GPS TRAILHEAD COORDINATES N36° 08.198' W82° 08.466'

126 CLIFF RIDGE

MODERATE | 3.6-mile round-trip | 2.5 hours

This hike takes you from the banks of the Nolichucky to a cliff above the river, which provides many fine viewpoints. The Trail follows Cliff Ridge for a mile. The walkway on the bridge over the Nolichucky River is named for Ray Hunt, a longtime trail maintainer, who served as chair of the Appalachian Trail Conservancy from 1983 to 1989.

THE HIKE

From the trailhead at the bridge, follow the road to the left and, shortly thereafter, climb the bank on steps. In 0.25 mile, the Trail begins to ascend on switchbacks. At mile 0.5, reach the southern end of Cliff Ridge. For the next 1.3 miles, the Trail continues to climb as it parallels the cliff. To the left, there are many fine views through the trees and from rock outcrops. To return, hike north on the A.T. to the trailhead.

TRAILHEAD DIRECTIONS

From I-26 in Tennessee, take Exit 40 (Jackson Love Highway/Erwin). Turn onto TN 36 South and turn right (immediately after the exit ramp) onto Temple Hill Road. Drive 0.8 mile; then turn left onto River Road/Unaka Springs Road, and drive 0.5 mile. Turn left onto Chestoa Pike, cross the bridge over the Nolichucky River, and the parking area will be on your right. Walk back over the bridge to reach the trailhead.

GPS TRAILHEAD COORDINATES N36° 06.330' W82° 26.806'

127 BIG BALD

MODERATE | 8.4-mile round-trip | 5 hours

B ig Bald is perhaps the finest example of a southern Appalachian bald mountain. From its treeless summit, the bald offers an outstanding 360° view. You can see an assortment of mountain ranges, including the Blacks, Great Smokies, Nantahalas, and the Unakas.

There are many theories about how the balds were created. Some have attributed balds to fires caused by lightning, Native Americans burning the trees to clear the mountains, settlers clearing pastureland, or even UFOs. Whatever the original cause, most balds have been kept clear at one point through grazing. Without being grazed or cut with mowers, the balds would become covered with trees in time, as plant succession does its work.

THE HIKE

From the dirt road in Street Gap (elevation 4,100'), hike north on the A.T. Follow the old road, continuing up the ridge for 1.0 mile before descending to a sag at 1.1 miles. In another 0.1 mile, you will reach a blue-blazed trail to a spring. At 1.4 miles, reach a dirt track crossing, 50 yards below the gap. In another 0.6 mile, you will pass a spring (2.0 miles into the hike). The Trail for the next mile has little change in elevation.

At mile 3.4 of the hike, reach the junction with another blue-blazed trail, leading to a spring, 100 yards downslope, on the left; in 0.1 mile, reach the junction with yet another blue-blazed trail on the right. This is an alternate trail for use in harsh weather, when the summit of Big Bald needs to be bypassed. From this junction, hike 0.2 mile, crossing small streams along a gentle grade. At mile 3.9, reach Slipper Spur, the southern end of a grassy bald and the northern end of a rhododendron thicket. At mile 4.2, reach the summit of Big Bald (elevation 5,516'). On a clear day, there is an unsurpassed view of many of the mountains for which western North Carolina is known, including Mount Mitchell, the highest peak in the East, to the southeast.

To return, hike south on the A.T. to Street Gap.

TRAILHEAD DIRECTIONS
From I-26 in North Carolina, take Exit 3 (US 23A/Wolf Laurel). Turn onto US 23 ALT South, and drive about 0.7 mile. Turn left onto Laurel Valley Road, and drive 0.2 mile; then turn left onto NC 1502/Puncheon Fork Road, and drive 5 miles. Continue onto Street Gap Road, and drive 0.6 mile to the trail crossing.

Note: If you are coming from the Tennessee state side, the road up to Street Gap is no longer drivable. You will have to get permission to park at the nearest farm to the trail on Higgins Creek Road and walk up the rutted road to the trail.

GPS TRAILHEAD COORDINATES N35° 58.136' W82° 32.414'

128 WHITE ROCKS CLIFFS, BLACKSTACK CLIFFS, AND BIG FIRESCALD KNOB

EASY | 6.4-mile round-trip | 3 hours

This hike offers spectacular views from three rocky ridges. The highest point east of the Mississippi, Mount Mitchell (elevation 6,684'), and the rest of the Black Mountains can be seen from this hike. There is little change in elevation on the hike because the drive to the trailhead brings you to the top of the ridge. If you're hiking in late summer, blueberries abound along the ridge near Big Firescald Knob.

Most of the rocks that compose these ridges are white quartzite, formed more than 500 million years ago. Keep in mind that exposed areas like these are very dangerous in inclement weather.

THE HIKE

From the trailhead at the Camp Creek Bald, take the fire tower trail (the fire tower is normally locked up) and hike 0.2 mile to the junction with the A.T. Turn left on the A.T. and hike north, descending 0.8 mile to an old logging road. At mile 1.9, reach a blue-blazed side trail, and in another 0.1 mile reach the junction with the short side trail leading to White Rocks Cliffs, composed of hard quartzite formed when this was an ancient beach. After enjoying the view at White Rocks, return to the Trail and continue hiking north. Hike another 0.2 mile to the junction with a short side trail leading to Blackstack Cliffs. In a turn on the trail there is a brown sign that notes that Blackstack Cliffs is on an unmarked spur trail up the hill. Continue through the rhododendron for about 75 yards to a stone ledge with a U.S. Forest Service benchmark. Take the big steps down and proceed through more rhododendron until you emerge at the cliffs, which offer views north and west into Tennessee.

Return to the A.T. and continue to hike north another 0.2 mile to a trail junction with the former A.T. route, now a bad weather trail for the exposed ridges. Bearwallow Gap is just south of here in a rhododendron thicket. In another 0.2 mile, you will reach the southern end of another exposed area of the ridge, which remains open for the next 0.6 mile until it reaches Big Firescald Knob at mile 9.2. At 4,500 feet, the ridge offers excellent views. There is an 8-foot vertical rock scramble here although you can stop before it, and finish your hike there, if you like.

To return, backtrack south on the A.T. to the 0.2-mile side trail leading up to Camp Creek Bald.

TRAILHEAD DIRECTIONS

From 1-26 in Tennessee, take Exit 50 (Flag Pond Road). Turn left onto Upper Higgins Creek Road, and drive 0.6 mile. Turn right onto Old Asheville Highway, and drive 2.1 miles. Turn left onto TN 352 West, and drive 4.2 miles; continue onto NC 212 South, and drive 8.5 miles. Turn right onto Duckmill Road, which immediately becomes NC 1307, and drive 3.1 miles. Turn right onto NC 208 North, and drive 3.8 miles; continue onto TN 70 North, and drive 0.3 mile. Turn right onto Viking Mountain Road, and drive 6.5 miles. Continue onto the gravel Bald Mountain Road, and drive 1.4 miles; turn right at the intersection, and drive 0.7 mile to the summit of Camp Creek Bald (elevation 4,844').

GPS TRAILHEAD COORDINATES N36° 01.490' W82° 42.930'

129 LOVERS LEAP ROCK

STRENUOUS | 2.8-mile round-trip | 2 hours

This short, sometimes steep hike leads to Lovers Leap, which provides outstanding views of the French Broad River and the town of Hot Springs, North Carolina. There is a 500-foot drop from Lovers Leap to the river below. The rock's name is said to date back to a Native American maiden who threw herself from the cliff after learning her lover had been killed by a jealous beau.

The hike begins in the town of Hot Springs, where the A.T. passes through town on a sidewalk alongside the main street. There is a 1,000-foot change in elevation from the town to the overlook, making this a difficult, though short, hike.

THE HIKE

From the junction of US 25/70 and NC 209 in Hot Springs, hike north on the A.T. and follow the white blazes down the sidewalk. At 0.4 mile, you will pass the Warm Springs Spa, which first saw use in the 1700s. Then you will cross Spring Creek on US 25/70, and then the French Broad River on a bridge. The trail passes several buildings, including rafting outfitters, as it follows the river's edge. At mile 0.9, from the bank of the French Broad (elevation 1,320'), begin climbing up to Lovers Leap on switchbacks. Reach an overlook with outstanding views in 0.3 mile. Hike carefully—loose gravel and rock fragments can be dangerous here. Continue another 0.2 mile to Lovers Leap Rock at the junction of the Pump Gap Trail, the former A.T. route.

To return, backtrack south on the A.T. to the U.S. Forest Service office in Hot Springs.

TRAILHEAD DIRECTIONS

From I-40 in Tennessee, take Exit 432B and merge onto US 25W South/US 70 East. Drive 28.6 miles, to the junction of US 25/US 70 and NC 209/Lance Avenue in Hot Springs. Parking is available along the main road in town.

GPS TRAILHEAD COORDINATES N35° 53.570' W82° 49.275'

Hikers marvel at Max Patch's open meadows.   *Photo: Leonard M. Adkins*

130 MAX PATCH

MODERATE | **1.6-mile round-trip** | **1.5 hours**

The Trail gently climbs up the side of the mountain to the treeless summit of Max Patch. There is an outstanding panoramic view of the Blacks, Balds, Balsams, and Great Smokies from this southernmost bald mountain on the A.T. On a clear day, you can see the highest point in the eastern United States, Mount Mitchell (elevation 6,684'), to the east. In the spring, there are many wildflowers in bloom along this section of trail.

THE HIKE

From the trailhead, hike north on the A.T. and pass over a stile. Enter the woods and descend 0.1 mile to a small creek, which is the head of the West Fork of Little Creek. Begin to ascend, slowly at first, and cross a gravel road at 0.4 mile. At 0.5 mile, the Trail climbs Max Patch on log steps cut into the hillside and then crosses the grass to the broad summit of the mountain (elevation 4,629') at 0.8 mile.

To return, hike south on the A.T. to the trailhead on Max Patch Road.

TRAILHEAD DIRECTIONS

From I-40 in North Carolina, take Exit 7 (Harmon Den). Turn onto Cold Springs Road (from I-40 West, a right turn; from I-40 East, a left turn), and drive 6.1 miles. Turn left onto NC 1182/Max Patch Road, and drive 1.5 miles to the parking area at the foot of the bald.

GPS TRAILHEAD COORDINATES   N35° 47.556' W82° 57.713'

You can see Mounts Kephart and LeConte from Charlies Bunion. *Photo: Victoria and Frank Logue*

131 CHARLIES BUNION
GREAT SMOKY MOUNTAINS NATIONAL PARK

STRENUOUS | 8-mile round-trip | 5 hours

Charlies Bunion, an exposed, rocky knob, is the destination of this hike. From this knob, there are several outstanding views—Mount Kephart to the west, Mount LeConte to the northwest, the gorges of the headwaters of Porters Creek to the north, Greenbriar Pinnacle to the northeast, and the Sawteeth Range to the east. Take care when climbing around the bunion: a man fell to his death here in 1990.

THE HIKE

From the parking area at Newfound Gap (elevation 5,045'), follow the A.T. from the northeast corner of the parking area east along a graded trail. Red spruce and Fraser fir (also called balsams) are common in this section. At mile 1.7, reach the junction with the Sweat Heifer Creek Trail, probably named for the cattle drives up this steep trail to the grassy balds where the livestock was grazed. The Sweat Heifer Trail heads down to Kephart Prong.

In another 0.6 mile, you will have good views to the southwest of Clingmans Dome (elevation 6,643'), the highest point on the A.T. Thomas Ridge and Oconaluftee River

Gorge are to the south. When you reach mile 2.4, cross Mount Ambler, hiking along the North Carolina–Tennessee state line, and descend from the 6,000-foot elevation to the junction with the Boulevard Trail in another 0.3 mile.

The Boulevard Trail heads 5.3 miles to LeConte Lodge and Shelter on Mount LeConte. You will take the right fork at this junction and skirt the North Carolina side of Mount Kephart. At mile 3, reach Icewater Spring Shelter. There is a good spring a short distance farther along the A.T.

From the shelter, continue 0.9 mile to the western peak of Charlies Bunion. You will skirt the left side of this peak by taking the side trail off the A.T. leading to the higher peak in another 0.1 mile. The lower, western peak is sometimes called Fodder Stack, for its similarity in shape to a stack of hay (or fodder).

To return to Newfound Gap, backtrack south on the A.T.

TRAILHEAD DIRECTIONS

From I-40 in North Carolina, take Exit 27 (US 74/US 19/Clyde/Waynesville). Continue onto US 74 West, and drive 3.7 miles. Take Exit 103 (US 19 South/Dellwood Road) and continue onto US 19 South. Drive 11.9 miles; then turn right, following signs for the Blue Ridge Parkway. Turn left onto the Blue Ridge Parkway, and drive 13.2 miles. Turn right onto US 441 North, and drive 16.4 miles to the Newfound Gap parking area on the right.

GPS TRAILHEAD COORDINATES N35° 36.675' W83° 25.521'

132 CLINGMANS DOME AND MOUNT COLLINS
GREAT SMOKY MOUNTAINS NATIONAL PARK

MODERATE | 7-mile round-trip | 3.5 hours

This day hike will take you to the highest point on the A.T.: Clingmans Dome (elevation 6,643'). On clear days, there are outstanding views of the peaks of the Great Smokies from the observation tower. Formerly Smoky Dome, the peak is named after Thomas L. Clingman, a Civil War general and US Senator. Clingman is known for his heated debate with Elisha Mitchell. The two argued over which peak in the state was the highest—Grandfather Mountain or Balsam Mountain. The debate took place

Backpackers cruise the A.T. just west of Clingmans Dome.   *Photo: Johnny Molloy*

through editorials in rival Asheville, North Carolina, newspapers. Mitchell died in a fall while trying to prove his claim that Balsam Mountain was the tallest. History proved Mitchell right, however, and the highest peak east of the Mississippi bears his name.

Clingmans Dome features an observation tower with signs identifying the distant mountains. The section of the A.T. from Clingmans Dome north to Newfound Gap was constructed by the Civilian Conservation Corps between 1939 and 1940; this hike will take you along the ridge from Clingmans Dome through a spruce and balsam forest and over the summits of Mount Love and Mount Collins.

THE HIKE

From the parking area at Clingmans Dome, hike 0.5 mile along a paved path to see views from the observation tower. Once back in the parking lot, it is a short walk along a side trail (rare mountain cranberry abounds here) to the A.T. From Clingmans Dome, you will descend steeply into a gap before climbing to the summit of Mount Love (elevation 6,446') at 1.8 miles into the hike. Descend moderately, 1.1 miles, to Collins Gap (elevation 5,886') at mile 2.9; then climb steeply, 1.1 miles, to the summit of Mount Collins, which offers good views as you climb.

A short distance before reaching the summit of Mount Collins (elevation 6,188'), you will have good views over North Carolina. Once you reach the summit, you are at the end of this hike.

Return the 3.0 miles to Clingmans Dome parking area by retracing your steps back along the A.T. and taking the side trail to the observation tower and paved trail.

TRAILHEAD DIRECTIONS

From I-40 in North Carolina, take Exit 27 (US 74/US 19/Clyde/Waynesville). Continue onto US 74 West, and drive 3.7 miles. Take Exit 103 (US 19 South/Dellwood Road), and continue onto US 19 South. Drive 11.9 miles; then turn right, following signs for the Blue Ridge Parkway. Turn left onto the Blue Ridge Parkway, and drive 13.2 miles. Turn right onto US 441 North, and drive 16.2 miles to Newfound Gap. Turn left onto Clingmans Dome Road (closed in the winter), and drive 6.9 miles to Clingmans Dome.

GPS TRAILHEAD COORDINATES N35° 33.418' W83° 29.688'

133 ROCKY TOP
GREAT SMOKY MOUNTAINS NATIONAL PARK

STRENUOUS | **11.6-mile round-trip** | **7 hours**

A steep hike up from Lead Cove leads to one of the finest views along the A.T. in the Great Smoky Mountains. The 360° view is all the more impressive because you should have few, if any, people to share it with. Of course, solitude in a popular national park comes at a price. In this case, that price is the steep, but beautiful, climb, which also takes you through high Spence Field. For hardy hikers, this is a hike not to miss.

THE HIKE

From the trailhead at Laurel Creek Road, ascend on Lead Cove Trail for 1.7 miles to a junction with the Bote Mountain Trail at Sandy Gap. Turn right following Bote Mountain Trail as it climbs to its junction with Anthony Creek trail in another 1.2 miles. Continue on Bote Mountain Trail and in 0.7 mile pass through a long tunnel of rhododendron. Reach Spence Field in 1.0 mile (at mile 4.6 of the hike).

Turn left on the A.T., hiking north as you follow the white blazes through Spence Field, and in 0.4 mile, pass the junction with the Jenkins Ridge Trail. Begin a steep ascent for the remaining 0.8 mile to the summit of Rocky Top (elevation 5,441'). The imposing peak to the east is Thunderhead, which is farther north along the A.T. There are views of Fontana Lake to the southwest. After enjoying the panorama from Rocky Top, backtrack to the trailhead.

TRAILHEAD DIRECTIONS

From I-140, take Exit 11A (US 129 South/Alcoa Highway) and merge onto US 129 South. Drive 3.6 miles; then keep left to continue onto North Hall Road (signs for US 411/Maryville/Townsend/Smoky Mountains). Drive 3 miles; then continue onto US 321 North, and drive 17.3 miles. Continue onto East Lamar Alexander Parkway/TN 73, and drive 2.2 miles. Turn right onto Laurel Creek Road (sign for Cades Cove), and drive 5.6 miles to the trailhead; the Lead Cove Trail Parking Area is 0.3 mile farther, on the right.

GPS TRAILHEAD COORDINATES N35° 36.410' W83° 44.696'

134 SHUCKSTACK
GREAT SMOKY MOUNTAINS NATIONAL PARK

MODERATE | 11-mile round-trip | 6 hours

This round-trip hike will take you through a relatively remote portion of Great Smoky Mountains National Park. While only a short portion of the hike is on the A.T., you do get the impressive views from the Shuckstack fire tower, while getting to take in an enjoyable walk along Twentymile Creek, including Twentymile Cascades, en route to the A.T. Be forewarned, though, that the fire tower has fallen into disrepair and may eventually be removed by the park service.

THE HIKE

From the gated road at Twentymile Ranger Station, follow Twentymile Trail for 0.5 mile, ascending along Twentymile Creek's falls and pools to where it crosses Moore Spring Branch on a wide bridge. After crossing the bridge, continue right on Twentymile Trail, passing the junction with Wolf Ridge Trail. In 0.1 mile there is a short side trail to the bottom of Twentymile Cascades, where Twentymile Creek falls over a series of stone slabs. Back at the main trail, ascend along Twentymile Creek, crossing the creek on bridges at miles 1.5 and 1.8 of the hike. For the next 1.4 miles (after the second bridge), ascend along a slope over the creek, crossing two bridges before arriving at Proctor Gap at mile 3.2 of the hike.

Turn right at Proctor Gap, staying on Twentymile Trail. For the next 0.5 mile, the Trail parallels Proctor Branch before ascending to the A.T. at Sassafrass Gap. You will reach the A.T. at mile 5.1 of the hike. Turn right on the A.T., following the white blazes as you ascend Shuckstack. In 0.3 mile, reach a side trail, which leads left 0.1 mile to the fire tower. From the fire tower, you can see the main crest of the Smokies towering over Fontana Lake.

Backtrack along the A.T. and Twentymile Creek Trail to the trailhead at Twentymile Ranger Station.

TRAILHEAD DIRECTIONS

From I-140, take Exit 11A (US 129 South/Alcoa Highway) and merge onto US 129 South. Drive 7.4 miles; then merge onto US 411 South/US 129 South, and drive 4.3 miles. Turn left to stay on US 129 South, and drive 32.8 miles. Turn left onto NC 28 South, and drive 2.9 miles; then turn left toward the Twentymile Ranger Station.

GPS TRAILHEAD COORDINATES N35° 28.017' W83° 52.667'

135 WESSER BALD

STRENUOUS | **2.8-mile round-trip** | **2 hours**

The spectacular views from Wesser Bald (elevation 4,627') are the highlight of this hike. In 1993, an observation deck was completed on the steel frame of the Wesser Bald fire tower. The old tower was burned by vandals in 1979. The new observation tower was funded by the Appalachian Trail Conservancy, North Carolina's Trail Grant Program, and the Nantahala Hiking Club (with matching funds from the U.S. Forest Service's Challenge Cost-Share Program).

THE HIKE

From the parking area at Tellico Gap (elevation 3,850'), take the A.T. north. Head left along a graded trail that parallels the gravel road that leads to the former fire tower.

From here, you will begin to climb Wesser Bald. Climb 1.4 miles to the top of the rocky ledge and reach the junction with a side trail that heads right a short distance to the observation deck, which offers great views of the surrounding mountain ranges.

To return, head south on the A.T. to Tellico Gap or take the gravel road that leads to Tellico Gap for a 3-mile loop.

TRAILHEAD DIRECTIONS

From I-40 in North Carolina, take Exit 27 (US 74/US 19/Clyde/Waynesville). Continue onto US 74 West, and drive 60.6 miles. Turn left onto Wayah Road/NC 1310, and drive 5 miles. Turn left onto Otter Creek Road/NC 1365, and drive 4 miles to the Tellico Gap parking area and A.T. crossing.

GPS TRAILHEAD COORDINATES N35° 16.085' W83° 34.338'

136 SILER BALD

STRENUOUS | 3.8-mile round-trip | 2.5 hours

Siler Bald (elevation 5,216') is this hike's destination. The bald was named after William Siler, whose great-grandson, the Reverend Rufus A. Morgan, helped establish the A.T. in North Carolina. The North Carolina Wildlife Resources Commission maintains the bald by keeping it cleared. From atop the bald, there are views back to Tray Mountain in Georgia and ahead to the Great Smokies.

THE HIKE

From the parking area just off NC 1310 at Wayah Gap, a hundred feet east of Wayah Crest (elevation 4,180'), pass through the picnic area. Pick up the Trail here, cross a dirt road, and begin the 900-foot elevation gain to

Siler Bald   *Photo: Johnny Molloy*

Snowbird Gap below Siler Bald. At mile 1.7, reach a clearing used for grazing by deer and other wildlife. Look to your right to view the open summit of Siler Bald. The outstanding view from the summit can be reached via a 0.2-mile side trail to the west.

To return to the parking area at Wayah Gap, follow the A.T. north.

TRAILHEAD DIRECTIONS

From I-40 in North Carolina, take Exit 27 (US 74/US 19/Clyde/Waynesville). Continue onto US 74 West, and drive 26 miles. Take Exit 81 (US 23 South/US 441 South/Dillsboro) and continue onto US 23 South. Drive 20.3 miles; then continue onto US 64 West, and drive 3.7 miles. Turn right onto Patton Road, and drive 0.3 mile; then turn left onto Wayah Road/NC 1310. Drive 9 miles to the trail crossing.

GPS TRAILHEAD COORDINATES N35° 09.232' W83° 34.864'

137 STANDING INDIAN MOUNTAIN

STRENUOUS | 4.8-mile round-trip | 3 hours

Standing Indian Mountain (elevation 5,498') is the highest point on the A.T. south of the Smoky Mountains. A 600-foot side trip on the Lower Ridge Trail leads to the summit and spectacular views, both north and south, of the mountain ranges the A.T. follows, including the Georgia Blue Ridge.

THE HIKE

From the parking area at Deep Gap (elevation 4,341'), follow the A.T. north along a graded trail that parallels two logging roads. In 0.75 mile, cross a small stream and continue to climb Standing Indian Mountain, reaching the side trail to Standing Indian Shelter at 0.9 mile. At mile 2.4, reach the junction of the blue-blazed Lower Ridge Trail, which heads 4.2 miles left to Standing Indian Campground. Follow this trail to the right 0.1 mile to the summit of Standing Indian. Cherokee legend says the mountain is named for a warrior who turned to stone when a bolt of lightning struck the top of the mountain, leaving the mountaintop bald. To return to the parking area at Deep Gap, follow the A.T. south.

Sunsets from Standing Indian Mountain can be quite spectacular.   *Photo: Leonard M. Adkins*

TRAILHEAD DIRECTIONS

From I-40 in North Carolina, take Exit 27 (US 74/US 19/Clyde/Waynesville). Continue onto US 74 West, and drive 26 miles. Take Exit 81 (US 23 South/US 441 South/Dillsboro) and continue onto US 23 South. Drive 20.3 miles; then continue onto US 64 West, and drive 14.5 miles. Turn left onto Deep Gap Road/Forest Service Road 71, and drive about 5.4 miles to Deep Gap.

GPS TRAILHEAD COORDINATES N35° 02.564' W83° 33.300'

138 RAVENROCK RIDGE

STRENUOUS | **9-mile round-trip** | **5 hours**

The cliffs at Ravenrock Ridge offer outstanding views of the Southern Nantahalas. Following the crest of the Blue Ridge, this hike offers views to the west of Shooting Creek Valley and Lake Chatuge on the North Carolina–Georgia state line. You will also pass through parts of the Southern Nantahala Wilderness on this hike.

THE HIKE

From the parking area at Deep Gap, follow the A.T. south by heading right, into the woods, and climbing Yellow Mountain. In 0.7 mile, the Trail switchbacks up to a rock outcrop and continues on to the highest point of this section at 1.1 miles (elevation 4,840'), providing a view to the north. Hike 1.0 mile to Wateroak Gap (elevation 4,460') in a small clearing. The A.T. continues up the ridge for another 0.9 mile to the junction with the blue-blazed Chunky Gal Trail, which heads 5.5 miles west to US 64. Head left on the A.T. for 0.2 mile to the edge of a large, grassy area at Whiteoak Stamp. An overgrown trail to the left leads to an intermittent water source.

Follow the A.T. for another 0.8 mile to Muskrat Creek Shelter just to the left of the Trail. Continue on the A.T. for 0.1 mile, cross a small stream, and reach the junction with a blue-blazed side trail that heads right about 0.5 mile to Ravenrock Ridge and its wonderful cliff views. Follow the side trail to Ravenrock Ridge.

To return to the parking area at Deep Gap, take the side trail back to the A.T., and the A.T. north to Deep Gap.

TRAILHEAD DIRECTIONS

From I-40 in North Carolina, take Exit 27 (US 74/US 19/Clyde/Waynesville). Continue onto US 74 West, and drive 26 miles. Take Exit 81 (US 23 South/US 441 South/Dillsboro) and continue onto US 23 South. Drive 20.3 miles; then continue onto US 64 West, and drive 14.5 miles. Turn left onto Deep Gap Road/FS 71, and drive about 5.4 miles to Deep Gap.

GPS TRAILHEAD COORDINATES N35° 02.564' W83° 33.300'

GEORGIA

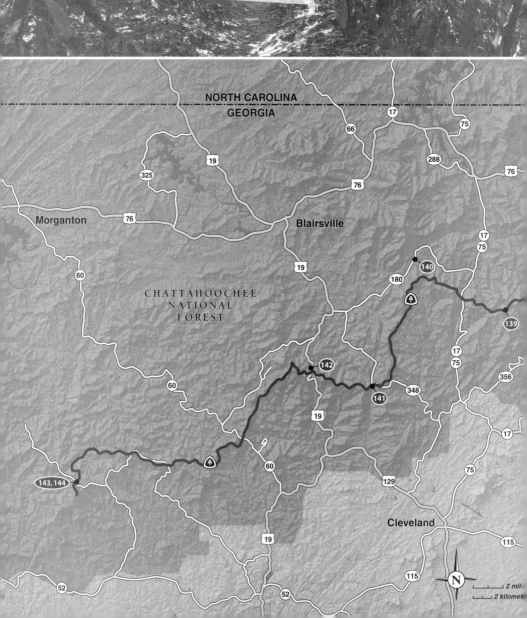

NORTH CAROLINA
GEORGIA

Morganton

Blairsville

CHATTAHOOCHEE
NATIONAL
FOREST

Cleveland

2 miles

2 kilometers

Hike	Page	Length (mi)	Configuration	Time (hr)	Difficulty	Features
139. Tray Mountain	216	1.6	↗	1.5	★★	🏔️ 🔭
140. Source of the Chattahoochee	217	4.8	↗	2.5	★★	🏰
141. Wolf Laurel Top Mountain	218	4.6	↗	2.5	★★	🏔️ 🔭
142. Blood Mountain	219	4.2	↗	3.5	★★★	🏔️ 🔭
143. Springer Mountain and Three Forks Loop	221	10.5	↻	5.0	★★	🏔️ 🔭
144. Springer Mountain	222	2.0	↗	1.5	★★	🏔️ 🔭

DIFFICULTY ★★★ strenuous ★★ moderate ★ easy   CONFIGURATION ↗ round-trip ↻ loop

🏔️ mountain peak   🔭 scenic view   🏰 historic area

GEORGIA IS THE LAST STATE on the Trail (or the first for most thru-hikers). Its more than 75 miles of trail are extremely popular year-round. The Trail traverses the Chattahoochee National Forest and is noted for its rugged wilderness areas and high elevations. Popular hiking spots include the Swag of the Blue Ridge, Tray Mountain, Rocky Mountain, Blue Mountain, Wolf Laurel Top, Blood Mountain, and Big Cedar Mountain.

Neels Gap, at the base of Blood Mountain, is home to Mountain Crossings at Walasi-Yi, a trail-gear store that is famous as the only building through which the A.T. passes. Springer Mountain is the southern terminus of the A.T. A bronze plaque created by the Georgia Appalachian Trail Club marks the mountain as the southern terminus of the A.T.

139 TRAY MOUNTAIN

MODERATE | 1.6-mile round-trip | 1.5 hours

This hike is part of the 10.8-mile section of the A.T. that passes through the Tray Mountain Wilderness from Tray Gap to Addis Gap. The climb up from the gap is a steady ascent on switchbacks that brings you to this outstanding peak. The summit is covered with low trees and shrubs, which do not obstruct the magnificent panoramic view of the north Georgia Mountains.

THE HIKE

From the trailhead in Tray Gap (elevation 3,847'), hike north on the A.T. and begin climbing the southern slope of Tray Mountain. The Trail ascends on switchbacks, climbing more sharply as you near the summit. At mile 0.8, reach the rocky summit of Tray Mountain (elevation 4,430'). Georgia's two tallest peaks, Brasstown Bald and Rabun Bald, are visible to the north. Brasstown Bald is the peak with the tower and buildings on the summit. The distinctive rock face of Yonah Mountain can be seen to the south.

To return, hike south on the A.T. to Tray Gap.

TRAILHEAD DIRECTIONS

From I-985 North, continue (past Exit 24) onto US 23 North, and drive 18.1 miles. Turn left onto GA 384 North, and drive 15.6 miles. Turn right onto GA 75 North, and drive 5.4 miles. Turn right onto Tray Mountain Road, and drive 7.8 miles to the A.T. crossing at Tray Gap, where there is a small dirt parking area.

GPS TRAILHEAD COORDINATES N34° 47.943' W83° 41.429'

140 SOURCE OF THE CHATTAHOOCHEE

MODERATE | 4.8-mile round-trip | 2.5 hours

This hike up to the A.T. via the Jacks Knob Trail takes you to the source of the Chattahoochee River. The mighty river, which supplies drinking water, recreation, and transportation to much of the Peach State, begins at a little spring along the A.T.

This section of the Jacks Knob Trail lies entirely within the 16,400-acre Mark Trail Wilderness, which is named for Ed Dodd and Jack Elrod's comic strip character, a naturalist who

Chattahoochee Gap   *Photo: Todd Ray*

protects the fictional Lost Forest National Forest. Dodd, who originated the strip, was a Georgia native who lived along a tributary of the Chattahoochee in Sandy Springs.

THE HIKE

From the trailhead at Jacks Gap (elevation 2,950'), on GA 180, hike south. From Jacks Gap, the trail ascends toward Henry Knob, but bypasses it, leading to a gap at 0.6 mile instead. Here the trail steeply ascends to Brookshire Top at 3,460 feet, which is the beginning of Hiawassee Ridge. After a short descent, the climb continues to

Eagle Knob at 4,560 feet before beginning the ascent of Jacks Kmob at 1.9 miles. After rounding Jacks Knob, it is an easy hike down to the A.T. at Chattahoochee Gap.

Follow the sign and blue blazes 200 yards downhill to Chattahoochee Spring. This little spring is the source of the Chattahoochee River, which flows 540 miles south to Florida and the Gulf of Mexico.

Backtrack to the A.T. and follow the Jacks Knob Trail back to the trailhead.

TRAILHEAD DIRECTIONS

From I-985 North, continue (past Exit 24) onto US 23 North, and drive 18.1 miles. Turn left onto GA 384 North, and drive 15.6 miles. Turn right onto GA 75 North, and drive 15 miles. Turn left onto GA 180, and drive 5.3 miles to the trailhead in Jacks Gap, at the intersection of GA 180/GA 180 Spur.

GPS TRAILHEAD COORDINATES N34° 50.905' W83° 47.927'

141 WOLF LAUREL TOP MOUNTAIN

MODERATE | 4.6-mile round-trip | 2.5 hours

This hike features excellent views from the summits of Cowrock Mountain and Wolf Laurel Top. There is a spectacular view from an open rock face atop Wolf Laurel Top. This entire hike is in the Raven Cliffs Wilderness.

THE HIKE

From the trailhead in Tesnatee Gap (*Tesnatee* means "wild turkey" in Cherokee, and it is not uncommon to see them in the North Georgia woods), follow the A.T. south and begin the steady, sometimes steep, ascent of Cowrock Mountain. At mile 1.0, reach the summit of Cowrock Mountain (elevation 3,842'). There are a couple of good viewpoints from the mountain. One is from the rocks just before the Trail reaches the summit. The other is to the left of the Trail just after the summit. The distinctive rock face of Yonah Mountain can be seen to the southwest, as can Brasstown Bald, the state's highest mountain (elevation 4,783'), to the north.

Descend Cowrock Mountain to Baggs Creek Gap (elevation 3,591') at 1.8 miles. The Trail from the gap to Wolf Laurel Top climbs 175 feet over the next 0.6 mile.

Reach Wolf Laurel Top (elevation 3,766') at mile 2.3. The outstanding view from the rocks is just to the left of the Trail.

To return, hike north on the A.T. to the trailhead in Tesnatee Gap.

TRAILHEAD DIRECTIONS

From I-985 North, continue (past Exit 24) onto US 23 North, and drive 18.1 miles. Turn left onto GA 384 North, and drive 15.6 miles. Turn right onto GA 75 North, and drive 4.7 miles; then turn left onto GA 75 Alt/GA 356. Drive 2.3 miles; then turn right onto GA 348. Drive 7.6 miles to the Tesnatee Gap parking area, on your left.

GPS TRAILHEAD COORDINATES N34° 43.575' W83° 50.858'

142 BLOOD MOUNTAIN

STRENUOUS | 4.2-mile round-trip | 3.5 hours

This hike is, without a doubt, the most traveled section of the A.T. in Georgia. On pretty spring and summer weekends, this section of trail is often crowded. The reason for the hike's popularity is twofold: it is easy to get to, and the rocky summit of Blood Mountain offers a superb view of the north Georgia mountains.

On the summit of Blood Mountain, there is a stone cabin built by the Civilian Conservation Corps in the 1930s. The two-room shelter, intended for overnight use by A.T. hikers, is listed in the National Register of Historic Places.

The mountain's name is said to date from a fierce fight between the Creek and Cherokee Indians. Also of interest in the area is Mountain Crossings at Walasi-Yi in Neels Gap. This hiking store sells a good selection of equipment and books on the outdoors and the region; drinks and snacks are also available here. The only covered section of the A.T. passes through a walkway at Mountain Crossings.

THE HIKE

From the trailhead at the Byron Reese Park, follow the blue-blazed trail 0.7 mile to the junction with the A.T. Turn right on the A.T. and hike south, climbing steeply on switchbacks and gaining nearly 1,000 feet in elevation in just over 1 mile. At mile 1.8, traverse an open rock face that offers an excellent view. Reach the tree-covered

The stone shelter atop Blood Mountain provides a cool respite in summer and warmth in winter.
Photo: Victoria and Frank Logue

summit of Blood Mountain (elevation 4,461') in 0.3 mile. There are outstanding views from the rock outcrops around the shelter.

To return, hike north on the A.T. to the blue-blazed side trail; then follow the side trail to the parking area.

TRAILHEAD DIRECTIONS

From I-985 North, continue (past Exit 24) onto US 23 North, and drive 8.3 miles. Turn left onto GA 52 West, and drive 6.2 miles. Turn right onto GA 283 South, and at the next intersection, make a slight right to stay on GA 283 South. Drive 2.3 miles; then turn right onto US 129 North, and drive 7.3 miles. Keep right to stay on US 129 North; then drive 20 miles, a little past the trail crossing at Neels Gap to the parking area at Byron Reese Memorial Park, on your left.

GPS TRAILHEAD COORDINATES N34° 44.556' W83° 55.268'

Seasonal wildflowers make the often steep ascent of Blood Mountain a pleasure.
Photo: Victoria and Frank Logue

143 SPRINGER MOUNTAIN AND THREE FORKS LOOP

MODERATE | 10.5-mile loop | 5 hours

This loop hike uses the A.T. and Benton MacKaye Trail (BMT) figure eight between Springer Mountain and Three Forks. The hike will take you to two viewpoints along Springer Mountain, which is the southern terminus of both the A.T. and the BMT. The BMT is named for the man who provided the inspiration for the A.T. in a 1921 article for the *Journal of the American Institute of Architects.* The BMT follows the more westerly route first proposed for the A.T. and was created to take some of the hiking pressure off the oft-hiked A.T. in Georgia.

THE HIKE

From the trailhead on Forest Service Road (FR) 42, hike south on the A.T. and begin the steady, gradual climb up Springer on a sidehill trail. At mile 0.8, reach the junction with the 0.2-mile side trail leading to Springer Mountain Shelter. Hike another 0.2 mile to the southern terminus of the A.T. There is a trail register in a mailbox on a tree near the rock face. After visiting the summit of Springer, head back the direction you came, traveling north on the A.T. for 0.2 mile to the turnoff for the BMT.

Descend Springer on the BMT, which is blazed with white diamonds. In 0.1 mile you will pass a memorial to Benton MacKaye before continuing the descent, which levels out in another half mile. After a quick ascent of Ball Mountain, you will pass a sign marking a view to the right of the trail. Continue along the BMT to FR 42 at Big Stamp Gap, 1.7 miles after starting on the BMT. Cross the Forest Service road and follow the trail, ascending via switchback through rhododendron and mountain laurel. At 3.5 miles into the hike, reach Davis Creek, the first of several stream crossings, before climbing again and reaching the junction with the A.T. at 4.4 miles. Remain on the white-diamond-blazed BMT, and in 2.7 miles, at mile 6.1 of the hike, the BMT rejoins the A.T., and the two trails descend together 0.1 mile to Three Forks, where Chester, Long, and Stover Creeks join to form Noontootla Creek.

Return by going back the direction you came, this time following the rectangular white blazes of the A.T. each time the two trails diverge. The Trail crosses Stover Creek before ascending along it for about 2.0 miles. A side trail, a mile from the creek crossing, leads to Stover Creek Shelter. The trailhead at FR 42 is 3.3 miles north on the A.T. from Three Forks.

TRAILHEAD DIRECTIONS

From I-575 North, continue (past Exit 27) onto GA 5 North/GA 515 East, and drive 25.6 miles. Turn right onto Greenfield Road (sign for GA 52), and drive 0.2 mile. Turn left onto GA 52 East, and drive 6.1 miles. Turn left onto Roy Road, and drive 6.9 miles. Turn left to stay on Roy Road, and drive 2.5 miles. Turn right onto Doublehead Gap Road, and drive 2.1 miles. Turn right onto Blue Ridge Wildlife Management Road/Forest Service Road 42, and drive 5.7 miles to the trail crossing. A parking fee is required.

GPS TRAILHEAD COORDINATES N34° 38.248' W84° 11.726'

144 SPRINGER MOUNTAIN

MODERATE | 2-mile round-trip | 1.5 hours

This short hike leads to the southern terminus of the A.T. A bronze plaque set into a rock face lies just past the southernmost white blaze. There is a fine view of the Blue Ridge range from Rich Mountain to the northwest, and the Cohuttas beyond, from this open rock ledge.

Leonard M. and Laurie Adkins head north from Springer Mountain at the beginning of one of their thru-hikes on the Trail.   *Photo: Warren Doyle*

Prior to 1958, the southern terminus of the Trail had been on Mount Oglethorpe. Real estate development in the area led the Georgia Appalachian Trail Club to move the terminus to this more remote mountain within the bounds of the Chattahoochee National Forest.

THE HIKE

From the trailhead on Forest Service Road (FR) 42, hike south on the A.T. and begin the steady, gradual climb up Springer on a sidehill trail. At mile 0.8, reach the junction with the 0.2-mile side trail leading to Springer Mountain Shelter. There is a spring just past the shelter. For those who wonder how the large beams of the timber frame shelter were carried up the mountain, they weren't. The beams were assembled and the framework was helicoptered to the shelter's present site in 1992. Another 50 yards along the A.T., you will reach the southern terminus of the Benton MacKaye Trail on your left. Hike another 0.2 mile to the end of the Trail. There is a trail register in a mailbox on a tree near the rock face.

To return, hike north on the A.T. to get to FR 42.

TRAILHEAD DIRECTIONS

From I-575 North, continue (past Exit 27) onto GA 5 North/GA 515 East, and drive 25.6 miles. Turn right onto Greenfield Road (sign for GA 52), and drive 0.2 mile. Turn left onto GA 52 East, and drive 6.1 miles. Turn left onto Roy Road, and drive 6.9 miles. Turn left to stay on Roy Road, and drive 2.5 miles. Turn right onto Doublehead Gap Road, and drive 2.1 miles. Turn right onto Blue Ridge Wildlife Management Road/ Forest Service Road 42, and drive 5.7 miles to the trail crossing. A parking fee is required.

GPS TRAILHEAD COORDINATES N34° 38.248' W84° 11.726'

APPENDIX: TRAIL-MAINTENANCE CLUBS

The Appalachian Trail owes its existence to the Appalachian Trail Conservancy, its 31 trail-maintaining organizations, the 1968 National Trails System Act, two federal agencies, and four dozen agencies among the 14 Trail states. Through ATC's agreement with the National Park Service, the clubs are charged with footpath and facilities maintenance. Together with ATC staff and agency partners, they also relocate the trail, manage its surrounding lands, help with land-acquisition negotiations and combating external threats, work with trail communities on both problems and special events, and recruit and train new maintainers.

If you are interested in local hikes or other activities in your area, check out the clubs and trail organizations near you. Volunteer opportunities can also be found on the ATC's website, appalachiantrail.org.

Mailing addresses are listed for those clubs with permanent offices or post office boxes. Occasionally these do change; in this case, please contact ATC headquarters for the address of the current club president or other appropriate officer (304-535-6331, appalachiantrail.org).

GEORGIA, NORTH CAROLINA, AND TENNESSEE

Georgia Appalachian Trail Club
PO Box 654, Atlanta, GA 30301
404-494-0968 (voicemail)
georgia-atclub.org
Springer Mountain, GA, to Bly Gap, NC

Nantahala Hiking Club
173 Carl Slagle Road, Franklin, NC 28734
nantahalahikingclub.org
Bly Gap, NC, to Wesser, NC

Smoky Mountains Hiking Club
PO Box 51592, Knoxville, TN 37950-1592
smhclub.org
Wesser, NC, to Davenport Gap, TN/NC

Carolina Mountain Club
PO Box 68, Asheville, NC 28802
carolinamountainclub.org
Davenport Gap, TN/NC, to Spivey Gap, NC

Tennessee Eastman Hiking & Canoeing Club
PO Box 511, Kingsport, TN 37662
tehcc.org
Spivey Gap, NC, to Virginia–Tennessee state line

VIRGINIA, WEST VIRGINIA, AND MARYLAND

Mount Rogers Appalachian Trail Club
PO Box 789, Damascus, VA 24236-0789
mratc.pbworks.com
Virginia–Tennessee state line to VA 670

Piedmont Appalachian Trail Hikers
PO Box 4423
Greensboro, NC 27404
path-at.org
VA 670 to VA 623; VA 615 to VA 612

Outdoor Club at Virginia Tech
www.outdoor.org.vt.edu
VA 623 to VA 615; VA 612 to VA 611; US 460 to Pine Swamp Branch Shelter

Roanoke Appalachian Trail Club
PO Box 12282, Roanoke, VA 24024-2282
ratc.org
VA 611 to US 460; Pine Swamp Branch Shelter to Black Horse Gap

Natural Bridge Appalachian Trail Club
PO Box 3012, Lynchburg, VA 24503
nbatc.org
Black Horse Gap, VA, to Tye River, VA

Tidewater Appalachian Trail Club
PO Box 8246, Norfolk, VA 23503
tidewateratc.com
Tye River, VA, to Reids Gap, VA

Old Dominion Appalachian Trail Club
PO Box 25283, Richmond, VA 23260-5283
olddominiontrailclub.onefireplace.org
Reids Gap, VA, to Rockfish Gap, VA

Potomac Appalachian Trail Club
118 Park St. SE, Vienna, VA 22180
703-242-0315
patc.net
Rockfish Gap, VA, to Pine Grove Furnace State Park, PA

PENNSYLVANIA

The Potomac Appalachian Trail Club also maintains the A.T. in Pennsylvania, from the Pennsylvania–Maryland state line to Pine Grove Furnace State Park.

Mountain Club of Maryland
7923 Galloping Circle, Baltimore, MD 21244
mcomd.org
Pine Grove Furnace State Park, PA, to Center Point Knob, PA; Darlington Trail to Susquehanna River

Cumberland Valley Appalachian Trail Club
PO Box 395, Boiling Springs, PA 17007
cvatclub.org
Center Point Knob, PA, to Darlington Trail

York Hiking Club
yorkhikingclub.com
Susquehanna River, PA, to PA 225

Susquehanna Appalachian Trail Club
PO Box 61001, Harrisburg, PA 17106-1001
satc-hike.org
PA 225 to Rausch Gap Shelter

Blue Mountain Eagle Climbing Club
PO Box 14982, Reading, PA 19612-4982
bmecc.org
Rausch Gap Shelter to Tri-County Corner; Bake Oven Knob Road to Lehigh Furnace Gap

Allentown Hiking Club
allentownhikingclub.org
Tri-County Corner to Bake Oven Knob Road

Keystone Trails Association (comprises 41 member clubs)
46 E. Main St., Mechanicsburg, PA 17055
717-766-9690
kta-hike.org
Lehigh Furnace Gap, PA, to Little Gap, PA

AMC Delaware Valley Chapter
amcdv.org
Little Gap, PA, to Wind Gap, PA

Batona Hiking Club
batona.wildapricot.org
Wind Gap, PA, to Fox Gap, PA

Wilmington Trail Club
PO Box 526, Hockessin, DE 19707-0526
302-307-4017
wilmingtontrailclub.org
Fox Gap, PA, to Delaware River, PA

NEW JERSEY AND NEW YORK

New York–New Jersey Trail Conference
600 Ramapo Valley Road, Mahwah, NJ 07430-1199
201-512-9348
nynjtc.org
Delaware River, PA, to Connecticut–New York state line

CONNECTICUT AND MASSACHUSETTS

Appalachian Mountain Club (AMC)
5 Joy St., Boston, MA 02108
617-523-0655
outdoors.org
The AMC is the umbrella organization for a number of trail clubs in New England.

AMC Connecticut Chapter
964 S. Main St., Great Barrington, MA 01230
413-528-6333
ct-amc.org
Connecticut–New York state line to Sages Ravine, MA

AMC Berkshire Chapter
amcberkshire.org
Sages Ravine, MA, to Vermont–Massachusetts state line

VERMONT, NEW HAMPSHIRE, AND MAINE

Green Mountain Club
4711 Waterbury–Stowe Road, Waterbury Center, VT 05677
802-244-7037
greenmountainclub.org
Massachusetts–Vermont state line to Vermont–New Hampshire state line

Dartmouth Outing Club
outdoors.dartmouth.edu/doc
Vermont–New Hampshire state line to Kinsman Notch, NH

Appalachian Mountain Club (AMC)
5 Joy St., Boston, MA 02108
617-523-0655
outdoors.org
Kinsman Notch, NH, to Grafton Notch, ME

Randolph Mountain Club
PO Box 279, Gorham, NH 03581-0279
randolphmountainclub.org
Edmands Col (north of Mount Washington) to just shy of Madison Spring Hut

Maine Appalachian Trail Club
PO Box 283, Augusta, ME 04332-0283
facebook.com/maineatc
Grafton Notch, ME, to Katahdin, ME

INDEX

LEONARD M. ADKINS

Photo: Laurie Adkins

Leonard has been intimately involved with the Appalachian Trail for several decades. He has hiked its full length five times and lacks just a few hundred miles to complete it for a sixth. He has maintained a section of the Trail near McAfee Knob and was a ridgerunner for the Appalachian Trail Conservancy. He has also served as an A.T. Natural Heritage Site Monitor, aiding the conservancy and the National Park Service in overseeing the welfare of rare and endangered plants. In addition, he has served on the boards of directors of the Roanoke Appalachian Trail Club and the Old Dominion Appalachian Trail Club. Among other long-distance trails Leonard has completed are the Continental Divide Trail from Canada to Mexico, the Pacific Northwest Trail from Glacier National Park to the Pacific Ocean, and the Pyrenees High Route along the border of France and Spain. In all, he has walked more than 20,000 miles exploring the backcountry areas of the United States, Canada, Europe, New Zealand, and the Caribbean.

Leonard is the author of 20 books on travel and the outdoors. His *Wildflowers of the Appalachian Trail* was presented the National Outdoor Book Award, while *The Appalachian Trail: A Visitor's Companion* received the Lowell Thomas Travel Journalism Award. He has also written more than 200 articles for magazines such as *Blue Ridge Country, Backpacker, Islands, The Roanoker,* and *Blue Ridge Outdoors.* Along with his thru-hiking wife, Laurie, he lives in Virginia, within easy striking distance of the A.T.

You may learn more about his adventures at habitualhiker.com.

VICTORIA AND FRANK LOGUE

The Logues hiked the entire Appalachian Trail in 1988 and have returned again and again to hike its many sections on day and overnight hikes. Frank has also served on the Appalachian Trail Conservancy's Board of Managers. In addition, they have continued to hike out west and abroad, including Israel, Jordan, France, Italy, Iceland, Ireland, Scotland, and England. They live in Georgia, where Frank works as an Episcopal priest and as an assistant to the bishop of Georgia. Victoria, a writer of fiction and nonfiction, recently published her fourth novel. Currently, they love visiting and hiking with their daughter, Griffin, in Arizona.

ABOUT THE APPALACHIAN TRAIL CONSERVANCY

The Appalachian Trail is well known around the world, not just among the diverse hiking and backpacking communities. Less well known is what put it on the ground in the 1920s and '30s and manages it to this day: the staff and more than 6,000 volunteers of the Appalachian Trail Conservancy, founded in 1925 by 22 pioneers.

The A.T. has been a part of the national park system since 1968, but part of the deal with Congress was that this small, private, nonprofit organization would continue to do the bulk of the work and raise most of the money to pay for that work. (The National Park Service does have a small A.T. office of fewer than a dozen employees working with us on major legal issues of environmental and historic preservation compliance and law enforcement.)

What does "take care of" mean? It means keeping the footpath of more than 2,190 miles open and safe for outdoor recreation of most nonmotorized types (including hunting for about half the area). It means maintaining in good condition overnight shelters and tent sites, absolutely necessary bridges, and other facilities. It means monitoring the health of more than 550 rare, threatened, or endangered species that call the trail lands home (we don't yet have a count on the animals)—more than almost any other national park. It means preserving more cultural artifacts still in place than in any other park. (Remember, these ridgelines were the Colonial frontier before the seas and the West, and they were the site of Underground Railroad stops and then dozens of Civil War battles, as well as farms taken over by freed slaves.)

It means working with the National Park Service, the U.S. Forest Service, and 14 states that hold title to those lands for the public—almost 100 agency partners in all. It means bringing into the fold for mutual benefit 85 counties' officials and the governments and businesses for almost three dozen places officially designated as Appalachian Trail Communities. It means watching for and combating threats from incompatible development. It means providing the public with timely, comprehensive, and useful information about the A.T.'s natural beauty and how best to enjoy it—for example, through books such as this, in which we are proud to have a role.

We consider it our job to conserve, promote, and enhance the Appalachian National Scenic Trail every day. We do all that for less than $6.75 in private funds per day per mile (and about $2.75 more in targeted federal contracts).

You can support that effort by going to appalachiantrail.org to learn more and/or become a member. Old-school (like us)? You can write to us at Appalachian Trail Conservancy, PO Box 807, Harpers Ferry, WV 25425, or call 304-535-6331.

Most of all, we hope that in some way you enjoy the People's Path. It is yours, after all.

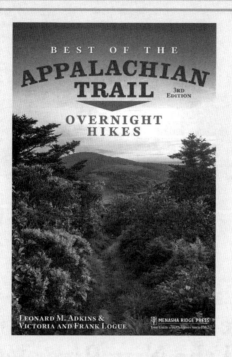

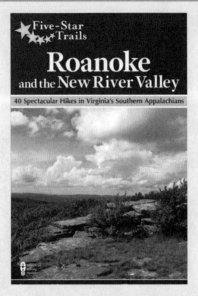

Check out this great title from
Menasha Ridge Press!

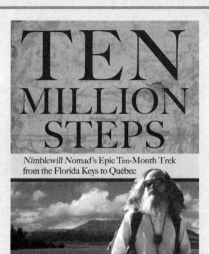

Ten Million Steps

By M.J. Eberhart
ISBN: 978-0-89732-979-8
$24.95

5.5 x 8.5, paperback
Full color, 544 pages
Maps, photographs, index

If every journey begins with a single step, then the culmination of M. J. "Eb" Eberhart's would bring that number to an estimated 10 million. In January 1998, the retired optometrist began what would become a historic 10-month, 4,400-mile journey on foot, from the Florida Keys to Cap Gaspé, Quebec.

In its original (2000) self-published edition, *Ten Million Steps* made Eberhart, known on the trail as *Nimblewill Nomad,* a hiking legend. In 2007, Menasha Ridge Press reintroduced readers to this vivid and honest account of his celebrated trek in a softcover edition.

In an engaging, inimitable style, Eberhart recounts his days and nights of deep joy, painful physical hardship, and exciting self-discovery on the Eastern Continental Trail, comprising the Florida Keys Overseas Heritage Trail; the Florida Trail; the Pinhoti National Recreation Trail and part of the Benton MacKaye Trail in Georgia; the entire Appalachian Trail; and the International Appalachian Trail in Canada.

 MENASHA RIDGE PRESS
menasharidge.com

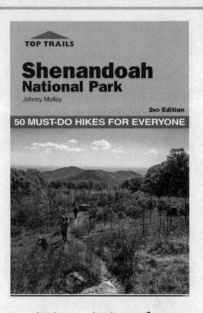

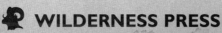

DEAR CUSTOMERS AND FRIENDS,

SUPPORTING YOUR INTEREST IN OUTDOOR ADVENTURE, travel, and an active lifestyle is central to our operations, from the authors we choose to the locations we detail to the way we design our books. Menasha Ridge Press was incorporated in 1982 by a group of veteran outdoorsmen and professional outfitters. For many years now, we've specialized in creating books that benefit the outdoors enthusiast.

Almost immediately, Menasha Ridge Press earned a reputation for revolutionizing outdoors- and travel-guidebook publishing. For such activities as canoeing, kayaking, hiking, backpacking, and mountain biking, we established new standards of quality that transformed the whole genre, resulting in outdoor-recreation guides of great sophistication and solid content. Menasha Ridge Press continues to be outdoor publishing's greatest innovator.

The folks at Menasha Ridge Press are as at home on a whitewater river or mountain trail as they are editing a manuscript. The books we build for you are the best they can be, because we're responding to your needs. Plus, we use and depend on them ourselves.

We look forward to seeing you on the river or the trail. If you'd like to contact us directly, visit us at menasharidge.com. We thank you for your interest in our books and the natural world around us all.

SAFE TRAVELS,

BOB SEHLINGER
PUBLISHER